THE 1855 MUDER CASE OF
MISSOURI VERSUS CELIA,
AN ENSLAVED WOMAN

Alexis Brooks de Vita

THE 1855 MUDER CASE OF MISSOURI VERSUS CELIA, AN ENSLAVED WOMAN

FAVIAN PRESS

Endorsements

"Dr. Alexis Brooks de Vita's storytelling is strong, sharp and goes straight to the brain but leaves you necessarily clear headed and sober after. This story dives into U. S. Black and legal history, and tackles a difficult tale made even more murky by euphemism, shame and secrecy, in the era of chattel enslavement. Dr Alexis Brooks de Vita approaches this story with strong insight and legitimacy, as an African Diaspora woman. She pieces together an alternative story to the one used to hang Celia, using facts allowed in the court case as well as considerations not allowed or stricken from the record. This is a bold reconstruction of history, with a stellar imagination, that shines where records (deliberately perhaps) failed. The resulting story reaches a very different conclusion and verdict from the prevailing assumptions about this case and challenges our faith in justice systems applied to unjust circumstances."

- Oghenechovwe Donald Ekpeki

Nebula, Otherwise, Nommo, Locus, Asimov's Readers, British and World Fantasy Awards Winner; Hugo, Sturgeon, British Science Fiction, NAACP Image Awards Finalist.

Author: *Between Dystopias: The Road to Afropantheology*, "Destiny Delayed," "O2 Arena," "Ife-Iyoku, the Tale of Imadeyunuagbon," and "The Witching Hour"

Editor: *Africa Risen: A New Era of Speculative Fiction, Bridging Worlds: Global Conversations On*

Creating Pan-African Speculative Literature In a Pandemic, *The Year's Best African Speculative Fiction: Volume 1, Dominion: An Anthology of Speculative Fiction From Africa and the African Diaspora*

"A poignant and intricate retelling of a historical injustice."
 Byron E. Price, Ph. D.
Dean of the School of Business Administration
Medgar Evers College, City University of New York, Brooklyn
Author of *Merchandizing Prisoners: Who Really Pays for Prison Privatization?*

"This is the poignant true history of Celia, who had no last name: a young mother enslaved and repeatedly raped, tried for a crime for which there was no evidence of her guilt, and condemned to hang by a justice system that—under chattel slavery—made only impotent motions to exonerate her. Celia, hardly more than a child herself, gave her life hoping against hope to save the children she had born to her hateful enslaver.

"The book is a depiction of heartbreaking heroism under insupportable suffering. I found it a stylistic triumph, displaying high poetry in spellbinding story-telling. Did Celia have a mini-stroke from pre-eclampsia when she was in labor? Celia's supervision of Miss Virginia's labor, despite Celia's being a young teen with no training or knowledge as a midwife, is a satiric critique of the labor scene in *Gone with the Wind* where Missy is forced to attend a birth by Melanie, despite having no knowledge or experience—graphic, since it was written by a woman.

"Dialog is just right; I especially like the fact that there is no difference between the slaveholders' speech and that of the enslaved people. That's truth. The narrative voice faithfully portrays the language, lifestyle, and even viands of that lamentable time. Expect to hear more of work by Alexis Brooks de Vita; writers of her genius are truly rare."

- Mary A. Turzillo, Ph.D.

Author of *Reader's Guide to Anne McCaffrey*, *Reader's Guide to Philip José Farmer*, *An Old-Fashioned Martian Girl*, *Mars Girls*, *Bonsai Babies*, *Dragon Soup*, *Cosmic Cats and Fantastic Furballs*

Nebula Award for Best Novelette for "Mars is No Place for Children"

Science Fiction Poetry Association Elgin Award for *Lovers and Killers* and *Sweet Poison*

"A brilliantly conceived project. *The 1855 Murder Case of* **Missouri versus Celia** explores a critically important event in American social and legal history. Brooks de Vita's careful attention to the detail of this narrative, as well as to its social reconstruction, offers a unique analysis that excavates the deep secrets and arresting circumstances of both the homicide, itself, as well as the trial and execution of the sentence. This is a book that urges our curiosity and our knowledge about an era as well as the circumstances it bred. It is as necessary as it is complementary to the growing body of scholarly attention to this grim chapter of American history."

- Karla F. C. Holloway, Ph.D., J.D.
James B. Duke Professor of English and Professor of Law Emerita
Duke University, Durham
Author of *BookMarks: Reading in Black and White*

"Dr. Brooks de Vita provides an eloquent and profound examination of the complexity of the 1855 murder mystery with its social and political contexts. She has the case re-tried in a 'textual tribunal' set up through her articulate and sensitive narrative, which will challenge each reader to become a jury of history and conscience."

Haiqing Sun, Ph. D.
Professor of Spanish
Texas Southern University, Houston
Author of "A Journey Lost in Mystery: *Death in the Andes* by Vargas Llosa" and Hong Lou Meng in Jorge Luis Borges's Narrative"

Dedication

For my mother, Dr. Johney Brooks, her sisters, Mrs. Willie Mae Johnson Young, Aunt Emma, Aunt Ellen, and Aunt Ruth, and for my children, Johnea Rose, Novella Serena, Ceschino Perry, and Joseph Michael.

Table of Contents

Table of Contents

"I perceived in this moment that when the white man turns tyrant it is his own freedom that he destroys. He becomes a sort of hollow, posing dummy [. . . .]"

George Orwell, "Shooting an Elephant"

Foreword

Alexis Brooks de Vita has found in the pitiable life and death of Celia, a slave convicted and executed in 1855 Missouri for murdering her owner, a chilling example of the injustice of justice in antebellum America. The abiding truth is that justice is often perverted in judicial proceedings in societies founded on egregious power differentials.

Any history that is more than a recital of bare facts is an exercise in historical imagination, and in her book, Brooks de Vita gives voice to the human actors who occasioned the court action but whose real thoughts and motives will never be fully known. The unspoken, the unspeakable must be spoken if we are to take the beams from our own eyes.

Dr. Ralph J. Hexter, Vice-Chancellor
University of California, Davis, 2011

Preface

Like a child in a new world, I have a lot on my mind and much to say.

W.E.B. DuBois wrote, "To be sure, behind the thought lurks the afterthought, some of them favoring chance might become men, and we build about them walls so high, and hang between them and the light a veil so thick, that they shall not even think of breaking through." So, just like a child, I stay in my place and create a world of my own, a world where my truths are appreciated, a world where I feel I am doing my part and playing my role.

To a young world, I spread knowledge of being an African American.

Opening one's mind is just as important as opening one's eyes or ears because just as many places as one's mind can take one, it can also confine one to limitations. The world as we know it has many dark secrets. Each race, country, region, and continent holds the unknown. They all have something that they are not proud of and keep undisclosed so that they would seem somewhat more humane. For some odd reason, though, African Americans seem not to have a dark secret, like the others. We have no dark secret because we are the dark secret. We are the bones in the closet that America keeps out of sight. We are America's lost diary that has been shuffled with other books in the library. This did not happen by accident but has been done to put away a haunting past.

Nelson C. Solomon, II
Texas Southern University, Houston, 2011

18

Acknowledgments

A loving thank you to my children, Joseph Michael, Ceschino Perry, Esquire, Novella Serena, and Johnea Rose. Thank you, Novella, for finding this book its homes.

Sincere thanks to Ralph J. Hexter, Vice-Chancellor Emeritus of the University of California at Davis, Karla F. C. Holloway, James B. Duke Professor of English Emerita and Professor of Law Emerita at Duke University, and Dr. Seetha Srinivasan, Director Emerita of the University Press of Mississippi.

Warm thanks to John Morrison, Dirk Blocker, Melody Mennite Walsh, Sean Allan Krill, Reagan Miller, Tedd Hawks, Brian Heaton, Alex Adams, Alexis Boudreaux, Rainee Hamilton, and Gabriel Walker.

Thank you, Dean Byron E. Price, Dr. Haiqing Sun, Dr. Obidike Kamau, Sister Akua Fayette, and Mr. Ronald Keys.

Thank you, Nelson C. Solomon, II, my TSU Literature classes of Spring 2010, and Novella's Spring 2010 Houston Community College – Central Campus Composition students, collectively named Sunrise English, Why English? and 1302 After the Googly Fall.

Particular thanks and sincere appreciation to Dr. Herbert Richardson, Founder and Editor-in-Chief of The Edwin Mellen Press and to the dedicated professionals of his publishing house, to Stuart Holland, Founder and CEO of Favian Press and Fiction4All, and to Dr. Mary A. Turzillo and Oghenechovwe Donald Ekpeki for their faith in and support of this book.

Prologue: Cornered
Fulton, Missouri 1855

August heat cooked the dusty streets of Fulton, Missouri so that Circuit Court Judge William Augustus Hall was not only disgruntled but already disheveled by the time he alighted from his horse. He flung open the delicate gate, stomped along the path through the brilliant flower garden, and hammered the brass knocker on Captain John Jameson's front door.

Jameson watched from his wingchair as the scowling figure flipped the horse's reins about the hitching post and hunched its way through his garden. He decided to pretend he had earlier closed the library's drapes against the late morning sun. Then he never would have seen the judge's arrival.

Judge Hall, more ambitious than the captain, was notoriously impatient. It would be no matter at all for Jameson to simply wait the younger man out. For Jameson already knew the purpose of Judge Hall's visit and was determined to have none of it.

But when Captain Jameson rose from his wingchair to draw the library windows' drapes, he lurched and slammed painfully against the edge of his mahogany writing desk.

Jameson whirled like a man under attack and looked in confusion about him.

What had caught his foot? He could detect nothing in the faded antique carpet that might have snagged him. Surely, he could not be drunk already.

Captain Jameson stumbled into his upholstered leather desk chair and grappled at the heavy mahogany quill drawer. Where was his silk scarf?

He was just knotting the fine cloth above his knee when the young housemaid scratched at the heavy library door even as she opened it.

Jameson could not look into her anxious wide eyes and chastise her. For it was perfectly obvious that it was the huffy judge behind her who was responsible for this rude intrusion.

"Ah, Judge Hall. Yes, thank you, Bess." Captain Jameson waved a hand in a gesture of resignation that the judge might have read as "Come in," or "Get out," or, perhaps most accurately, "What else should I have expected of you?"

Jameson returned to fumbling at the recalcitrant knots at his knee and in his mind. How could a man of his years, his experience, his stature in the Black Hawk War, his three terms in Congress, a former speaker of Missouri's state legislature, be brought to hide from callers in his own home?

"Ah, yes. Good morning, Captain Jameson. Is it still morning, sir? I heartily hope I haven't invited myself to your home at dinner time," Judge Hall said.

Jameson did not look up from his task, but it occurred to him that his obvious difficulties in tying the silk scarf were to his advantage. His back, at his desk, was to the lovely leaded glass library window. Clearly, the judge would have to believe that the captain had been so absorbed in the challenge of getting the swollen joints of his fingers around the fine silk that he had not noticed the arrival of his uninvited guest.

Hall need never know I was hiding, he realized and immediately began to consider how to turn his retreat into attack. *Like a cornered animal. Like that slave girl he wants me to defend.*

Jameson's opportunity came when he heard the judge say, "May I join you, sir, in a seat and in that fine whiskey?"

Before he could think, Jameson had pulled himself to his unsteady feet and pronounced, "That would be rude of me, Judge. It would be best if I join you in standing before you depart." His returning volley was only partially marred by the stagger and clutch at the desk's edge that saved him from tumbling to the floor.

"Let me help you, John." Immediately, humiliatingly, the judge was by his side and eased him past the desk chair, back to the encasing arms of his wingchair and little deal table, laden with its crystal decanter and shot glass.

The judge himself bent to raise Jameson's flimsily tied leg to the needlepoint ottoman before the fireplace, murmuring, "Is it the rheumatism or that old war wound acting up again, Captain?"

Before he could stop himself, Jameson's mouth had produced the habitual, "It is immaterial."

He could have bitten off his tongue. The judge was not five minutes in Jameson's own home, and already Captain Jameson was plunged back into the deceptions, the lies, the intimidations, feints and counter-feints of that long, illustrious, loathed career as a man of the law and the legislature,

23

rushing to hide his shame behind the flag of his honor as a would-be Indian fighter.

He must not surrender to the old weaknesses.

"I will have none of it, Judge Hall." Jameson's voice was, at last, strong. His gaze clear. He stared at Hall.

But now it was the other man who would not look at him.

Hall straightened from his ministrations. Bent to the deal table to pour out another shot of whiskey neat for his opponent in this contest of wills.

Then he moved swiftly, smoothly, without a stumble to the sideboard. There the judge selected a large crystal glass, unstoppered a decanter of water, watched the clear liquid pool at the glass's faceted bottom as he poured it, refracting the blaze of sunlight through the leaded window panes.

A loud splash of whiskey followed. Hall must have found another decanter ready for Jameson at the sideboard. Jameson watched as Hall threw back his head and downed the drink, reset the glass, and turned to face him again. "Thank you, Captain Jameson, for your unfailing hospitality."

The sarcasm meant nothing to Jameson. He must keep his mind fixed on his purpose. He must say no and keep saying it until this brutal man bringing these unwelcome memories of an inglorious past was finally quit of his home.

Jameson made a mental note to himself. He would instruct all the enslaved members of his household, as well as his wife and daughters, to never again open the door to this judge but leave it to him to deposit his calling card in the mail slot, if he chose to, and depart.

Jameson repeated, "I will not defend that girl, Judge Hall. Find her other counsel."

Judge Hall approached the fireplace and seated himself in Mrs. Jameson's favorite upholstered velvet chair. He did not ask permission again to be seated but toyed with the tassels of a Kashmiri shawl she'd draped there, letting the strands waterfall between his fingers. "You will be pleased to learn that I have found the suspect other counsel, Captain, as you've requested. I have retained your own apprentice, young Nathan Chapman Kouns, a member of one of Fulton's finest families."

"Eldest son of Dr. Kouns? But he is no scholar, Judge! And he has no trial experience, whatsoever. He cannot handle a case of this magnitude."

"Nor will he have to. I did not say that I have released *you* from the case, Captain. Though your aversion and your shock and outrage at the heinousness of this slavegirl's crime have my sympathy. But the law must be allowed to run its course, Captain Jameson. Even the likes of Celia have rights in the fine state of Missouri."

"You misunderstand me, Judge. Deliberately, I suspect."

"Not at all, Captain Jameson. It is you who misunderstand. And you are unfair to your young apprentice. For he has earned a degree from St. Charles College, has he not?"

"Neither he nor I are scholars of the law, Judge. You know that."

"I know you believe that, which is why I have gone so far as to appoint you yet a second assistant

25

in this case, Captain Jameson. Young Isaac Boulware. There. I thought that would get your attention."

For Jameson had reached for his glass in his anger but, upon hearing Boulware's name, left it untouched. His hand faltered before he withdrew it to stare open-mouthed at the judge. "Not Reverend Theodorick Boulware's son?"

"The same. Youngest sons have such a fire in the belly to prove themselves, don't you think?" Smiling now, Hall elaborated. "Not only is young Boulware from one of the most well-respected families in all of Callaway County, in all of Missouri, as far as I am concerned, but his scholarly excellence is uncontestable. He has earned not only his bachelor's degree from Transylvania College, one of the finest in all of the South, but his law degree, as well. Did you know that, sir? He has passed the bar as a scholar, John, not as an apprentice, as we all have done. Young Boulware is probably the sharpest legal researcher in all of Missouri. I look forward to hearing the case he shall help you and young Kouns prepare." Hall rose.

His smile was smug. "So there, sir. Your concerns are addressed, Captain. I will brief the three of you tomorrow morning in my chambers. I am not an early man." He chuckled. "If memory serves, neither are you, for that matter, John. But I suspect a fire-eater such as our young Boulware might be. We shall have to rise to his standard and present ourselves at my chambers at nine sharp. Ten, at the latest." Hall made as if to depart, saying,

"Will your girl have my hat ready for me at the door, do you suppose, Captain? She seems none too accustomed to handling your visitors for you."

Jameson stopped him with, "I shall not be there, Judge."

Hall, arrested with his face to the closed library door and his back to Jameson, stood still. When his voice came, it was grave. "Yes, you shall, John. I suggest you push me no further on this matter. You shall come to my chambers of your own free will and be briefed on this case, or you shall come to my chambers in chains and be briefed in a jail cell shortly thereafter. Perhaps we can accommodate you with a cell near to that of your client. You will not defy me in this, John."

Jameson's answering silence was absolute. His mind reeled over each word the judge had just said. He pictured himself led by the deputy into the judge's chambers with his wrists and ankles shackled, ridicule attending his every step as clerks, attorneys, criminals jeered his progress down the court hallway, his wife and daughters wailing as neighbors rushed to comfort them, rushed from them to spread ugly rumors about the town.

Finally, as if having thought better of his threat, Judge Hall turned back to the incredulous captain.

And against his every resolution, Jameson was reduced to pleading. "Judge, listen to me. I am an aging man. I have put the law and war and their rigors and their defeats and their injustices behind me. I am not the same man who camped on the banks of the Des Moines River at Fort Pike and waited futilely for my regiment to be deployed. Nor am I the man who once railed on the House floor against that young Whig Illinois upstart, Lincoln, the man who so brashly called him out as a coward for opposing the war with Mexico." Jameson stopped himself and muttered in confusion, "That damnable speech destroyed my good name in Congress," his mind wandering, his train of thought utterly lost to him.

"Captain." Hall's voice rang like a pistol shot, pitiless.

Jameson looked up at him as if he'd just realized the other man was still there.

Hall said, "This is not about the Mexican War, nor about Abraham Lincoln and your Congressional defeats at the hands of Benson. I am now the one who must deal not only with Benson's proslavery contingents and the isolation of Missouri as a Western slaveholding state but with the backlash from the events of this passing summer. Which, I may add, seems remarkably reluctant to pass and get itself over with."

"Judge—"

"Enough!"

It seemed to Jameson that Hall was suddenly across the room, leaning down in his face. The slender young judge loomed, blocking out the brilliant sunlight as he became the only thing Jameson's bleary eyes could see.

"Make no mistake, John." As drunk as he had thought himself only a few moments ago, suddenly the reek of the fresh whiskey on Judge Hall's breath nauseated Jameson. He withdrew as far as the comforting shelter of his wingback chair would allow. "I was born in Maine, as you may know, John, but I was raised in Harper's Ferry, Virginia. And I take slave rebellion to heart." Jameson registered the judge's gritted teeth, the spittle as he spoke. Again Hall seemed to make an effort to speak reasonably. "But my concerns go beyond Benson's factions. He may have driven you from the House and from the bar, but he will not drive me from my bench. Because I believe in the law as it stands, and this case, as savage and shocking as it is, is neither complex nor to be protracted. That girl has confessed. She had no accomplices. The case is clear. She killed her owner, and there is no defense for such an act in the state of Missouri." By now, the judge had recovered himself. He stood straight again, smoothed down his rumpled suit jacket, smoothed back his hair.

Light and air struck the dazed Jameson. He returned to his senses. What had Hall just said to him? Was this to be a sham trial, is that what he had just been instructed?

Hall said almost gently, "You have thirty years before the bar, John, three terms in Congress, as distinguished a family name as your two apprentices, and an impeccable reputation as a trial lawyer."

Jameson said, "I have tarnished all of those." He shook his head as if to clear it. "And what is more to the point, I have put them all behind me, William. I am ordained now as a minister of the Disciples of Christ. I have moved on to matters of the soul. This girl needs a practicing attorney, man."

29

Hall's next words were precise. "A practicing attorney cannot afford to jeopardize his record with a case that cannot be won, John. Have some humanity. Will we spark a war at the borders between Missouri and Kansas over this chit? Kill our finest young white men, like Kouns and Boulware, in their prime, over these cursed blacks? We're lucky the papers have taken little interest in this bloody business. May we lay it to rest before they take notice of the uproar." The word seemed to recall to Hall that he himself verged on roaring.

And once again he lowered his voice, as if concerned that servants or Jameson's womenfolk might come to check on them. "As you point out, Captain Jameson, you have withdrawn from the practice of law and built yourself a new career. A final lost case cannot hurt your record. Nor can it hurt those of your two young apprentices, for they are only assisting you with research, and this need never count against their records. Bear up, man. None of the three of you have anything to lose."

Jameson was incredulous as the contents of their conversation rushed in upon him. Now he remembered what they had been discussing. "Nothing to lose but that girl's life, William! And moral decency. You know how she lived with Newsom. Is this what slaveholding has become? Not a matter of work and care as compensation, but brute misusage? That girl deserves real counsel. Surely, given the circumstances—"

"The only circumstance is that she has confessed. I ask you what is one miserable slavegirl's life when weighed against the peace and stability that all of Missouri stands to gain, when this distressing incident is finally laid to rest?" Hall's voice rose at the last, despite his best efforts. He broke off, clearly forcing himself to remember civility.

Perhaps it was beyond him. For Hall shoved his way through the clutter of heavy Victorian furniture all the way to the door before he paused again.

"Peace at the cost of justice, William? Think how that girl lived." Jameson detested the whine, the feebleness in his voice.

"She will have justice. For you will be at my chambers tomorrow morning, Captain Jameson. How you get there is the only choice I leave you. Don't test me further. I swear to you that I am a man of my word." He pulled the door open and gave a start. "Ah, Mrs. Jameson. Perhaps you will be so kind as to help me recover my hat from your girl at the door?"

Jameson heard his wife's gentle murmur in the hallway before the judge turned again to him with a courteous, vacuous smile. "Thank you for the refreshing whiskey, Captain," he said, too heartily. "I'm afraid our conversation about all these recent political events, as much as this unseasonable heat, certainly required it." Another chuckle of camaraderie between gentlemen. "But we'll get through all this, as you say, sir. Please don't trouble yourself. Mrs. Jameson has offered to see me out. Your leg, you know. Good of you to take the case, notwithstanding. Good day, sir."

And he was gone, sliding the heavy door shut

behind him with a whispered click.

Mouth still agape, Jameson could not say how long it took him to turn from the door closed in his face to his pathetic leg and its useless disguise.

The ridiculous kerchief and his pitiful hope that the rumor of his old war wound could mean anything to young Hall disgusted Jameson now. He gouged at the slippery silk bandage until it untangled, snatched it savagely from about his leg, and flung it toward the cold fireplace. It fluttered in the air like a butterfly hesitant to land. Remembering how he'd confessed his history of frauds and failures to Hall, desperate to get out of appointment to the murder case, sickened him.

Jameson registered the musical tinkle and faint slosh of the whiskey he'd forgotten on the table at his side. Had he backhanded his untouched drink to the floor when he threw the scarf, without realizing it?

Dazed, Jameson looked around and spotted the shot glass and the crystal decanter rolling on the hardwood between the carpet and the fireplace. He bent forward as if to rise and fetch them from the floor.

He wobbled, lightheaded, and fell back, helpless.

Not helpless.

Jameson clutched the table and swung again, deliberately this time. He sent the finely carved deal table splintering against the fireplace bricks.

It was this sound of shattering wood that Jameson thought of three months later when Hall's gavel pounded down his carefully constructed closing arguments.

"Counselor, you will not instruct the jury to consider an enslaved woman as a woman in the state of Missouri with the right to protect herself from rape!"

"But the law states, Your Honor—"

"The law states a woman may defend herself against rape, counselor. But if an enslaved man is not a real man and subject to the protections of the law, then neither is an enslaved woman a real woman and subject to such rights and protections. Modern science tells us that these Africans are talking beasts of burden, counselor, the half step a gracious God took between animals and humans. Ask your young assistant there. Mr. Kouns?"

"Your Honor?"

"I'm sure your father, the learned Dr. Kouns, has read extensively on the talking animal status of the African. Inform your senior colleague, if you please. And Mr. Bartley?"

"Your Honor?"

"Strike all the above from the record."

And so it went, the judge's gavel hammering down each aspect of the brilliant defense Boulware and Kouns had labored at breakneck speed to help Jameson assemble in the month and a half they had to prepare a case for the stone-still, honey-soft teen who sat silently in court with them.

Doggedly, Jameson turned again to the jury, farmers all, slaveholders, most of them. Judge Hall had just snatched from Jameson his assistant, Boulware's, finest argument, sure to appeal to all the fathers of teens who sat on the jury.

Kouns had spent the month of the trial reminding Jameson that he could read a jury like an open book, better than any attorney alive in the United States today.

Jameson knew it was true. But he also knew that with the loss of the rape defense, Judge Hall had just dealt Celia's case a mortal blow.

Still, Boulware's argument for defense of life itself remained. Jameson scrambled to shore up his image before the men of the jury, to re-assemble his thoughts and instruct them.

The case had forced him to give up his whiskey. He still suffered shakes and unwelcome voices when the stress of the trial overwhelmed him. He wished he could call young Kouns to the floor, or even the brilliant, belligerent, unpredictable Boulware, in his place. The jury would admire Boulware, even if it feared him a little. Boulware was of the grand old school and would go down in defeat as proudly as if he had triumphed.

But Jameson reminded himself that, if Hall meant to doom the case, it was up to him, Jameson, to protect these young men from ruined legal reputations.

But he had to look away from Celia to gather his thoughts. He could not afford to remember all he had learned about this awful case, what she had been through, what she would not say.

Jameson began to instruct the jury again. "Gentlemen of the jury, you must remember that the state of Missouri allows an enslaved girl, such as Celia, to defend herself against threat to her life. And when Newsom came at her, in her cabin, on the

34

night in question, when he reached for her after she had begged him to leave her alone, she had no way of knowing how far her life was threatened."

The judge's gavel rang out like rapid fire from a squad of rifles. At the same time that prosecution shouted, "Objection," the judge was already shouting, "Sustained! Prosecution has already instructed the jury that self-defense is not under consideration in this case."

Jameson whirled and faced the judge's bench. "Then Your Honor," he shouted, "you have utterly destroyed my defense of my client!"

"Then I suppose you are prepared at last to rest your case." Judge Hall turned to Bartley. "Strike the counsel for the defense's last comment, too, from the record."

Jameson surged toward the bench just as Boulware and Kouns leapt from Celia's side to restrain him.

"It's all right," Kouns urged him.

"We've got another plan," Boulware whispered.

"I know, I know. Appeal," Jameson wailed. He noticed that, even in the young men's firm grip, his hands trembled from the wrist down.

Soon his body would be shaking. If the young girl ever looked at him, ever took notice of him, this shaking and trembling would do her faith in him no good. If she had any faith left in him.

He found himself praying, for once, that the honey-gold, spun-sugar-soft-voiced Celia would continue to sit in her catatonic silence, as if he didn't exist.

The three men took their seats together. The young men each put a hand on the older man's broad, bent back. "Just put in the appeal," Boulware hissed. "Hall can't get away with denying us defense against rape and even simple self-defense against mortal assault. Get the appeal underway. Ignore the verdict, for the moment. We can handle this. Hall will not make fools of us and a mockery of the law. We are better men than that, Captain Jameson."

"She can't sit in prison in this town now, Isaac. Have you seen the attitude of the mob? They're growing violent. Hall's rumors and machinations have whipped them up to this."

"The outrage at Harper's Ferry has whipped them up to this."

Jameson was on the point of breaking into sobs. His jaw shook, perhaps with rage, frustration, or withdrawal from the alcohol he'd given up to prepare himself for this trial. "You don't understand. We're out of time. Celia's lost that baby, boys. She's not pregnant anymore, and Judge Hall is in a hurry to hang her and put this incident behind the town of Fulton and the state of Missouri."

Boulware said firmly, "We're aware of that, Captain Jameson."

"But if Judge Hall can't execute her fast enough, the townsfolk will lynch her, now that he's forced a guilty verdict, Isaac. She won't live long enough for us to appeal."

Kouns insisted, his whisper loud enough to carry throughout half the courtroom, "We're taking care of that too, Captain."

And then Kouns silenced under Boulware's warning look.

Isaac Boulware didn't let Nathan Kouns say anything else about their plans to save Celia from Judge Hall until after they'd seen Captain Jameson safely home. "You discuss it with your father, and I'll discuss it with mine, Nathan," Isaac said as they closed the delicate wrought iron gate on Jameson's dying flower garden. "We can't afford to wait any longer. Judge Hall will be perfectly content if a mob breaks into the prison and lynches Celia, following today's verdict."

"What is it, do you think, Isaac, that's driving the judge to persecute Celia?"

"Don't be naïve, man. Hall grew up in Harper's Ferry. He knows the chaos that all our lies about slavery and the talking animal theories have engendered. We're always walking the tightrope over our own destruction, lying to ourselves about what lies at the bottom of the pit below us."

Nathan Kouns held open the carriage door for his colleague. "You're always talking like a college man."

"Excuse me, Kouns. I'd heard you graduated from St. Charles, yourself."

Nathan Kouns held up his free hand in a gesture of surrender. "I can't out-parry you, Isaac. Just let me know when you're ready to answer my question. All I want to know is why Hall has it in for Celia. She's so little. And she was pregnant and sick the whole time, Isaac. God help us, but I know Judge Hall is fully aware that Celia couldn't have done

37

what she's confessed to."

Isaac sighed and took the carriage door handle from his friend. "Look, you go on home, Nathan. I'll walk. I need to clear my mind."

Nathan paused before entering the carriage. "Why don't you get in with me? Come on over to my father's. We'll have some dinner and some of his fine brandy and talk with him. He's a physician, as the judge keeps pointing out. I still think we should have called the judge out on that challenge and had my father testify that, even if Celia could have knocked the old man out, she couldn't have done the rest of it."

Now it was Isaac who held up his hands in surrender. "Nathan, thank you. And give my greetings to Dr. Kouns when you ask him about what we can do with Celia. I have to figure out how to approach my own father about this. I need—" But Isaac broke off and began to walk briskly away. He tossed an offhand wave over his shoulder at Nathan Kouns as if driving him back from any further pursuit.

In truth, it was difficult for Isaac to go home with Nathan because of Nathan's lovechild. The young woman who'd been bought for Nathan's pleasure and learning experience seemed well taken care of, as far as such women's circumstances went. And the toddler seemed as healthy and as happy as any small child, loved by his very own mother and too little to be broken into his enslaved status.

The Kouns' father and son's mistresses masqueraded openly in daylight as housemaids, just as Celia had been disguised in the daytime on the

Newsom farm as a cook. Like Celia, the Kouns' mistresses had been allowed to keep their youngest children with them, tumbling about the place. The toddler picked up kindling from the trees in the gardens and fetched and carried knickknacks for household members, and the seven-year-old ran errands about the house and close by in town.

Isaac thought that the Kouns' tableau of wife, sisters, and mistresses all in the same household probably upheld the peculiar institutions' fondest fictions about its level of civilization. And wasn't Nathan getting engaged soon? Isaac Boulware was sure that the potential fiancées and their parents were all served at table by Nathan's mistress and her toddler dressed in a clean little white shirt that reached to his knees. As in every wealthy household, the guests and the Kounses most likely smiled and ignored Nathan's first family—and the doctor's most recent one—in unison.

But the death threat always hanging over Celia's neck had finally dropped like a guillotine today. One more visit to the outwardly genteel, profoundly duplicitous Kouns house seemed impossible to Isaac tonight, disturbed as he was even without the scrutiny into the secret structures of his own life forced by every visit to the Kounses.

Isaac was convinced that he could bring justice to Celia if he focused on that goal alone and shut out the nagging, yapping dogs of his painfully sensitized conscience.

He let himself into his father's house with his own large key and shouldered his way through the rosewood-paneled hallways to his father's study.

39

He knocked and shoved the door open, unannounced. "May I speak with you, sir?"

As Reverend Boulware looked up, his spectacles glinted in the lamplight.

Reverend Boulware had established the Baptist church in Fulton. Isaac saw the familiarly scratched reams of curling paper, the stilled quill pen poised above one of the many sheets that signaled that his father was, eternally, composing another sermon. "Yes, Isaac?" Reverend Boulware prompted.

"The judge condemned her. He sustained objections to all our closing arguments. It was unconscionable, sir. May I do as we discussed, father?" Isaac's habitual eloquence, learned from and shared in common with his father, had deserted him. He wanted an answer, and he wanted to get out of his father's presence so badly that he felt allergic to the man who had given him life, education, opportunity.

Reverend Boulware was a rapidly aging man who had done well by each of his eight children. His gaze upon his youngest was wary, tired. Patient as is only the man who has already glimpsed his own infinity.

Reverend Boulware said carefully, "There is no law higher than the law of God, though obedience to man's laws implies truthfulness and the shouldering of responsibility for our brethren, which reflect our obedience to God's laws."

Isaac waited. He had said all he could to his father. It was as much as he could do now to stand quietly in the doorway and listen.

Reverend Boulware sighed, much as his son

40

had done earlier. *I've got to become more aware of the ways in which I imitate my father if I'm going to learn to live with myself,* Isaac thought.

"Very well," Reverend Boulware said. "Protection of any society's weakest members is a sacred trust from God to man. Perhaps you rise now to your highest calling, Isaac. May God guide you."

"Thank you, sir," Isaac murmured, already backing from the threshold.

Reverend Boulware's voice hardened. "Only until the appeal has run its course, Isaac. Whatever the final verdict."

"You have my word, sir."

Reverend Boulware held his youngest child's gaze but could think of nothing further to add to this precaution except, "Good luck, son. And may God bless your efforts with justice for this girl. But remember that—"

Isaac forced himself to wait as his father intoned that hated phrase that had shaped and haunted his growing years, "God's ways are mysterious to the mind of even the most intelligent man."

"Yes, sir," Isaac said a shade too soon for courtesy. He added, "I will remember that, sir," as if he had heard the phrase tonight for the first time, to make up for his discourtesy to the old man who had made his own life possible and powerful.

His father sighed again and rebuked his beloved youngest son with no more than, "Your sisters have supped, and your mother is waiting to sup with me, but I am still working. Why don't you excuse us

41

and sup alone, so that you may go to bed and get the rest you so obviously need? Old men sleep but little, I'm afraid. I work best when the household is at rest and there is no noise, as you know."

"Good night then, sir. I do thank you for this."

"Good night, Isaac."

Isaac made his way through the fragrant hallways, both relieved and uncomfortable that his father no longer even tried to ask him what it was that had triggered his distaste, his impatience, his desire to flee the very people who had made him all that he was.

A woman as sultry in shade as the shadows from which she materialized brought Isaac's supper to the dining hall. The slices of venison and piles of potatoes, peppers, and onions were warm from the oven.

As the savory steam rose about him, the woman bent to light the candelabra on the table. Isaac seized her wrist as she curved above him to blow out the taper.

He could not look at her. "Madeleine, I need to ask you something."

Madeleine looked at him with only the mildest curiosity and, as he hesitated, growing pique. Soon, if he didn't ask his questions, she would remind him that she'd had a long day, and perhaps he could search for his tongue and his courage on the morrow.

His other mother. Like most men of his class and race, Isaac had always taken it for granted that every true gentleman had, in effect, two mothers. The acknowledged mother was the European one

42

who sat in parlors decked in the family's finest spoils. She represented the family's gentility to the outside world and translated the world's expectations and demands to her family.

But the other mother, the unacknowledged African one, fed that gentleman's family her milk-spouting nipple, the food she'd saved for her own children at the end of the day, the fine cuisine she'd labored over in a smoke-filled kitchen. This African mother sat on floors and walked barefoot and stood laboring for hours in heat and cold, endlessly soothing, scolding, and spanking in equal measure until she had produced another scion of society.

For Isaac, this was Madeleine. And yet there was one thing more that Isaac had long expected of her.

As if on cue, the swinging door from the direction of the indoor and outdoor kitchens flung in at the man and woman caught in their face-off at the table.

"Mister Isaac!" A teenager threw herself across the room and wrapped her slender copper arms about his neck, dislodging his hold on Madeleine.

Before Isaac could respond with more than a bemused smile at the girl's wild show of affection, Madeleine snapped, "Now, Lise, you know better. *Master* Isaac, honey. And keep your hands to yourself."

The lithe Lise slid away from Isaac and stood straight, pouting. "But, ma'am. I haven't seen him in two or three days." She threw her delicate oak-colored fists against her hips and faced him, tapping one bare foot. "All right, you. Out with it. Where you been keeping yourself, and why don't you come say something to me when you get in at night?"

"Lise," Madeleine warned.

Lise plowed on. "You don't want me to know what time you get in, that's why. I know you, Isaac. Out there tomcatting around the town, I bet."

"Lise, I'm going for my strap," Madeleine said and made as if to execute the threat.

But, "No, Madeleine," Isaac interrupted, forced to indulgent laughter even as he snatched to catch Madeleine by the wrist again and keep her in the dining room. "Lisette is right. I've been working late, Lisette. And it's made me forget my manners."

"I'll say. Don't think you're fooling me, young man. I'm watching you."

"Lise, now that's enough," Madeleine insisted, even from her position of helplessness in Isaac's grasp. "Master Isaac may be inclined to tolerate your sass on occasion, but that occasion will never arrive for his father. And therefore you better learn to talk to young master like you got some sense and some upbringing, girl. And that quick." Madeleine threw an uneasy glance at the door that led out to the main hallway, as though expecting the Reverend Boulware at any moment.

Isaac reached for Lise with a freed hand, so he could pull both women at once into an embrace. "No, Madeleine, don't scold. Or rather, if you must scold, I am the culprit. Scold me. Lise is quite right, you know she is. Lise, accept my sincerest apologies. I have been neglectful of my old friend.

44

How are you, dear?"

"That's better," Lisette said, mollified enough to fold her arms with a satisfied smile. Then she frowned. "I'm lonely, Isaac, and I'm mad as hornets. Home alone with nobody but my ma'ammy to talk to and nothing but work to do all day. Ma'ammy's no fun, and you know it."

"Lise! Really, Master Isaac, let me get her out of here. She'll land herself in terrible trouble if your father hears any of this." And Madeleine broke away at last, pried Lise from Isaac, and began to shoo the vivacious Lise out of the room.

As she departed amid a tangle of giggles, blown kisses, and threats of fury if further scorned and neglected, Isaac called after Lise, "I'll make it up to you soon, I promise."

"You'd better. How, Isaac?"

"Master Isaac! Lise!"

"How do you want me to make it up, Lisette?" Isaac laughed as he asked the question, but his heart was choking his throat.

Lise whirled out of Madeleine's grasp to call back, "Cherry taffy. Or lavender bath salts. Yes, lavender bath salts. Or perfume of violets. Yes, perfume of violets to put behind my ears. Oh, Isaac! Have you seen my hair when I take off my headkerchief and take down my braids, lately? It's very long and needs pomade." And Lise reached up to begin unbraiding her hair.

"Cherry taffy, lavender bath salts, perfume of violets, and pomade," Isaac repeated dutifully as Madeleine gave a final shove and pronounced, "Oh, for shame."

45

Madeleine latched shut the swinging door against any more intrusions. "Master Isaac, I know she's your childhood friend, but really you shouldn't tolerate Lise's talking to you like that, sir. You have to help me keep her in line. Just think if your father hears any of this."

But this was just the point, Isaac thought. Lise was the only person in the world who knew him well enough and loved him in just the right way to talk to him like that. He would shrivel inside and die of creeping loneliness again, as he had done daily throughout that last grinding stint away at college, without hearing Lise talk to him like that.

Isaac quipped lustily, to hide his torment, "On the contrary, I'd better make a lot of money on this case if I mean to buy Lisette's good temper back, at the end of it. And she's not my childhood friend, Madeleine. You know that very well. I'm hers. I myself was well nigh past childhood when little Lisette was born to you."

And here it was again. His question. Always there. It would have to be asked someday. He must know.

Or maybe not. Was it possible to return to the bliss of mindlessness once a man had been awakened to his society's barbarity?

For if Isaac had always assumed, until this case with Celia, that the well-born European-American gentleman had two mothers, he had also assumed without examining that thought that the well-born European-American gentleman had what amounted to two wives.

Just as with his two mothers, he had an African

wife and a European one.

"Madeleiene, how would you feel if I were to buy Lisette from Reverend Boulware?" Isaac blurted.

The woman was silent. At first Isaac thought that she had not fully understood his question. But as her silence became her answer, gradually, horribly, he understood.

She might as well have cried out, "Isaac, how could you?"

And he would have loved to ask the same of her.

For didn't Madeleine already know with every fiber of her sanity all the twisted, tangled skein of their labyrinthine society that Isaac had just spent the last three months unraveling, for Celia?

If a man of wealth and position loved a woman of Lise's race, what could he offer her better than the protection of his ownership?

It was ironic that men such as Isaac and his father had structured their society so that it would be illegal for him to propose any relationship to Lise other than that of rape.

Isaac felt sickened. What did Madeleine honestly expect of him? Didn't she realize that buying Lise was the best he could do by her?

"Madeleine," he said. His voice caught, and he thought miserably that it was just as well that he could not say the first words that came to his mind. *Why didn't my father teach me against our customs, teach me a way out of this conundrum? How could he leave me trapped in the heart of such traditions?*

I was an innocent.

47

Isaac said, "I have learned that we are enslaved every bit as much as you are by this institution that we have constructed to feed our ungodly greed. Your bodies are captive and brutalized, but so are our souls." His grip on her wrist must be painful. He let it go.

But as she pulled away and stood straight, he seized it again. "No," Isaac said. "Don't go before I tell you, Madeleine. . . ." But it was not so easy to tell her what he wanted to say.

He tried again. "I want to tell you something. But you must wait when I have finished, for I want to ask you something, as well."

Still, Madeleine said nothing.

Isaac forged on. "We think that we want pleasure, but we learn that we want love. But power and love are antithetic, Madeleine, and the pleasure we have taken from the helpless, those who have no choice, earns us an irrevocable hatred that we deserve but do not understand. Do you understand me, Madeleine?"

At last she spoke, and her mellifluous voice soothed him. "Yes, I understand very well, Master Isaac."

"Don't ever call me master again, Madeleine, unless my father forces you to," he amended. "But when we are alone, I am no one but Isaac, the boy you nursed and cleaned and spanked, who grew up and was just on the verge of doing such an unforgivable thing to you, in return. I want your forgiveness, Madeleine, though I don't deserve it."

Her silence again.

"Don't forgive me if you cannot," he said.

48

"Just know that I regret what I always thought I had the right to take from you. From Lisette. I thought it would have been an honor, for you. For her. I am ashamed. I should have been taught better."

Still nothing.

"For all my learning, I cannot figure another way out of this, Madeleine." He looked her fully in the face, yearning, as when he was a child, for her to fix this.

"But now I must ask you my question."

She waited, her face devoid of any emotion he could discern.

"Did my father or my brothers, I mean, did the Reverend Boulware or his sons ever. . . ." His courage faltered.

Not a word. Did she know where this was leading?

Isaac's voice was low when he resumed. "Did my father or his sons ever do what men in our position assume they may with women such as you?" He begged her to hear the unsaid question behind the ungainly, spoken one. But her silence said he could not be sure she had heard or understood anything.

Like Celia.

So he blurted, "Is Lisette my sister? Or my niece?"

"No, sir," Madeleine said.

And then recklessly, thoughtlessly on a rush of exhaled breath before he could think, "When I was away at college, both times, I was gone for years, Madeleine. While I was gone, did anyone force Lisette?"

49

Only once the question was finally out did Isaac recognize its myriad flaws. Perhaps before he left, perhaps when Isaac was home from college, before he went back to law school, perhaps at any of those times, his father, her lawful owner, the most obvious person with a right to….

"No," Madeleine repeated. And then, mercifully, "Never."

Only as the relief from jealousy and hatred ebbed from the seething edges of Isaac's mind did she add, "Sir," and Isaac fully felt the dreaded contempt that her delay implied.

Isaac's relieved, belated admiration of his father for his restraint, perhaps for the old man's embracing of those annoyingly simplistic ideals he espoused from the pulpit, curdled again to resentment and envy.

Easy for his father to abstain. He had never loved either Madeleine or Lise. Love was Isaac's torture.

And though Lise was thankfully not Isaac's sister, still she could never be his lawful wife. What was he to do? Spend his life looking at her, adoring her with his eyes and loving her with all the force of his heart, but never with the passion of his body?

Not unless he chose to destroy her high regard and his own self-esteem with his desire.

But what good was restraint?

For whether or not Isaac ever let himself take Lisette, she could never stop any other man from doing so. Celia's case had driven that point home to him.

And what would Isaac do if he spent his life

loving and sheltering Lisette but never making love to her, and then some other man did it?

Isaac would kill him. It was as simple and inescapable as that.

Isaac felt his father had raised him wandering blindly in a labyrinth until he slammed, innocently and unprepared, against the roaring minotaur at its center.

Evidently, his father had known enough to resist the temptation that men such as he had written into law. So why hadn't he educated his lonely, precocious, temperamental youngest son to also recognize and outwit their society's most precious, most pernicious vice?

Isaac released Madeleine's wrist for the last time that evening. He rose from the table, flung down his napkin, and strode from the room and from the rear door through the early blackness toward the stables. Nowhere along the way did he espy Lisette.

Thank God.

He saddled up his horse himself, snatching the bit into place, acting out with his loyal horse the impatience and punishment he felt his world directed daily at himself.

But Celia still needed him to come through. Isaac would deal with the demands of love, devotion, and conscience when he had done all he could to assure Celia justice and all the protections that a civilized society should afford its weakest members.

But was his society at all civilized? This, his first case, had brought Isaac to the full realization that he doubted that. Not civilized, not rational. Not even humane toward its most powerful members.

For the thing that writhed at the bottom of the pit they all traversed on a tightrope was their collective discarded soul. Theirs was a corrupted community.

Isaac whipped his horse to a canter down the alleyway to the street, and then to a gallop through the moonlit streets to the Kouns house. As he rode, he wondered if Celia had ever been as happy, as lighthearted as his Lisette.

And would his Lisette ever come to know misery such as Celia's?

As if he had been watching for Isaac, the younger Nathan Kouns threw open his bedroom window over the street just as Isaac's horse drew up and reared.

"What is it, man?" Nathan called.

"Get your carriage. The time has come."

"Tonight? But, Isaac, we haven't discussed the case with Jameson."

"Stop shouting down to me in the street, Kouns. Let me in and we'll settle it."

Nathan's head disappeared from the window, followed by the light from his room's lantern. By the time Isaac had wrapped his horse's reins about the hitching post, the door was opened by the larger of the two enslaved boys most likely fathered by the Kouns men.

Lecture and recrimination had been tamped down in Isaac by his attempted conversation with Madeleine. He looked down at the two blue-eyed

52

enslaved boys, their milky skin barely tinged by their mothers' gold and bronze. "Have you eaten, Isaac?" Nathan asked him, arriving with his bedroom lantern lifted high.

"No," Isaac said. "No time for that. We have to move on this case."

"You look a little wild, if you will allow an observation," Nathan said. "And you don't sound quite rational, either. Let's sit like civilized men and make a plan that we can actually execute. I learned that strategy from a friend who went away not only to college but to law school."

Isaac could not quite smile at the sally. Still on edge, he waited silently to see which of the household mistresses Nathan Kouns would summon to serve the men something to eat at this hour.

Nathan chose the youngest boy, the one Isaac suspected was his own. "Go tell your mother to heat something warm and hearty for Mr. Boulware and me. Can you remember all that?" Nathan ruffled the golden curls atop the wide-eyed boy's head before the tot ambled off to find his mother.

Isaac caught the glimpse of reserve, of envy and desire in the older boy's eyes before his gaze shifted with surprise to Isaac. "Sir?" the boy asked hesitantly.

"You go fetch that brandy Mr. Boulware prefers," Nathan intercepted, and Isaac fished in a pocket to toss the boy a coin to make him smile before he disappeared.

Nathan mumbled, "You know father doesn't like them to get their hands on money. He thinks it will make them inclined to steal when they get

53

older."

Isaac led the way down the hall toward the dining room, making himself at home in his colleague's house. "Steal? You mean keep for themselves some of the money they will earn for you someday, if you hire out their labor?"

They had had too many of these debates before. Nathan said, "Tonight is not the time to pick up on this thread again, Isaac. But I have thought of the many points you've made when we've discussed these issues before. Perhaps the French had it right, old man. You know, they used to buy their lovers' freedom and put them in houses of their own, send the little pickaninnies home to France for a college education before setting them up in a shop or making them overseers on the plantation, or some such trade. That is, before the U.S. got our hands on Louisiana, made it a state, and executed all those Frenchmen's grown black children by firing squad." Nathan shook his head ruefully.

Isaac turned on him and snapped, "Executed? Is that your prognosis for Celia?"

Nathan set his lamp on the dining hall table. "Isaac, I'm here, and I'm with you, and I'm going to help you do everything we possibly can to assure Celia and the Newsoms justice in this awful case. I'm not the enemy, Isaac. Have a seat while I get us a board and chalk from the old schoolroom, to start drafting a plan."

Isaac folded his lanky form for the second time that evening into the confines of a dining room chair. He smoothed his dark hair back out of his face just in time to catch sight of Nathan's golden lover as she drew cautiously into the room.

Isaac was struck by her timidity even before her quick, soundless withdrawal as she caught sight of his eyes dead upon her. He could still hear her breath like a frightened animal's as she waited beyond the door, safely out of sight in the back room that led outside to the kitchen. Obviously, she was waiting for Nathan to return before she re-entered the room.

Nathan's mistress had never been alone in a room with Isaac, as far as he could remember.

The older boy bounded into the room juggling a decanter of the Kouns' exquisite brandy and thumped it onto the table before scooting out again. The little tike was drawn out of hiding with his mother to chase after—his cousin? No; the older boy was the little one's uncle, or perhaps even his great-uncle, technically, Isaac reasoned—to help fetch the snifters. Clearly, the boys were excited by Isaac's electric mood and the odd intensity of Nathan's rising at night to work.

Nathan brought noise and bustle into the room with the slate and chalk that he clattered to the tabletop. He whipped out a flint, struck it against his shoe, and lit the candelabra as his mistress came in with the food tray.

Isaac watched her set down two bowls of stew and two steaming slabs of fresh-cut bread rich with melting butter. He wondered if she had produced this meal so quickly because it was her own and the other housemaid's supper.

"Thank you," he said to her, and she bobbed her head but said nothing before she withdrew.

Nathan raised his eyes from pouring the brandy into two snifters to tell her, "Put the boys to bed, Hattie, and get some rest yourself. You can clean this up in the morning. We won't require anything further tonight." He watched her go.

Isaac said, "Nathan."

Nathan shot him an agitated look.

"Have you thought of what you would do if you found out that your father had taken an interest in your woman, Nathan, while you were away at college?"

Nathan straightened up, his face more sober than Isaac had ever seen it. Nathan said, "Do you have a reason to ask me that?"

"Of course, I do. Or what would your father do, if he had such a woman, and he learned that you had shared her without his consent?"

Isaac saw that Nathan relaxed. More theory, that was all.

Nathan asked, "Why bring this up now?"

"Because we have never figured out who Celia thinks she's protecting with her silence, Nathan. I'm still banking on the youngest son, David Newsom. How could he live in the house with his old man doing Celia down the hall every night and never want her for himself?" Isaac shook his head. "And that sister of his, Virginia, her behavior when the posse was closing in on Celia was just too peculiar. Shouting all those hints about how the body ought to be found at the creek. As if she were telling her younger brother David where to hide it, trying to provide him a way to be found innocent of murder."

Nathan drawled, "Miss Virginia's been through a lot, Isaac. I find Mrs. Waynescott and that younger Miss Newsom, that Miss Mary, both a bit peculiar, myself. Don't you?"

Isaac was in no mood for gossip or jokes. He said, "Perhaps it's still possible to get Celia to talk to somebody and either name an accomplice or retract her confession."

"Perhaps, Isaac. But as you've said, the first goal is to keep her from getting lynched as we go through the appeals process."

The men worked through the night to draft the appeal for Jameson, so that his gifts as a trial attorney could remain all that he would have to contribute to the case. Only as dawn woke them, and they raised their heads from their arms on the dining table, did Isaac's questions of the night before blossom and fulfill his plan.

Once they were closeted in the washroom, he said to Nathan, "If Celia won't confess to us what really happened, why not get her someone a little less threatening to talk to?"

Nathan yawned, stretched, and pulled his trousers down to step into the tub of warm water Hattie had brought him as he answered. "I hear that Virginia Waynescott keeps going by the jail to try to get in and talk to Celia, but Celia refuses to see her. Just as she refuses to see anyone else the law doesn't force her to see."

Isaac rubbed his borrowed washcloth over his teeth, having finished sponge-bathing his own body. "So Virginia Waynescott is not the one Celia will confide in. Not us and not the daughter of the man

57

who owned her and raped her. Who else can we try?" he said before he filled his mouth with salted water to rinse.

"No one white," Nathan said. "And therefore no one who can testify in court for her."

"Is there an enslaved woman, perhaps, we could get her to open up to? She can tell that person who can then pass the statement on to someone white who can speak up in court. Hearsay, but better than no statement in her own defense, at all."

"Not Hattie." Nathan's voice was harsh.

Isaac waved Nathan's nascent upset aside. "Not your woman, fine." He slicked his hair with lavender-scented oil as he wondered if he could persuade Madeleine to wheedle confidences out of Celia.

But then he thought of Madeleine's silence at the end of last night and doubted that she would do anything for him, thinking of his desire for her daughter, newly confessed. Would she do it just to save Celia, a stranger, from hanging? That was doubtful, for the threat of lynchings and hangings terrified the enslaved and the free, alike, into self-protective silence.

"Is there a woman of either race already imprisoned with Celia in Sheriff Snell's jailhouse?" Isaac asked.

"None at this time. Look, Isaac, it's a good idea, but let's get this appeal filed, first. I'm afraid that Jameson may not be at his best, the morning after yesterday's defeat."

"It was cruel of Judge Hall to flush him out of retirement and force him back into court."

"Want to bet when we go to pick him up he'll have that silk scarf wrapped around his knee again today?"

Isaac took a careful look at himself in the lightly fogged mirror above the washbasin. "I thought of pointing out to him that he should try to figure out, when he ties it on, if the weather favors the illusion that his rheumatism's acting up."

Nathan chuckled as he rose from his tub of dirtied water and reached for a towel. "Good old 'immaterial John.' You know that's what they used to call him when he practiced law. 'Oh, John! Is your old war wound acting up again, or is it the summertime rheumatism?' 'Gentlemen, my pains are immaterial.'"

Nathan had to laugh at his own joke, for Isaac couldn't even work up a smile. Isaac was wondering, as the housemaids brought them razors, suds to lather up, and clean white shirts in the washroom so they could shave, dress, and head back to court with Jameson, what his own father's weakness might have been, all these years.

Immediately after filing the appeal, Isaac and Nathan escorted Jameson safely home and went by the jailhouse to talk with Celia and Sheriff Snell, themselves. Jameson still had only limited knowledge of their plans, so that he could in no way disrupt or prematurely reveal them.

Nathan, as always, wanted to hurry out of the jailhouse. He hadn't even seen Celia, this time. He could rarely bear it.

Isaac held her still, coppery hands in his own and gazed at the lids of her downcast eyes in the

59

stygian grey of her cell. "Don't be afraid," he told Celia. "Things will change suddenly, and you may wonder what's happening. But you have friends, Celia, and we're working on your behalf. You're safe, for the time being, and everything we're doing is for your safety. Do you understand me, Celia?"

Nothing. Isaac hesitated in the stink and the gloom of the airless cell before he raised the still, soft hand to his lips in a gentleman's salute to a real lady. Then he let himself out of the unlocked cell.

Celia never made any effort to escape or defend herself. Her situation made Isaac hate the society whose laws he had spent his young adult life studying.

Isaac moved over to the neighboring cell. He stood ostentatiously outside it, filling and rolling a cigarette paper with aromatic tobacco, waiting to get the attention of the other inmate.

Soon, a young man drew near the bars.

"Good afternoon," Isaac said and held the rolled cigarette toward him. "Hold on while I strike you a light. So, what did your owner put you in here for?"

When Isaac returned to the sheriff's office at the door to the jailhouse, he found Nathan waiting impatiently, having finished his assigned talk with Sheriff Snell.

The sheriff smiled unctuously at Isaac. "Well, Mr. Boulware, Mr. Kouns has just been apprising me of plans on behalf of little Celia, in there. I'll be ready whenever I'm needed, gentlemen. Whenever I'm needed."

"Thank you, Sheriff," Isaac said as he slid a

60

rolled bundle into the other man's hand. "Something for your extra work, Sheriff," Isaac said.

Nathan didn't wait for Isaac to decline a ride in the carriage a second time, today. He scrambled into the carriage and threw himself back into the seat with real exhaustion.

Isaac watched the carriage being driven away, wondering if, for the first time, Nathan disliked him as much as he often disliked Nathan.

Isaac had not walked far when he saw an uncovered wagon rattle to a stop at the edge of the gapped boards cornering the sheriff's jail.

Virginia Newsom Waynescott was rumored not to have left her father's house unescorted since she'd come from her husband's homestead, years ago, to watch by her mother's deathbed. But now she whipped up her dusty skirt in one fist, braced herself with the other hand, and leaped from the wagon to the ground like the punch-throwing tomboy people still said she'd been as a child.

Before her skirts settled around her ankles, Virginia had turned and slid a roughly hammered box out from under the driver's bench. She stomped with it up onto the splintering sidewalk.

Sheriff Snell rose from his desk, where he'd been stuffing the roll he'd just received from Isaac Boulware. He didn't make it to the door before Virginia shoved it open with her shoulder.

"Morning, Miss Virginia." He touched where the brim of his hat should have been, forgetting that he didn't have it on in the jailhouse. This woman made him nervous.

61

"Morning, Sheriff." Virginia did not slacken her stride toward the barred cells.

So the sheriff stepped back and put out an arm to block her. Her neck bumped up against his filthy sleeve. He cringed and lowered the arm to the level of the buttons opened at the top of Virginia's bodice.

With everything coming out about this family in court these days, everything the judge had to keep that crazy defense attorney from forcing witnesses to admit, it was becoming hard for the men of the town to look at the Newsom women. Harder still to look away.

But being near Virginia, trying not to think about all the things hinted at in court, hotly denied in court, shouted down in court, was enough to make shadows squirm up out of the secret places in the sheriff's mind. He was only human.

The sheriff beat the shadows back. Now was not the time to wonder. To stare into the V from throat to ribcage where her heartwarmer shawl should have been, getting ready for the late autumn chill. "Miss Virginia, ma'am, we've had this out before. I done told you, now. That little gal in there ain't got many rights. But due process and all the protections of the law during that process, yes, ma'am. She's got that."

Virginia waited before she located his eyes with her own as though she'd just noticed him. "Meaning, Sheriff?"

"Meaning she's got the right to refuse to see anybody she don't want to see. I'm right sorry, ma'am, I'll give you that. That gal don't know who

62

her real friends are. But that's the way it is."

Virginia shifted the box before her. The sheriff's closeness made the sharp wood dig into her pelvis, thin and tender from the last few months' anxious worry and nausea, and the resulting sudden loss of flesh and fluid. "Sheriff, I didn't come here to bandy words with you today. That girl in there is killing herself. And it isn't right. You talk about what she doesn't know. Well, you and I know she'll get herself killed if she doesn't start defending herself. And she doesn't know that she doesn't have to die. She's still scared of my father, Sheriff, and I'm here to tell her that he's dead, and she can break his rules now and talk to people." Virginia moved in on the Sheriff, startling him. "Somebody's got to get her to accuse the man who really did murder my father, Sheriff."

The sheriff shook off his unease with this fragile, disturbing woman and tried to look as if he'd recovered his composure and gained control of the situation. His shoulders went back. He put an authoritative hand on the butt of his holstered gun. "Ma'am, you can rest easy. Them three attorneys of hers done hit that courtroom like a tornado hitting a barn."

Virginia said nothing.

When she was sure of his attention and his silence, she raised the box up under his gaze. "Sheriff, look."

His eyes dragged from the soul-battered beauty of Virginia's face to the unwilling softness of her exposed throat and chest to the clutter of charred bones nestled in the box.

There, he thought he saw the jagged black seam joining rounded dark cream skull plates.

Virigina went on. "Sheriff Snell, I look into this box every day. I keep my father's bones in this open box on my bureau, and I look at them first thing every morning. That's the way I know he's dead and why he wasn't at the supper table the night before. It's how I fight off the nightmares and come back to myself." The sheriff saw confusion hit Virginia's face like a slap. She frowned and looked away as if struck with wonder at what she'd just said. Her arms trembled and lowered to rest the box against her hip.

He had just thought to himself, *No telling what them Newsom women been through*, when the sagging box tumbled to the jailhouse's pine floor.

The bits of Robert Newsom's charred skeleton scattered along the boards as if they meant to gather momentum and reassemble themselves to flee.

Virginia clicked her tongue and squatted like the harried homemaker she was to right the upended box. She leaned around in a jerky circle to snatch up and toss in the puzzle pieces of her father's remains, as though they were her children's abandoned toys.

The sheriff turned his back to face the corridor to the prisoners' cells, his nose and mouth suddenly buried in his dirty sleeve. Some things, a man never got used to. "Miss Virginia, ma'am," he ventured, "you really ought to give your father a decent burial."

"A decent burial is due every decent man," Virginia quipped before the words were quite out of the sheriff's mouth. It struck him that this was probably a handy phrase she said to family and neighbors several times each day. She stood.

She gripped the box at the end of her tired arms so that it rested against her legs. The sight of her skirt pressed against the contours of her thighs, the old lecher's bones sticking up above the edge of the box as if scrambling for a last contact with his daughter's private places, overcame the sheriff's self-control. To his embarrassment, he retched into his sleeve.

"Sheriff," Virginia said gently. "William."

He looked into her face.

"Sheriff, that girl in your jail cell doesn't have what I have to tell me every day that my father is gone, and his rules no longer apply. Celia's still scared of my father, Sheriff. She's scared to say anything to anybody. And they're men, Sheriff. My father wouldn't let her talk to men. Or listen to what men had to say. You've been in court. You've heard all this. I've got to be the one to tell Celia she's free to speak to her attorneys. Or she won't. She doesn't know any better than this silence, and her silence is going to get her killed."

The sheriff felt Virginia draw close. She had left the box behind on the floor. The sheriff relaxed into the comfort of her nearness.

She put one of her freed hands on the sheriff's arm, holding him still, arresting his attention, and lowered her voice to a murmur. "When Celia kills herself obeying my dead father, in the end, no matter what your deputy's posse did, no matter what the judge did, no matter what Celia's attorneys

65

didn't do, Sheriff, her hanging will be on your head."

Virginia drew nearer still to whisper, "Celia thinks she's doing the right thing. She thinks she's dying to save someone who tried to save her. She thinks she's protecting someone my father himself would have wanted her to protect."

When the implications of this last hint sank in, the sheriff gave a start. He threw up his hands as if to ward off any further divulgences. "This sounds like something for the lawyers, Miss Virginia. You'd better not tell me any more, ma'am. I don't want no part of family secrets."

Virginia reached up, seized the sheriff's arm and squeezed it tighter, pressed it down to her chest and whispered relentlessly, "She thinks she's dying for my brother David, Sheriff. He was going to buy Celia from my father. She thinks David lost his patience and killed Father, instead. Of course, you and I and the whole town know who really murdered my father. But her attorneys won't think to tell her that everybody knows, that she can tell now, that my father can't whip her for talking to men now, that nobody's after David because everybody knows the killer was—"

The sheriff snatched his arm away. He threw up his hands as if Virginia had drawn a gun. "I can't hear this, Miss Virginia. You better stop right there." He backed away.

Virginia did not pursue. He was relieved to feel the caress of her skirt against his leg as she drew away. He even let himself admire the curve of her back as she bent to retrieve her box.

66

The slender swell of what hips she still had melted his reserves. He wanted to be gentle with her, wanted her to like him. Maybe when all this court business was over.... "Miss Virginia, I mightn't ought to tell you this."

She straightened, holding the box and listening with her cheek tilted toward her shoulder.

"You confided in me, Miss Virginia. I'll confide in you, ma'am. And we'll call it square and not tell any more secrets, after today. You going to give me your word on that, Miss Virginia?"

She said nothing, but neither did she move away. He came close. Was hit by the mellow sultry scent that rose like a dusty cloud from her skin laced with spider web-fine wrinkles. His fingertips brushed at the wisps of hair that escaped a clump of braid at the back of her head, as if to clear her ear for his own whisper. A ruse. He let his lips brush the ear. A stolen kiss, now that she had no husband and no father to get in his way.

She wouldn't go back to her husband, would she? No. How on earth would she explain the baby she'd had two years after she left her husband to come home and tend her mother?

Even the census takers had shaken their heads over the baby. What to do with such a scandal? In the end, they'd counted him but didn't try to account for him.

The judge, tough as nails, had just decided to pretend Virginia's youngest child didn't exist. "Irrelevant to the case," he'd flung at Celia's newly dried-out attorney, Captain Jameson. "Stick to facts pertinent to the accused."

"Your Honor, the sexually charged atmosphere in that house and on that farm is pertinent to the crime of which my client is accused."

The bang of the judge's gavel had been like a pistol shot before it was leveled at Jameson's face. "Do I have to charge you with contempt of court, counselor, and have you hauled out of here? I encourage you to ask yourself if you're acting in your client's best interests, probing into these family matters."

The judge had almost daily addressed the furiously scribbling transcriber with, "Bartley, expunge these unfortunate proceedings from the record."

And now the sheriff stopped his hand just short of dropping to the modest swell of Virginia's breast. The cotton of her bodice was so worn that it was almost no covering at all. And she had gotten so thin that she had evidently ceased to tie herself into a corset.

Her breast was just there, visible under the thin veil of her bodice, the nipple warm under his hovering palm.

And still she didn't move. Listening. Waiting to save Celia. Did she love a little slave girl that much?

Or was she lonely? Hard to believe, with all her own kids and her sister Mary still at home. And all the fuss and bother of the court case. The sheriff feared she must be too busy to welcome a man's attention.

But still. Maybe. Before some other man got there first.

"There's plans afoot to save Celia, Miss Virginia. You don't have to fret. It's good citizens of this town might just give the law time to do its duty by this gal of yours."

"How?"

He'd always heard widows were lonely. Was a woman who'd lost a father like Robert Newsom technically almost a widow?

"When?" she said.

He wanted to say, "Now," say, "Whenever you want, whatever you want," but dimly he remembered that this had to be done right. There were important people in this town who meant to save this little slave gal but without outright defying the law.

Bending it a little. Helping it along. Like he meant to bend and help Virginia along. He couldn't afford to mess up their plans. Or his own.

He didn't realize he hadn't answered her question about when the jailbreak would take place until she'd shoved her way out of his near embrace, hoisted her father's makeshift coffin between them like a barrier, and turned to go.

He watched her into the sunlight. How she slung the box of bones under the seat like a sack of flour before she pulled herself up onto the driver's bench, lithe as a young man. Every move she made said she disdained the sheriff's help.

She'd already been rescued by that helpless teenaged slave girl shivering and still bleeding from her recent miscarriage, in his prison. And all Virginia wanted now was to return that favor.

As he watched her slap the reins against her

horse's shoulders and jerk back in her seat against the wagon's lurch forward, he thought how sad, how foolish, how pitiful that all the most important words in his own life had always gone unsaid.

When Miss Virginia was out of sight, Sheriff Snell headed to his desk, snatched open the top drawer, yanked out the roll he'd received from Boulware, and shoved it deep into the pocket protected by his holstered pistol.

He made himself take the time to go back to the cells and lock them up.

"Celia," he said. "Everything's going to be okay, now."

Nothing from the huddled figure on the straw pallet.

He paused before the cell of the imprisoned man and sniffed appreciatively at the aromatic smoke of his cigarette.

"Remember, Wayne," he said, "you don't have nothing to be afraid of, if anybody breaks in here tonight. Ain't nothing going to happen to you that you need to fight off, boy. You got my word on that."

"Yes, sir," Wayne called as he drew near the bars to murmur, "Sheriff, why they doing this, sir?"

The sheriff said, "You and me don't know nothing, Wayne. Why is who doing what, boy?"

He tapped the bars and nodded in the direction of Wayne and Celia as he returned to drop the cell key on its heavy ring atop his desk.

Wayne listened and identified what was happening based on the sounds that echoed back to him through the darkness of the jailhouse's windowless interior. He heard the keys thrown down on the desk before the sheriff's big show of latching the jailhouse shut without locking it, outside.

The glowing cigarette tip had lit and cleansed the gloom and stench of Wayne's and Celia's cells for as long as it took to burn down to ashes. The familiar curl of the grey smoke cheered Wayne, the sight and smell of it reminding him of when he was hired out at the river to work with the longshoremen.

Those big brawny men had loved nothing better than to break from the long day's labor, collect the clinking coins of their pay, and spend away the bit of it that they'd earned extra. The longshoremen shot the part of their pay that their owners would never know was missing, the odd job tips that went to tobacco and cigarette papers first, dice and card games next. Only if the gambling went well enough for a man, his winnings, his fists, and his switchblade might get him some time with one of the favorites among the river walk's women.

Wayne had always hoped and believed he'd grow to be one of those men someday, bigger than life and brighter than the sun, tossing cargo that it took four or five ordinary men just to lift. It was thanks to them that Wayne had learned to fight like a wildcat, which is why he was always in the sheriff's jail these days.

It turned out to be all for nothing that Wayne showed up to work the docks in the dark long before dawn, sweated errands for tips while the men rested and gambled, and never wasted a cent of his

71

hard-earned coins on tobacco, gambling, or even the cheapest woman. Wayne handed every halfpenny to his owner to convince him that keeping Wayne working at the river would earn him more money than selling the teen. But Wayne had just not grown big enough to produce the work of a real stevedore. His owner had sold him away from the work at the river, and he'd ended up out here in pioneering Missouri farm country.

Wayne had been miserable and too fast with his fists, ever since.

When Wayne in deep nostalgia took a drag of the lawyer's cigarette, he gagged and coughed until tears ran. Not big enough, and he'd never even learned to smoke.

So, in the end, he'd just held the burning stick and enjoyed the red gleam and fond memories of the dock.

Now Wayne wished he had asked for food from that lawyer. For a drink, maybe. For another cigarette, even, to help him stay awake and wait. Wayne savored the heady buzz and sense of alertness from the tobacco's smoke perfuming the air around him.

It didn't matter that he knew there was supposed to be no danger, when the break-in happened. No enslaved man lived to be his age without knowing that jail drew accusations like carrion draws flies. Maybe that slick-haired, smooth-talking lawyer was telling him the truth. And maybe he was just setting Wayne up for the sport a bunch of townies could make of a passive enslaved teen grinning and welcoming a lynch mob.

Wayne reasoned that, if they were a lynch mob, there was little he could do but fight, anyway. At least he'd had his first—and possibly final—cigarette. That was more than most enslaved men got when they were sentenced to death.

He called out softly into the darkness, "Miss Celia, I don't know what's going on. But I'm here with you. You ain't alone. I'm keeping watch, if you want to sleep." He didn't know how much she knew. And he wasn't sure if he should warn her.

Nothing.

There was never anything from Celia. Wayne wasn't even sure that she could talk.

He settled down to watch and wait.

But he must have drifted off to sleep. For Wayne woke with a start when he heard scratching at the latch to the front door, the hiss of whispers, and the sibilant scrape of shoes stealing across the office's hardwood floor.

Beyond the stealthy figures approaching, Wayne heard the whinny of antsy horses and remembered a man left dangling from a tree branch when the horse had been whipped out from under him.

He shot upright on his pallet. Curled into a small dark ball in the corner. "Celia," he whispered and decided to hush.

Why had he trusted a white man? What was this game they were playing with him now?

He would play possum and not explode, swinging and kicking, until he felt hands on him. It was a plan. It gave him hope that they might pass him by, leave him alone.

Of course, if they seized him, by then it would be too late for him to put up much of a fight. But here he was in a cage. It was too late for him, anyway.

And then smothered lantern light outlined black-caped figures that rushed upon Wayne, clanging open his cage, shouting low muffled instructions at him, at each other. Or were those threats?

He thought he heard a woman's high thin scream.

"Celia," Wayne called.

Hadn't the slicked-back lawyer told him to protect her, quiet her, settle her down if she got distressed? But he was caged, himself. How could he protect her?

He heard her scream again just as heavy hands seized him. He struck out soundlessly with both fists.

Whenever he let loose of that pent-up rage, that tightly leashed power, it was impossible to stop it. He thought wretchedly as his fists connected, now with one body, now with another, that he'd rather they shot him than do what they tended to do if they got their hands on a man they could get away with lynching.

There was only one explanation for why they'd come after him. His owner must have given him over to the state to pay the debts for his keep at the jailhouse. No one was going to speak up for him or interrupt the sport of cutting, burning, and dragging to make him scream. No one was going to claim him.

One of the black-caped men he'd just struck whipped up the barrel of a rifle and poised it in the air before he brought it down on Wayne's head.

Only as it connected with his head did he realize that the man had been shouting, "It's us, Wayne! Are you all right, Kouns? Damn it, Wayne, we're no lynch mob!"

Wayne felt himself fall to the floor, stunned and unable to make his arms strike and his legs run. He flailed in a welter of confusion, commanding his body to resist, to fight, to flee. But he felt himself clamped in powerful hands that hauled him to his feet and dragged him through the blackness to the starlit night outside.

The beauty of the black sky ripped with stars awed him as it terrified him. His last sight before the awful pain that would finally, thankfully, leave him senseless?

And here was the rope lowered around Wayne's neck, more rope looped about his wrists, more tied from ankle to ankle. Wayne stared up from the ground at the blazing black sky.

"I was told he goes wild," Wayne heard a voice say. "But I thought I'd made it clear to him."

"Damn it, Isaac. Fool near about broke my jaw with that last one."

"I'm sorry, man. But what can we do? He's all we had. The sheriff says he's been on good behavior. Maybe he didn't understand—"

"Shut it, Boulware. I want to get to the house and get some cold water on this jaw. Do you think that sullen wench who opens the door at your house might at least give me a wet rag?"

"How's Celia doing?"

"I think she's fainted."

"Oh, God."

"Oh God is right, preacher's son. The way this is going, I'd say we'd better start praying before a real lynch mob catches wind of this and hangs us all right here in the street."

"Shut up, Kouns. Let's get the two of them out of here."

Wayne felt himself hauled to his feet.

"You're not going to put him in the carriage with Celia, are you?"

"What the hell else can we do with him?"

"He's crazy, Kouns! What if he wakes up and goes after her in there?"

"What do you want me to do? Wait with him here outside the jail until you come back for us? Are you crazy, too?"

Wayne felt the rope around his neck yanked tight. He gagged and stood straighter to ease the pull as the rope at his neck was knotted to the rope at his wrists.

"We'll tie him to the carriage and let him run behind it."

"And hope to heaven no one sees us and reports us to the judge tomorrow."

"Shut up, Kouns, and get in the carriage with Celia. I'll ride up on the box with my driver."

Wayne's feet were quickly freed by the caped figure before it swung up into the sky at the front of the carriage.

Within seconds, Wayne was yanked to a stiff trot as the carriage took off, jerking him along by his tethered wrists.

If he fell forward, unable to keep up with the pull, he would be dragged to his death.

Better not to think about it. He knew he never should have trusted a white man.

Mindlessly, Wayne trotted, woozy and sore, toward what, he could not say. When the carriage lurched to a stop, Wayne tumbled forward against it before crumpling to the cobblestones beneath his feet.

Wayne came to tied outside an outbuilding in a quiet courtyard. He struggled to rouse himself, sure he needed to fight, to run. But his wrists and neck were still tied.

He yanked helplessly against whatever they'd been tied to, but he was disoriented and could tell nothing except that he was on his back, kicking out. His head pounded, and his tongue was thick in his mouth with thirst.

"Water," he called, snuffling about him for a bowl of water such as he'd found now and then in his cell back at the jailhouse. "Water!" he called more pitifully still. His mind, blank in the darkness, now filled with the image of that lynching he'd seen when he was only beginning to grow out of childhood, when the burning man's charred face had turned, eyeless, in his direction and mouthed one last time, "Water."

"Oh, God, have mercy," Wayne mumbled around his own thick, motionless tongue. "Water."

A rat-a-tat pounding sounded on a door next to his head. He realized he was tethered to a large brass ring on the door of what looked like a cookhouse. And a woman's voice—or a girl's?—from just inside called out softly, "Do you want water? I'll see if I can open the door. Hush. Don't make them come back."

It creaked slowly open to show him Celia.

Her face was twisted with fear in the hazy grey of the unlit courtyard. In her hands she held a wooden bucket.

She lowered the bucket to the ground as Wayne worked himself to his knees. She raised the bucket's dipper to his lips again and again until his thirst was slaked.

At last, Wayne sat back against the wall of the cookhouse and looked at Celia. "Was that you talking from inside the cookhouse?" he asked and jumped with alarm when she answered, "Yes."

"I didn't know you could talk, Miss Celia."

"I can. I don't. Not to most folks. And especially not now. But you put me in mind of somebody special I used to sneak and talk to, back at the farm." Her voice was low, her words slow, as though she had to work to choose between them.

"Don't tell anybody I talked to you," she said.

"I won't live to. They going to hang us," he explained to her. "They do it for sport."

"I don't think so."

"Why else they bring us here? They going to bring the townfolks out here to see us die."

"I don't think so, Wayne. Your name is Wayne?"

"Yes, ma'am."

"I'm not no ma'am, Wayne. I'm nobody."

"Why they doing all this, then? What you done

78

to them?"

Celia was quiet.

Wayne started to roll to his feet.

"No!" Celia reached for him and tugged him back to a seated position. "Don't go. Don't run. You'll only make them chase you down."

"Stay put and wait to be killed? Why? If you scared, untie me and run with me."

"Where? Do you know how to get out of town and back to the farms? My children are at the Newsom farm."

"I don't know nothing about getting somewhere special. All I know is how to run."

"They have dogs."

"I don't want to burn, I don't want to be cut, and I don't want to die at the end of this rope."

Celia shook her head. "Wayne, these are my attorneys. They told me they want to keep us safe."

"You believe them."

"Up to a point."

"Why they doing this?"

"I don't know."

"White men don't steal black men out of the jailhouse to do nothing but cut them, burn them and hang them. I'm running." He raised a foot from the ground and kicked with his heel at the ring anchored into the cookhouse door. "Soon as I get this ring free," Wayne mumbled between hits.

"Stop, Wayne. Listen to me." Celia laid a hand on his arm. "You hungry? They brought me bread and a bowl of milk. If I bring it to you, will you eat? And stay still and quiet? Don't make them come out here again, Wayne. Please."

79

Wayne lay flat on the ground, exhausted. "I'll eat. And you tell me why they brought us here. And if it don't make sense, I'm kicking that ring out that door and running. They ain't tied you. You can run with me. I can show you how to get away."

Celia withdrew into the cookhouse and came back with a copper basin of milk, as promised, and a large hunk of bread.

She sat on the ground to break pieces from the bread, dip them into the milk until they softened, and feed the soothing morsels into Wayne's mouth.

Wayne felt the edge of his terror blunt with the feeding of his raw hunger. When the bread was done, Celia poured the last drops of milk into his mouth and set the basin on the ground between them.

"Promise not to tell anybody I talked to you, Wayne. And please don't ever tell anybody what I say. If you promise, then I'll tell you everything," she said. "When I'm done, you still won't know anything. But maybe it will help you sleep."

When her words started, they were like a flow broken through a dam. They began, they released everything, and Celia watched in wonder as memories long lost tumbled into her mind with her own words. Fresh, brightly lit, and aching with numbed emotions reawakened, her story spun itself out through the night.

Chapter One: Rain
Missouri, April, 1850

The day Newsom came to get me, I knew something was wrong. Nobody would look at me. Not even the old woman who took care of me and was teaching me to cook.

We got up as always before the clang of the bell called the men to the field. I heard her move around in the dark of our cabin, pouring well water for me to wash. She mumbled my name like every morning. "Celia."

But that was all. No "rise and shine" or "look lively, girl." When I got up off my pallet to wash and pull on my dress over my kitchen petticoat, she wouldn't look at me.

She kept it up all the way to the kitchen, which was in the big house in winter. She kind of hunched along in her stoop-shoulder way, old and tired. The men started up singing with the strike of the stones they were chucking from a newly cleared field.

I thought I knew what was wrong. But it was too evil. I tried to put it away from me.

But still, I felt the fading start. How you start to forget things soon after you get sold and have to move on. People's faces and where buildings used to be at. Voices that woke you in the morning and sang you to sleep at night. Forget how they teased you when you made mistakes, trying to learn the skills they had to teach you.

Forget everything but the work they taught you

to do.

Already in the kitchen, the old woman looked distant from me. Like, if I didn't look at her good and close, from one minute to the next I just might disremember her face. Her voice started to sound new and strange, not like a part of my thoughts, like it had sounded all these years since I was ten.

Four years now, the old woman was my family. Everything. I never even talked to the men in the fields, ever since mistress said I was not to take them their bucket of water.

So why did I have to go? Surely, the old woman not looking at me was a sign that I was getting sold off again.

It must be the bleeding. Evil thing, a woman's blood.

And you, who've been called a girl all your life. Suddenly you show the blood for the first time, don't even know why or what happened to change you. Don't feel changed inside.

But suddenly everybody's calling you a woman, and the mistress is looking at you slant-eyed.

The old woman warned me this would happen. "Mistresses don't never have a kind thought for negresses old enough to bear."

Babies. Bearing is all about increasing the master's property. "And it starts and ends with your blood." And you don't never have no say. "Mistresses think negresses of bearing age is filthy and evil. Keep your eyes cast down and speak to them in a soft way, so they can't take no offense."

All of which I did, even before the first blood.

Because the old woman didn't never want to lose me. She said so when I first came here. She was teaching me not to be offensive to the sensibilities of a lady. I did my best.

It must have been something I did the last time I took water to the men in the field. Did I raise my eyes to look at anybody? But I never would have done such a bold thing.

I sucked in my breath. Already, I couldn't rightly recall the faces of the men in the field.

The fading.

By the time the master called me to come from the kitchen to the parlor, where Newsom was waiting, I was already looking at the old woman like a stranger.

She wouldn't look at me. She knew I knew.

Despite everything she had taught me about how to keep my eyes and my voice down, and to keep my feet clean so I wouldn't need clogs in the house and make noise and draw attention to myself. I was going.

I asked her in the minute I still remembered her name, Mama Something, "Tell me something to take with me. Teach me something to get by on, ma'am."

She shrugged. "Do as you told, Celia. Try to please them as is kind to you. Look for little things to be precious to you. Little kindnesses. Your own children, someday soon now. Love your little ones while you still got them with you. Cherish what you got. Hold on to it while you can. Remember everything pass, no matter how good or how bad. Just wait it out. Be quiet. Be grateful. Be good,

83

like I taught you. Go on, now. You keeping your new master waiting."

That's when I knew, for sure, she knew all along. That's why she wouldn't look at me that day.

But how much did she know?

My new master was waiting in the parlor with my old one. I didn't see anything but dark great coats. It was cloudy outside. Wind was moving a storm in. But too warm for snow.

I didn't have anything to take with me but the dress and apron and kitchen petticoat I wore every day. The old woman didn't have time to braid my hair up tight, so she'd bound it in her own head rag. I was still wearing that, too.

So that's what I took with me to Newsom's covered wagon.

Nobody said good-bye. They never do.

But it mattered to me. I felt like I was leaving something behind that cost me too dear. My whole life before the blood was staying behind with the old woman.

Newsom's covered wagon looked rickety in the drive, tattered and old. He made me climb inside, under the cover. He sat up front to drive.

Inside the wagon was a mattress and quilt on the floor. They were thick with dust and leaves. They smelled like they hadn't been aired in a long time.

There was a carpetbag like my old owner would have me and the old woman pack for him when he went off for days at a time. It hadn't been closed right, so I could see the mess of shaving things jammed in there so you could cut yourself trying to unpack Newsom's bag for him. Next to the carpetbag was a box with bundles wrapped in rags that I guessed was food somebody had packed for his trip. Besides those, there was a canteen and a rag on the floor. I sat on the floor and stared out the back of the wagon at the gray storm coming.

I was cold. I wished I'd wrapped up in one of the old woman's heartwarmer shawls, like when I did yard work in the fall. If I had to, I could maybe brush this quilt with the rag on the floor and wrap myself up in that. Wouldn't draw as much attention as trying to shake the quilt out the back.

And just when I had made my mind up to do this, the wagon rocked and swung to a stop by the side of the road.

The horses shied under the storm clouds. Newsom took some time to calm them.

I looked for him out the front of the wagon, craning my neck to see past the driver's bench. But he was climbing in the wagon at the back.

"Hey, gal. You looking for me?" In that little space of light at the back, Newsom looked big.

And he was older than my old master, whose face had already faded from my mind. So it was just a feeling I had. Someone I used to see but not to really tell you how he looked.

Newsom pulled off his dark rough great coat. "Lay down, girl. Let's see what I got for my money."

All of a sudden, I couldn't understand a word he said.

He said something a couple more times. He

85

stared in my face. I panicked.

I had all of a sudden forgot everything the old woman ever taught me. I stared straight back with my mouth open, like I was just about to say something.

I think I did say something. Over and over again. Newsom slapped me and said to shut it.

And when he had pushed me to lay down on the mattress, he said he'd been told I wasn't one to smart off and talk back, and he didn't ever want to hear that again.

The crackly leaves and mold-smelling dust rose up all over my face and Newsom's. I remember thinking I was glad I still had the old woman's rag on my hair, or it would stink from this.

Newsom yanked my dress skirt and my nice new kitchen petticoat right up to my stomach. He covered my face with the skirt and petticoat and put something over the cloth on my mouth. Probably his hand. I was screaming.

I screamed into the fingers.

I didn't know why. I couldn't see anything. But I had seen his eyes. Watery and red veined.

I felt his weight fall on me. I couldn't breathe between that and the cloth in my mouth. I was sure I'd choke.

Split rough fingernails scratched inside my thighs. A hand shoved one thigh up and caught it behind the knee. My knee got pressed into my chest. I gagged.

And then something hard and hot just burned its way into me, deep inside me, like I was being broke open. Shoved open. First one shove. Then another. And another.

Each one landed harder and deeper.

I was bleeding for sure now. I was torn and broke. I could feel it. I just knew Newsom had pulled out that razor from his carpetbag and cut into me to see if he could kill me, slicing up in here where nobody would see.

Hadn't I overheard once, a long time ago and a long way from here, that your owners could do anything to you but kill you?

For sure, Newsom had bought me just to kill me, all of a sudden and ugly and deep inside, this way.

The bones in my hips felt like they split apart from how heavy he was. Stuff was going to gush out of me as soon as that razor blade or whatever Newsom was ramming into me, plugging me up, was gone.

Newsom cried out in my ear.

Maybe whatever was killing me was killing him, too. But that seemed too much to hope for. He loved this pounding his razor into me so much it hurt him was all.

I wondered if I'd live through it. Why this was better to Newsom than to let me live and cook.

Now Newsom hollered in my ear so it rang. His one shoulder went straight into my throat. His head mashed into my cheekbone and scraped my skin so it burned. His hips drove mine flatter and farther apart, so I screamed too.

I lay real still.

Then Newsom pulled the skirt and petticoat down from my face. I heaved in air. Everything looked too bright and ugly.

I couldn't see past Newsom's shoulder where his shirt was bunched up and his arm was raised. His arm still pinned my leg up so the foot was stuck on the edge between the wagon and cover. I could see his hair and the flakes of skin caught in it. And the dirty, faded wagon cover stretched and curved on its old twig frame, high over us.

I thought for sure now he was dead. But then I felt how hard he breathed into my chest and stomach. I felt how his chest and stomach on mine were scratchy and hard and wet with hot sweat.

He was alive.

He lay flat and still and dropped my leg.

It hurt, coming down. All along the hip and the thigh.

All of a sudden, he pushed himself up off me and the mattress. He raised that same leg and looked at what the old woman had told me was my shameful part, and I was to keep it to myself.

And that was the clearest thing about her and the four years she took care of me that I was ever going to remember.

She faded.

Newsom said, "Virgin, all right. Nothing feels like a virgin. Let's wipe that up with this." His voice was rough like he had trouble breathing.

He took my kitchen wench's petticoat, my first ever, and it made me feel so pretty, and he wiped between my legs in big hands full. Then he pulled the petticoat off me, working it down my hips.

"I'll keep this." Newsom waved it under his nose.

Body smells. Private, like when you're sent to carry the master and mistress's laundry out back in the yard to be boiled and beat and hung to air and dry. And you turn your head away from the basket because you feel shamed at the smells.

So this was what happened to negresses who showed first blood.

Newsom balled my petticoat into a corner of his shirt. He buttoned up his breeches. He turned and jerked his head at the canteen and rag near him on the floor. "Take those and wash up. You'll be coming into a house with decent womenfolk. My daughters. Try not to make all that noise next time."

I couldn't understand a thing he said. All I could think of was death and if I could get clean of what had just happened. I got to my knees and crawled to the open back end of the wagon.

It had started to rain.

My legs burned. My bloody part was on fire. I lifted my legs careful over the edge of the wagon. I got down at the edge of the road and looked up at the falling rain.

Somewhere, men were singing in a field and an old woman pulled bread I had kneaded from an oven.

I raised it the skirt of my gown. Something warm and sticky ran down my legs. I thought it must be more blood. But it wasn't. It looked like snot and smelled private, like laundry from the master and mistress, but sharp, like what Newsom and I had just done.

I hated this smell.

The rain fell on my legs, where the stinky snot stuff ran. My legs shook. The rain couldn't wash the smell and the runny stuff off fast enough.

Newsom came up behind me. "Girl, what are you doing?" He grabbed my skirt from my hands and yanked it back down over my legs.

I doubled over and threw up on the ground.

When I had washed my mouth with Newsom's canteen and he had splashed the rest of the water on the bloody snot on my legs, he told me to get back in the wagon. He swore at me for a troublemaker. He said his youngest daughter was just my age exactly, and she was a troublemaker too.

He tried to get me to ride in the wagon by the mattress. I don't know why I couldn't. I should have been used to its stink and dust by now. But as soon as the wagon rocked and tipped and the horses clopped it back onto the road, with Newsom's voice rolling out, "Get up," I crawled on all fours to the driver's bench and eased my legs over it, so I could sit there.

Newsom turned to me, surprised. "Good girl, Celia. You go ahead and get used to me." But I only wanted to get soaked enough by the rain, even through my ruined gown, to feel clean again.

Cool hard drops pattered the rough cloth and pressed it to my thighs. Water pooled in my burning, bleeding lap.

Newsom reached behind me into the wagon to grab the quilt and pull it over me. "We've got a full day's ride ahead. You'll catch your death sitting in the rain."

Even with the quilt around my shoulders, I

90

managed to push it back and even raise the hem of my gown until the rain ran free and washed my legs and my lap clean of the ooze if not of the pain and the memory of what had happened to me.

After what seemed a long, rocky ride, Newsom drew up the wagon alongside the road and told me to crawl back inside. I didn't want to go. He took hold around my waist and shoved me.

I fell near the carpetbag and had to be careful to stay away from that razor. It felt like it wasn't just sitting in there anymore. Ever since what had happened between Newsom and me, I had the feeling the razor in the bag was watching me, thinking about coming out after me again.

I had seen people get like that after a particular bad beating. Scared of their own shadow, we used to call it. Jumpy. I eased away from the carpetbag and the dusty mattress both that stank worse than ever now, full of sweat and glop drying sticky.

Newsom crawled into the wagon after me and started pulling rag-wrapped bundles out of the food box. Passed me a couple of dry rolls and pickled hard-boiled eggs out of a clay jar. He peeled off strips of dried venison for himself. He swore when he found ants had gotten into his bundles of dried fruit.

He handed me some dried apples and told me brush them off. He cracked some walnuts for himself and ate those, instead. Then he drank from another clay jar and told me to rinse my mouth with a swig of it. It looked like water, swirling clear against the dark clay, but it stank and burned in my throat.

Then he lay down on his dirty mattress. "Come here, Celia."

I had thought that what was done was done once and over forever. It hadn't occurred to me it might happen again. When he said that, "Come here," I felt my dinner start up. The ants hadn't helped any.

I leaned out of the back of the wagon. Newsom made me stand out back in the rain and catch mouthfuls of rainwater to rinse out, this time. When he felt I ought to be done, he told me to crawl back in the wagon and strip out of my wet clothes.

I didn't like the way he watched me strip. No matter how I looked away from him, I felt his eyes running up and down me. I could feel that burning and the weight of him. Wherever I turned my head away from Newsom, I saw the mattress waiting for me or the razor looking ready to jump at me.

I kept gagging. He kept shouting at me to be done with all that and come lay down next to him. He would warm me up.

So I got on that mold-smelling mattress again. If I hadn't already been sick as I could be, I would have been sick now.

The rot. The dead leaves. The stink soaking in all this time we had been on the road.

This time I could see that what Newsom had stuck in me before wasn't his razor. It was part of him where the old woman told me not to look when I used to take water to the field and the men would turn their backs to pee.

On Newsom now, it looked like a giant tomato worm crawling out of a bunch of hair and didn't look like it could hurt anybody. He kept trying to poke it into me, with my leg up on the runner of the wagon's side again, but it didn't want to go.

I was still burning from what he had done before, but that was all that hurt. I could tell nothing he did now hurt because I watched.

He laughed. "Getting old. Should a got a young thing like you fifteen years ago after my Mary was born and her mother kept taking sick." But I couldn't help wondering again if maybe he had used that razor the first time, after all. It didn't make sense that what hurt so much before shouldn't feel like anything but fumbling and prodding now.

He fell asleep and napped off his dinner. I listened to the rain that kept falling. I was out of the wagon and waiting on the bench as the sun went down. When Newsom joined me on the bench, he grabbed up the reins, clicked to the horses, who'd been grazing on the cropped grass at the roadside, and we jerked back onto the road. "I don't take to waking up alone, gal. Don't hie off and leave me sleeping again unless you want a good hiding." The sun set on one side as his wagon made its slow way along.

Then Newsom said, "Best tell you something about your duties and the folks waiting for you at your new home." Virginia, Newsom's oldest daughter, was back home "where she should be" since Newsom's wife died, along with "her husband's" three children. It sounded odd to me that Newsom thought his married daughter and her husband's three children should be "home" with him instead of with her husband. But I wasn't invited to ask questions. This daughter, Virginia, would explain to me "all my duties."

I was afraid of Virginia. The old woman had made it very clear that slaveowning ladies looked viciously down on slaved women, especially if the master had his eye on them.

It was clear to me today that I had become the kind of slaved woman that the master had his eye on. To have Miss Virginia teaching me my duties was going to be nothing like the hot, hardworking, shared laughing days of cooking in the old woman's kitchens.

I remembered the old mistress sewing thread through the seamstress's hands to make her remember something the mistress had said, or spitting in a tureen of soup to punish the old woman for having me cook it. I dreaded Miss Virginia.

Then, Newsom said, was his son Harvey. Lazy, big old cuss who needed to finish working off some debts to his father, so he could get his own land and wed some little woman he had his eye on.

And son David. Young scrapper, seventeen. I was to have absolutely nothing to do with David. I was not to be seen so much as talking or raising my eyes to sons Harvey and David. Ever. For any reason. Miss Virginia could carry my messages to them, if indeed I had a reason to have any messages for them.

Then there was Newsom's "child." Mary. My age. Fourteen. I was to say nothing to Mary, neither. Not a word.

I pondered on how, if Mary was a "child," I must be a "child," too. And I thought of how, back

94

at some other plantation I couldn't remember, when I'd been called a "child," my workload had been gathering kindling. Slopping hogs. Fetching and carrying and no one to mind much about time spent lazing and playing in between chores. Not much to eat though.

I was still wondering what it meant for Mary, at my age, to still be a "child" and what she did all day that I wasn't to speak to her, when it came to me that Newsom was saying real sharp, "And mind. There's a handful of hands at my place. Big buck negroes, four of them. Only one of them is a little nipper. You're not to be seen anywhere near any of them, for any reason. Ever. Got that, gal?"

"Yes, sir." Then, for good measure, I repeated all the people I was to go nowhere near. Which was easy, seeing as how Miss Virginia was the only one I was to talk to besides Newsom, himself.

I must have dozed and dropped my chin just about onto my chest. The rain had let up, and Newsom must have slipped that quilt back around my shoulders. He shook me awake just as the wagon pulled off the road and headed under a copse of trees on its way to a spreading log house in the dark distance.

You could see scattered outbuildings and a fire left crackling under a cook pot outside the barn. That must be where the hands cooked their supper and maybe sat up talking until we pulled off the road. I could see some of them coming up to the wagon path, walking slow among the trees, watching us.

I lowered my eyes to my hands folded on my

lap, under the quilt. It wouldn't do to have Newsom angered with me already.

But I was itching curious to take a peek around me at the house and see where I'd be staying in some shack somewhere. Getting away from Newsom. Sitting right up under him all the time was starting to make my chest heavy, like when you've got a bad cough and somebody needs to make you a poultice before it kills you.

The men, just brown and black shapes in the woody shadows under the trees, drew alongside the wagon. Newsom called out to them. "Get on away with you, all of you, till I done left this wagon outside the house. Plenty time to get and curry these horses. Get on away from here, now. Don't make me fire off my gun."

But the "little nipper" Newsom had told me about kept coming, running right up to the wagon's side. Newsom shouted and cracked his whip at him, but high above his head. And one of the men who had already turned back now turned and shot out after the "little nipper."

He snatched the little boy up. The boy had started crying from fear of the whip and confusion about how to get away from it. The man looked up at our faces. He looked worried. And surprised to see me looking back at him and the boy. When had I ever looked into the eyes of a slaved man?

His eyes stayed with me, bright, dark, and steady, recalling something in me that wouldn't quite come.

Newsom hollered out as soon as he unlocked the door and let us into the house. It was dark except for a lamp left burning on the fireplace mantel. A woman opened a door down a hallway and stood in it watching us, a shape against soft lantern light.

Two other doors opened. A man came out of one and called out, "So, Father, we had some rain. It catch you, too?"

But the other man stayed behind in his doorway and watched. He was very young, just a tall boy. He must be that David I was not to talk to. He had his eyes dead on me.

I remembered myself and looked away.

Chapter Two: Red Ribbon Round Her Neck

Miss Virginia took the lamp from the mantel over the fireplace. "Father, I'll take the new girl to her room, now." Her voice was firm. Even cold.

Newsom said nothing to her. He just went on talking to his oldest, Master Harvey, about the drive and the money spent and an offer somebody had come to the farm and made for one of the bulls while he was out.

I followed Miss Virginia to a small room that she told me on the way used to be Master David's. But he could share for a little while with Master Harvey, who should soon wed and get out on his own again, anyway.

That is, if Newsom ever anted up for the overseeing Master Harvey had done, so he could buy him and his second bride some land to start their own farm. "The bride's all picked out." Miss Virginia's lips went thin. "But Father's not paying."

I didn't know what to say to all this chatter. I said nothing till I saw Master David's old room and caught my breath. "Oh, Miss Virginia." For the room had a fluffy mattress on a real bed, up off the floor, with a pretty quilt somebody had worked hard on. And even pillows in clean embroidered cases.

There was a little wooden table and a straight back chair. There was a pitcher and bowl on the table, like ladies get for washing.

Miss Virginia set the lamp on the table, so she could see to light the lamp that was already there. "I didn't realize, Celia, that you'd be bringing nothing of your own. I think for tonight, after you wash, I can give you one of Mary's gowns to sleep in. And I have my mind on a dress of my own I can give you that will be more suitable than the one you're wearing." She straightened and smiled. "You may save that one against a rainy day. But it won't be suitable to wear in the house."

"Miss Virginia, thank you, ma'am." How sweet and small her voice had got, now when she wasn't talking to her father.

Miss Virginia herself went to the indoor kitchen and came back with a kettle of hot and a bucket of cool water to mix in the basin for me. She carried gowns and a long torn strip of rag draped over her shoulder.

As Miss Virginia put them down, the kettle, rag, and gowns on the table and the bucket on the floor, she reached for her back. "I'm afraid, Celia, there'll be no more of that kind of fetching and carrying for me till this baby is born. Else it'll be born too soon and none strong enough."

I could see, as she stood, that she was odd-shaped about the stomach. Like some old slaveholding men get. Like all the wealth they ever made just went in and sat in their gut for the world to see.

I had never had a mistress with child, that I could recall. "Ma'am, thank you. But I could have fetched my own wash water."

She smiled. "For sure, you will, Celia, after tonight. But I thought to welcome you. For you are very welcome here, you see."

I felt tears sting my eyes. Welcome! It was like being a farmer's wife met at the door, coming to call for a tea party.

Miss Virginia stretched her back and turned away while I undressed and washed. She said we would have to wait until morning to talk about my duties, for we must both be tired. "Father likes his breakfast early."

Miss Virginia showed me how to tie the little bow strings high on the nightgown she had brought me from Mary. As she tied them, her face close to my face in the dark, her fingers busy under my chin and her eyes carefully on her hands, she said, "Don't forget, Celia. You're to speak with no one of the household but me and, of course, Father, who owns you. It goes without saying that under no circumstances are you to exchange even the least little word with any of the hands. Nor with my brothers. Particularly not Master David, who is quite young and might be unaware of all of his duty to our father. Any messages you need passed, you must tell them to me."

Miss Virginia's breath was little puffs of milk and bread dough scent in the air between our faces, sweet like a child's. "Yes, Miss Virginia."

When she had finished with the bows, she took the basin of dirty water and poured it into the bucket, careful never to look at it. Then, despite what she had said about not fetching and carrying, she took both the bucket and the kettle as she left.

I knew a little about praying. So, after I'd closed the door behind Miss Virginia, I put out the lamp she'd left behind and knelt in the middle of the floor and said a blessing on my new mistress, for her kindness. I thought to say something about Newsom. But I was afraid I had nothing to say that sounded like what one ought to share with God.

I got off my knees and into bed in my stiff, warm gown. The bed rose up around me and comforted me like a mother does a child.

And just like that, for no reason, I broke down and cried.

I woke up in the dark. I could hear a branch scratching at the outside wall of my room. Inside, I heard somebody working at the latch of my door.

I lay still and thought about Newsom's razor.

This had to be Miss Virginia at the door. It could only be Miss Virginia. Surely, I was done with Newsom's tomato worms and razors for good and forever, after all I had been through today.

The latch gave. The door opened.

Newsom in a white nightshirt drifted in.

At first, I couldn't be sure it was him. He looked so big and bulky in all that white against the soft black of the night shadows all around me.

But after he closed and latched the door and came close to the bed, I could see it was Newsom for sure.

He climbed into the bed and on top of me. I whimpered. He put a hand over my mouth. "Quiet, girl," he said, even though he was breathing louder than my crying. He started his fumbling and scratching and poking. This time, when the burning

101

came, I thought I had it figured out.

The problem was the tomato worm could turn into the razor blade with no warning.

So sometimes I'd get one. And sometimes the other. And no way to tell which or when.

Except one thing.

There was no longer any question that this was a big part of why Newsom had bought me. This worm and razor thing. And I'd be living with this as long as he lived, I guessed.

Newsom's grunts exploded in a groan and he collapsed and lay still on me, cutting short my cries. I lay there, my face wet and stinging with his sweat, blubbering.

A memory came to me. I snatched at it before it faded. Newsom looked about as old as my old master's father. And that gentleman had passed away only last year. Maybe Newsom couldn't live much longer, either.

The thought helped me sleep, even with the cramps in my legs from being caught up and bent at the knee, tangled in Newsom's nightshirt so I couldn't let them down.

When Miss Virginia allowed me questions in the morning after she explained my chores and duties, that was the first thing I asked her. How long did she expect her father to live.

She looked away.

We were in the kitchen where the sunlight came right in through the open shutters over the cutting table. The streams of light turned Miss Virginia's brown hair into maple and honey colors along the edges. Her lashes, lowered to cover her

102

eyes, paled to the color of good oak wood.

Miss Virginia was not the kind of woman that my old mistress would have called handsome. But to me, her kindness made her soft on the eyes.

I was sorry if my question hurt her. I said so.

Miss Virginia said, "Father is hale. We've none of us any reason to expect he won't outlive us all."

And then she started in on the most peculiar instructions.

All about how a good woman hopes for one man to claim her body and with it, her soul and her life.

But it can happen that another man may come along and lay claim to her body. If that happens, that woman can no longer be as good a woman as she used to be. Ever. So forget about it.

But if she would still strive to be as good as she can be, then this is what she must do.

The woman who has been unhappy enough to draw the eye of a second man must cling to this new man, if he manages to claim her. For she would dishonor the first man, to go back to him with another's man claim clinging fast to her body.

And this woman must renew her honor by her bravery and her commitment to serve the second man and think no longer ever again of that first one, even if she still loves him most dearly.

"But the most blessed kind of woman is the one who has known only one man." Miss Virginia's voice was tight like a fishing line before it breaks. Her hands shook. "And to show God how grateful she is for having been so honored as to be touched

103

by one man only in all her lifetime, this happy woman must cling to him and never have another man for the rest of her life as long as he lives."

Her eyes and her voice wavered. "A woman who passes herself from one man to another shows herself to be a wanton and a whore, undeserving of pity or protection. She will die without honor and go burn in hell forever. Which will be no more nor less than she deserves."

She stared at me, shaking. All I could think to say was, "What does all that mean, Miss Virginia?"

A new little frown cut her brow. I'd asked exactly the wrong thing. I scrambled for something better. But this wasn't like learning to pat biscuit dough or turn a cobbler. What could you say to such talk?

A whisper hissed out of Miss Virginia. "I would crawl on my knees, dragging this monster by its umbilical cord around its neck, all his babies marching beside me to remind him I was a good wife before my fall, if it would make him take me back."

Her eyes blazed like her father's.

I stared at Miss Virginia open-mouthed.

Just then Miss Mary, hostile as ever, came into the kitchen and took up a bucket of beans to snap. I turned to her like as if for help or understanding, but she was gone, flinging back over her shoulder her fear of her father's temper if all our meals were to be delayed today.

Miss Virginia looked at where Miss Mary had flounced out of the kitchen. Her eyes cleared. Her shoulders sagged. Her voice calmed like a layer of syrup spread on griddlecakes. "Celia, it's like this. What you need to understand is that, if your lot feels a little heavy to you, you are more blessed than you know." Little tears started in the corners of her eyes and swam to redden the centers. "You are fortunate to be claimed by a man who will be loyal to you and take care of you and your children. Should you ever allow another man to touch you, which is unthinkable, you will lose all that you have. You will lose your children. Which may mean nothing to you today, as you sit here, my sister's age, in this kitchen. But when you have children you will understand that their loss makes your whole life meaningless."

My stomach, uneasy since meeting Newsom the day before, cramped. Back in some lost memory, a woman screamed for a child.

I tried to make up for hurting Miss Virginia. "Ma'am, I can see what a blessing it is to your father that you came home to him after you had been claimed by your own husband. It was good of you to do it, Miss Virginia."

Miss Virginia threw her apron up over her face and clutched it there. I went down on my knees by her chair. I rubbed her back and told her how sorry and stupid I was.

A voice cut in from the doorway. "Why, sister. What kind of instruction is this? I daresay that negress won't be fit for a thing after you get done turning her against her master."

I looked up to see Master Harvey, a graying, glowering man, in the doorway. I dropped my eyes for he glared at me though he spoke to his sister.

105

Miss Virginia swiped her apron down her face. "Sit down, Celia. I'm fine. One is overcome sometimes, that's all."

I climbed back into my seat. She put on that smile. But her voice was cold as it had been last night for Newsom. "Harry, you'll learn more about women when you're married again. God willing, this new wife may even survive your early days together."

Master Harvey didn't bat an eyelash. "The Good Book teaches me all I need to know about women, Ginny."

He waited. But Miss Virginia seemed through answering back. She kept her peace. He left.

Miss Virginia had given me a really pretty apron with a little ruffle around the edge, boiled bright white. I offered the tip of it to her after Master Harvey left.

She waved it away and got up. "We can talk some more about women's duties some other time, Celia. Time to get that dinner cooking."

When we had the bread rising and the gutted rabbits roasting, I looked over at Miss Virginia from where I scrubbed potatoes across the table from her shaping a piecrust. "Miss Virginia, maybe my being here will make it so you can take your children and go back to your husband. I expect you're a good woman, like you said, and you miss him. Please plan on it and don't cry no more."

I had been about to suggest that, when she went, she might consider taking me with her. But her face crumpled and she choked. We both froze as she fought to keep tears from dripping into the

106

pie.

Cherry, it was going to be. Her father's favorite. She'd made it from cherries preserved last spring and gone a little tart. It couldn't take no extra salt. She wiped her eyes on her sleeve.

I wondered as I mashed my boiled potatoes in silence how much Miss Virginia missed her husband. Being away from him couldn't be that bad if, well. . . . Did all men do that worm and razor thing?

I doubted it. For one, I had never seen a slaved man allowed to get his hands on a razor.

I wondered if I could ever cry for Newsom like Miss Virginia cried for her husband. I doubted that too. Even if he had a razor, Miss Virginia's husband had probably never used it on her. But even giving him that, her talk made little sense.

First off, if you had to cling to the man who claimed you, what was Miss Virginia doing here at her father's house? When had Newsom said his wife died? Going on a year, now?

None of what Miss Virginia said stood to reason, if you looked at it with a level head.

Must be that Miss Mary's fault.

Lazy and unpleasant "child," as they styled her. If she would take over and be mistress, Miss Virginia could go on back to her husband, where she and her children belonged.

Odd how I liked Miss Virginia, who I had kind of feared when Newsom described her, and had no use for Miss Mary, though I had looked forward to meeting her.

And that Master David. Turned out I was to

107

spend a lot of time fleeing Master David around that house.

The duties Miss Virginia laid out for me were nothing, really. Learn to look after my own and Master Newsom's clothes and clean our rooms and help out a little in the kitchen.

But don't go for no water nor take any washing to hang outside, unless I could see clear all the hands was off in the fields and wouldn't nobody bother me. And be on hand in the kitchen to help with cooking. Except breakfast.

I was that let down Miss Virginia didn't want me around to help with breakfast. Cooking breakfast would have got me away from Newsom a solid hour earlier every morning.

I offered myself to come in and start the bread rising. But she wouldn't hear of it. Wouldn't look at me either, as she turned me down. Almost like she knew what I was trying to get away from.

If she knew, she was also clear on what was my first duty around that house. It didn't take me long to figure out that any and every chore I had as cook or washerwoman could wait on Newsom and what he wanted from me.

Sometimes, shoved off to my room in the middle of the day because the notion took him, I wondered if the whole household knew that this was what went on between us. And if everybody but me had known from the day I got here why Newsom bought me.

I took to planning my daily chores so I could be harder to find when Newsom came early from the fields for dinner.

I would take my washing, once dinner was cooking good, out back to boil and pound. I was out too long one day, I guess. Because Master David came in from the fields and asked me to get him some wash water so he could scrub for the table. I went for it without thinking.

My first few days at Newsom's farm, I had been very careful of Master David. Of all the people not supposed to talk with me, he tried the hardest. I had to be on the listen and lookout for him and make my getaway as soon as I espied him.

He always had a smile for me, though, and even left me little treats on the table in my room. The first bright wildflowers of the season, brought fresh from the woods and floating in water in my washbasin. A ribbon I wished I could put in my hair. A whittled doll with a smile cut into its face as pretty as you please. You could even see the ruffle around its little apron. Must have taken Master David great care to carve that ruffle.

I expected Master David wasn't supposed to leave me treats.

So I tried to hide them just enough so that when Newsom woke in my room with the morning's light shooting in between the shutters, he wouldn't see my little gifts.

It worked with the ribbon and the doll, which I tied together and hid in my apron pocket, and with the flowers till I spread them across the hearth to dry. When Newsom asked where I got them from, I lied and said I had gathered them while hanging my wash. He growled something and kicked the drying flowers into the banked embers on his way out of my room.

I promised myself to be more careful. And I was.

But then anyhow one day after supper I heard shouts. Newsom demanded to know what Master David had been doing in "Celia's room." He had heard it from Miss Virginia's oldest son, Coffee.

The family disappeared from around the table except for Master Harvey, who took off running down the hall and stood behind David, like to hold him. He didn't touch his younger brother, but he blocked the way and forced David to turn back and face their father or get caned on the back.

Master David said, "Seeing as how it used to be my room, Father, every now and again I go into it when Celia ain't there, just to be on my own. I don't have nowhere else to go."

I stood in the hall, watching. Master Harvey, behind Master David, moved his eyes to glare at me. "Come now, Father. You know what a sulky brat David's been since his mother's death. He likes to be alone to brood. But he means no harm by it."

I looked away and put my hand in my apron pocket, around the doll with her pretty red ribbon round her neck. I held her and went away into the kitchen like to hide.

I was looking for walnuts or peas to shell or corn to shuck against the morrow or milk to churn the butter from or anything I could do to get busy and get my mind off the men in the hallway outside my room.

But soon Master Harvey followed me into the

kitchen, like he was keeping watch on me. He didn't move until Newsom came and stood in front of me where I sat, working. And then Master Harvey came and stood close behind his father.

Newsom said, "Celia. You wish to tell me why you're letting my boy David in your room?"

I looked up. "Sir, I don't tell nobody round here what to do and not do."

Newsom grunted. I felt embarrassed for him to make that sound right out in the kitchen in front of Master Harvey.

But Master Harvey just stood still.

Newsom said, "Celia. It's like this. You better make it your business for nobody to go near your room but me and Miss Virginia. You understand me, girl?"

I lowered my eyes again. "Yes, sir, Master Newsom." Now, just what did he think I could do if anybody did go near my room? Me, who couldn't even talk to anybody to tell them to get away?

I sat and worked and fumed. Newsom not only made me sick with his fumbling and scratching and his worm and his razor. He was stupid, too. He didn't even think but what he wanted. Not what you had to go through to do it for him.

But just because he didn't think was what made him so dangerous.

The very next time Master David tried to sneak into my room, Master Harvey caught him at it and dragged him away, to the parlor. Master David struck out, struggling to get away from his brother, and Master Harvey balled up his fists and struck him back. Miss Mary had come running and now set in to screaming. The noise brought Newsom, and this time Newsom beat Master David with his walking cane.

Across his back. Right in the family parlor, where everybody was arguing and shouting and overturning their few good crystal and china pieces.

Newsom and Master Harvey left Master David there, when they were finished with him. They came and found me in the kitchen where I'd run to hide under the cutting table, which didn't make any sense and just went to show how scared I was.

Master Harvey dragged me out. Newsom promised to cane me, too.

Miss Virginia came in the doorway, holding her back in one hand and a bloody dry rag in the other. Miss Mary must have called her to tend to Master David's welts. She looked on her father. "If you and your son cane that girl, it won't be me who buries her baby, if she loses it. I can't bear to. You and Harvey will have to do it." She pushed herself away from the doorway, shaking her head and mumbling.

"Celia, what's this I hear? Why the devil didn't you tell me you was knocked up?" Newsom sounded proud. "Damn, girl. Harvey, drop that chit and let's get on back to the fields. No telling what them hands is got up to, all this ruckus going on."

They left me alone, crying at the news that I was going to have a baby. It couldn't be true. Maybe Miss Virginia had lied to get Newsom not to cane me.

But then I thought back on Miss Virginia watching my washing and asking about my monthly rags. She didn't even say anything when I told her it seemed I'd gotten too sick to bleed and wasn't that a joy.

I'd never stopped being sick from the first minute Newsom laid hands on me. So I just naturally figured that, with all that sickness, you soon can't eat and then your body can't bleed for babies nor do much of anything else.

But I must have been wrong.

When I crawled up off the kitchen floor and went to find Miss Virginia in the parlor, I asked why she hadn't told me I was having a baby.

Master David jumped under her hands, like the salt water must have stung him. Miss Virginia pressed his cheek with a damp hand, to keep him from turning to look up at me. She said, "Because, Celia, until the time of sickness passes, you might not greet the news with fitting joy. Besides, many babies are lost at such an early time. No point getting your hopes up for nothing."

Master David bowed his head and didn't move now. She patted his pale, red-striped back dry. She said, "But now that you know, you might as well try to be careful and work light and easy. And remember that babies give their mothers new life, as much as their mothers give it to them."

"Virginia," Master David started but she cut him off.

"Your life starts new each day, Celia, when you see it through the eyes of your babies. How much they need you. How happy they are for every little thing you do for them."

Her brother tried again, his voice more soft, his

113

head still down. "Ginny. Please."

Miss Virginia wouldn't let up. "Every sorrow you thought you had disappears in caring for your babies."

Then why did she cry all the time, I wondered.

She said, "Besides. The birth of your baby means your man has to leave you alone for a little while afterward. Every doctor and midwife will tell you so."

David turned sharp to her, and now she smiled at him. He turned full and she let him look up at me. But I turned away, excused myself, and went back to my kitchen work.

But now my baby became precious to me, after all. At first, for the time free of Newsom that the baby's birth would get me. But, after a while, also for the new life it was supposed to bring me. Like my wood doll from Master David, I thought. Maybe even better.

I could use a new life.

So when Master David came up behind me outside one day hanging my laundry, so close I could feel his hot sweaty chest and belly right through the rough cloth on my back, hidden between the damp cool clothes, and asked me again to get him some wash water, I just went in the kitchen and passed his message on to Miss Virginia, like I was supposed to.

And then I sat and finished churning the butter that lazy Miss Mary must have left. I was going to stay there until Miss Virginia told me to serve the table for her. My heart pounded, and I wasn't going near Master David, if I could help it.

So Miss Virginia herself went for a bucket for Master David to fetch himself some well water to wash in. But then she thought better of the time it would take him, leaving Newsom to wait and fret for his supper. Instead, she scooped some of the kitchen water into the bucket.

Only, when she went to lift it, she doubled over and dropped to her knees, crying out and clutching at herself between her legs.

Dark water gushed from under the skirt of her gown and spread around her on the floor.

I ran to her and pushed her to lay down. I dipped my hands in the bucket of water she had tried to lift and patted cool drops of it on her forehead. I called to her, "Miss Virginia, Miss Virginia, everything's going to be all right, ma'am."

She started screaming. I hollered out for Miss Mary and the men.

Miss Virginia's oldest boy, James Coffee, made it to the kitchen first. He was only about seven, and when he saw his mother, his eyes bugged and he froze.

I could talk to him because sometimes he ran errands and messages between his mother and me. And nobody had thought to tell me not to talk to him. So I said now, "Master Coffee, go get your grandfather or your uncles or somebody quick. Miss Virginia needs help and I don't know what to do."

Coffee ran.

He must have run around in circles outside the house, shouting the news. Because, the next thing I knew, Master David came in from the back through the kitchen door and Master Harvey and Newsom bumped into each other, coming in through the doorway to the dining room.

Finally, with her head in my lap and the dark hot spilling liquid staining both our skirts, they got Miss Virginia to say that her baby was coming.

So Master Harvey said he would go for the doctor. And Newsom told his son was he a fool.

Newsom said Master Harvey would do no such a thing. Did he want people to talk and ruin the family's name?

Master Harvey started in out of nowhere talking about somebody name of Lot who had daughters. So I asked, looking at Newsom, if one of this Master Lot's daughters couldn't come help Miss Virginia have her baby.

Master Harvey said she already had. He laughed.

Newsom shouted at him to shut it up. Then Newsom looked at me like he just had a thought. "Since you having a baby someday soon, Celia, you might as well learn here and now what it's all about. You can tend Miss Virginia's lying in."

Harvey made a choked sound. Newsom turned on him. "If the baby lives, the doctor can come then and check it over. Hell if I'll have him in here now, pestering Virginia with a lot of damn fool questions. It's a crying shame to chance the birth this a way, I'll grant that. But damn it, Harry, ain't a woman alive can keep her mouth shut when it counts."

Chapter Three: Strange and Blessed Night

Master David and Master Harvey went and fetched hay from the barn to make Miss Virginia comfortable on the kitchen floor. Newsom nailed up a quilt at the dining room doorway and another over the back door, so the hay the men gathered could be slid in under the quilt without anybody seeing Miss Virginia.

With her head on my lap, I was steady trying to get her shed of those tight buttoned clothes.

Her dress bodice was hiked up high these days over her big belly that had dropped till it poked way out at you like a prized watermelon strapped to her tummy. But riding up that bodice was all she had done, really, to make room for the baby growing in her belly, as she told it to me.

And now it seemed that, with the tight bodice and the hard work and the heavy breathing that had set on her all at once, Miss Virginia was turning dark red and pale pasty and panting like a dying dog.

I thought, with all that running blood, both our gowns were ruined anyway. And it would never do for the mistress to appear with baby birth stains on her clothes.

The dress was a goner.

So I reached up behind me on the cutting table, felt for a knife, and sliced the gown open from the collar to the rise of Miss Virginia's straining belly.

And then I thought, Newsom ain't yelled and Miss Virginia hasn't said a word, either.

So then I slit the gown to the hem, so it could fall away from her and I could finally see what I was supposed to learn to help her with.

Her knees were up and apart, and I didn't see anything but how her belly would rise to a sharp point, like the baby meant to get pushed out through the top.

And when it rose and pointed like that, Miss Virginia would cry out.

Then she'd hold her breath and turn colors. Her hands would clutch at the straw her father was shoving under her at every side.

And finally she'd bust and wail or scream again.

And her belly would go softer and lay a little flatter and lower under her ribs.

It was hot in the kitchen from cooking the dinner. The fire in the fireplace wasn't even banked. I couldn't think, though, how to ask Newsom to take care of it.

I couldn't bear to look at him.

I felt like something awful was happening to Miss Virginia. And even if nobody ever explained to me how it was his fault, still, I knew it was all Newsom's fault.

I kept dipping my fingers in the bucket of water that had started all this present trouble and dribbling cooling drops on Miss Virginia's forehead and lips. When she wasn't crying out or holding her breath, she licked at the drops and even once asked for more. So I knew it was helping.

Only, I didn't know how else to help.

As soon as Newsom got the quilts nailed up and the straw under Miss Virginia, he said he'd go watch her children and free Miss Mary up to serve whatever was prepared for dinner. Then he stood at Miss Virginia's feet and stared at where she had told me I'd have to help her baby come out.

Miss Virginia had started passing out now and again when her belly did that pointy mountain thing. So she didn't seem to see her father down there, just staring.

But I got to where I couldn't take it real fast.

So I flipped the cut sides of her gown together over her belly and legs and that wet patch of hair that had Newsom's eyes bugging out.

When I saw him start out of the corner of my eye, like he might be going to correct me or something, I said, "Sir, I'm guessing you don't want Miss Mary 'the child' to see so much of her sister's state."

And he left, flinging aside the dining room doorway quilt so bad until you could hear it rip a little on the nail.

There wouldn't have been no reason to hide a thing from Miss Mary.

When she came in, red-faced from crying, she worked so hard not to see her sister in the straw on the floor, turning her face as she stepped over and around Miss Virginia, that you would have thought it was a brood sow giving birth down there.

Miss Virginia kept her eyes closed, though, whenever Miss Mary was in the kitchen gathering together the dishes we'd finished.

Miss Virginia only opened her eyes once to tell Miss Mary that if the dinner table looked spare, she might put out some cheese and maybe some pickled and preserved goods to fatten it up. But none of the pickled meats, please.

Miss Mary went for the larder without a word.

And when the next pointy squeeze came to her belly, Miss Virginia bit down on her screams and held her breath without crying out till the tears ran down her nose and the sweat trickled right into her hair.

I took to patting at her forehead and face now with my apron and blowing a little from her face down to her belly to cool her off.

After a while, I heard grace being said in the dining room. Newsom told Miss Virginia's children to remember to pray that their mother and the new baby would be safely delivered from their trial before the night fell. And God, please make it a boy.

Because it was so costly and it did no good, anyway, to marry off your girls. Seeing how Eve had set them off on the wrong foot for all time.

And somebody, sounded like Master Harvey, laughed after everybody said their amen.

After dinner, Mary brought in the dishes. Still without looking down at her sister.

She washed them with her back turned to Miss Virginia. Finally, without turning, Miss Mary said over her back to her sister, "Sister, if you don't think you can help with supper, I'd like to just make some quick bread and serve it with buttermilk. It's easy and it helps the children get to sleep."

120

I said, "Miss Virginia's nodding her head yes, Miss Mary."

And so Miss Mary was gone again.

The day dragged through hay dust and sweat and the heavy grunting of a tired woman.

After a while, it occurred to me that I might close that back door, take down the quilt and put it under Miss Virginia.

I had to ease myself out from under her. It was a chore. My legs had both fallen asleep and prickled with needles as I crawled backwards.

When I finally stood, my knees gave out from under me. I caught the edge of the cutting table in both hands, and that's what kept me from falling. I dropped into a chair and waited, rubbing my legs till the needles made me weep.

But then they got so I could straighten them and stand.

And once the quilt was under Miss Virginia, she was so pleased that I was glad I had gone to all the trouble.

She was laying on her side and opened her eyes to say, "Celia, maybe we'd best get ready for the baby. Let's have some hot water to wash the knife you'll use to cut the cord. And you can boil up a little twine in that water, too. Just dip it so it won't fall apart on us. And a basin to catch the afterbirth. We'd better have that ready. I feel so much better on this quilt. Almost like being in my own bed back with—"

She cut herself off. But I thought she was thinking of the three babies she gave birth to back in her husband's home.

Was this his baby? Was anybody on their way to let him know he had a fourth child coming into the world?

When Newsom came into the kitchen again late that evening, I asked.

I was down at the end where Miss Virginia said the baby would come out. The little slit of her private part had stretched till you could have slipped a lemon in there, if it hadn't been for the bulge of baby head coming out at you.

Miss Virginia had nothing left in her to help her push, so every time her tummy knotted up hard to push the baby forward, I had to press my hands against the skin and hair that was blocking his way out, trying to spread them back and out of the baby's way.

She was tearing a little, down between her private and her bottom. And I was thinking that if this was what was ahead for me and the new life I was carrying, I wanted no part of it.

Was there no other way?

I had a damp rag pressed to Miss Virginia's tearing, bloody bottom when Newsom came in to check how his daughter was doing.

"Sir," I said, "has someone been sent to tell Miss Virginia's husband?"

He was a little behind me and to one side. But I could swear Newsom jumped like I'd thrown a ball of fire at him.

"Her husband?" he bellowed at me. "Why should anybody do a dag-blame fool thing like that?"

I looked around up at him. "Sir," I said. "The

baby. Shouldn't he be told?"

Then something passed Newsom's face that I didn't like at all. And he said, "Mind your own business, chit. And I'd better not hear of you mentioning that baby to anybody for any reason. You're here to help, not to spread gossip and hurt people's reputation."

And then he was gone again.

I could have sworn Miss Virginia was asleep, she kept her eyes lowered so they were almost shut.

But when Newsom left this time, Miss Virginia said with more force than she was putting in her pushing, "Celia, don't ever mention my husband to <u>him</u> again."

This was the first time I ever wondered if, just possibly, Miss Virginia hated her father near on as much as I did.

We went on alone, Miss Virginia pushing and me spreading the tight pale private skin and pushing it back along the baby's head.

Every now and again, Miss Virginia would let me leave her to go fetch her chamber pot and prop her up on it, or empty it with water into the latrine, or bring her a little sip of her father's stinking, burning whiskey for the pain.

But mostly she wanted me to fan her or blow on her skin and her face and dribble that water on her lips, between pushes. Since nobody was offering me leftovers from dinner, or anything else, for that matter, I took to cupping Miss Virginia's water into my own mouth, as well.

The screams had stopped. But the grunts came more often.

We sat in the cool dark as night fell outside.

After another while, Miss Mary came in, still red-eyed and stiff-faced, to make up some pan bread and scoop up some buttermilk. She carried this over to the dining room quilt, still hanging.

I saw pale hands reach in to take the food from Miss Mary and carry it to the table. And I heard Master David's voice say, "Celia, how is she?"

Now here was a dilemma.

Miss Virginia could hardly answer Master David for me. And Miss Mary, when I asked her to tell their brother that Miss Virginia was getting along like a brave lady, didn't say a word. Neither to him nor to me.

So I called out myself, "She's fighting the good fight, Master David."

And no sooner were the words clear of my mouth than I heard Newsom's bellow. "Boy, what have I told you? You are one hardhead young buck, ain't you?"

And I heard that cane slicing the air.

Miss Mary put down the plates and bowls she'd washed after dinner and had been gathering for supper. She went and sat in a straight back chair and put her head in her lap and threw her apron over her head.

And she didn't move again until the sound of the caning stopped.

Then Miss Mary got up slow and gathered up her dishes and cutlery and made her way out of the kitchen, still stepping around her sister without looking at her.

The whole time, Miss Virginia had been

124

squeezing at my hands till I heard the little bones inside pop and felt them slide over each other. I guessed she didn't want to scream with the belly squeezes and draw her father's attention. I thought I might have to scream for her, if she didn't let loose of my hands.

But the caning stopped, and so did the big squeeze that had arched Miss Virginia's back and shot her belly up like a mountain into the air.

The mountain slid flatter and she sagged into the quilt and the straw.

And it struck me she had passed clean out.

Next time the squeezes came, Miss Virginia didn't do a solitary thing to help them.

While I listened to the family at the table saying grace and then trying to keep up their spirits with a little laughter as they supped, I set to work to get a grip on that baby and pull it out of its mother.

I didn't know if you should do this or not. I didn't know anything.

But the only person who might have told me anything was beyond talking to me now. Miss Virginia was passed out so cold until I couldn't even slap her awake with water or threats that her baby would suffocate if she didn't help it out by pushing.

I pushed up her knees and let them flop open.

I spread away all the bits of her gown and put down a big clean rag to catch whatever I dragged out of her body, at last.

And I started pressing apart and stretching and pulling on that private skin till it was a hairy cap that I could slide right down to her baby's ears. I

125

didn't wait for belly squeezes any more. They hadn't done any good for a while now.

That ugly tear between her private and her butt hadn't but gotten uglier. I figured, if her husband ever saw it, he would want to have me horsewhipped.

But I hoped Miss Virginia would take up for me, since it was her life I was trying to save by dragging this baby out as best I could without her help.

When the hairy cap slid down to rest on her baby's ears, I fell back, sweating, on the straw to think of what I might reach in and grab to get myself a good handle for pulling.

I didn't know if the baby could be alive, going through all this. Somehow, I doubted it.

But I tried to think if I'd ever seen a baby, and where you find places on them that you might not break off by hauling on them hard.

I figured I didn't know enough to think ahead that way. I'd just have to reach in and feel.

I wet my fingers with my own warm spit and slipped them in between Miss Virginia and her baby's head.

Ears, just like I thought. Which made me feel better, since I'd figured out something right.

Then a tiny little face, smashed flat. Tiny hot mouth felt like it slipped a little open as one of my fingers brushed by.

The head was glued to a thin short neck. No, I could never grab hold of the head to pull, though it felt big and firm. If the baby was alive and screamed when I snapped its neck, I'd have the devil after me.

I couldn't reach in further. So I eased my hands out, inching that tight private skin and meat down past the baby's ears now.

And as the dark swooped and I thought I should have asked for a lamp to be lit, how foolish of me, and the last sunlight fell away from the part-opened shutters where a breeze from the woods was to be let in to stir around in the hot, frightened air of the kitchen, the baby's head came free of Miss Virginia all the way down to its chin.

I knelt and stared down at it.

It stared back up at me, still, through tight squinted eyelids.

I reached down, afraid now of this real person, strange and still, and slipped my fingers inside Miss Virginia.

Behind the head, still trapped, was a real little body. And there, not inches from the head, were armpits. I slipped my fingers under the arms and pulled.

First there was nothing.

And then the laziest little tummy squeeze happened. And the strange sunset-colored baby made a squishing sound in my hands, like sometimes between me and Newsom in the dark.

And it slid right out against me.

It was a strange color and not breathing nor moving. It flopped in my hands and was warm and slick and covered with slimy stuff. It wasn't all the way out of its mother. Because even though I could see its feet, some long thick cord with a beating heart making it leap with blue and red colors was

127

still reaching out of the mother, like to take the baby back.

So I went for a cutting knife and splashed it with the water I had simmering in the kettle.

A little splashed me and I cried out from the burn.

And the little sunset-colored live thing I'd left between Miss Virginia's spread knees jumped at the sound of my cry.

And then it went like to stick its thumb in its mouth. Only the thumb didn't quite get all the way there.

And it lay still again, curled up and not breathing.

I took the knife and crawled on my knees to where the live--maybe--thing that was a baby lay still. I reached with my knife for the heartbeating thing that tied the baby to its mother's insides, thinking to cut it and save one of them if not the other.

But I looked down and saw how my hands were shaking.

So I sat back and put down the knife and picked up the baby to hold it and cry if I had killed it somehow.

And with the tug on the heartbeating cord, all of a sudden a giant wad of Miss Virginia's insides just slid right out of her.

Even in the dark, I could see it.

I had killed her.

Now I had to try to save the baby.

Blood was flowing everywhere. No need being careful. With the baby held on my shoulder by one hand, I took the knife and sawed at the heartbeating thing, which I now knew was nothing but her tripes, until it finally broke and fell away from the baby.

And still, the baby didn't breathe.

I threw down the knife and raised the baby over my head with both hands. I whispered to it, "Live, baby. They're going to kill me because I've killed your mother. Now, live, you. I did everything I could. I'm so scared."

As I held it and hissed at it, its oversize head flopped on its tiny neck. First down to the tiny chest. Then back. Its eyes stayed swollen shut.

Then I had an idea. I remembered how, when I stuck my hands in Miss Virginia to try to pull the baby out, it had opened its mouth to suck at one of my fingers. After all that birthing, it should still be hungry. Hungrier.

I stuck my finger between its lips and tried to wiggle a way in.

The baby's head moved a little away from me on its tiny neck. Its lips stayed pursed pretty tight. In fact, it was fast fading from sunset colors to gloaming ones.

Getting to night like when you sleep.

And that couldn't be an all right color for Miss Virginia's child.

I got more and more frightened. I thought of tossing the dead baby and the lump from inside Miss Virginia into the bucket that had started this deadly birthing and dumping it all into the latrine.

Then I could run to the creek in the woods before anyone found Miss Virginia's body, the creek where Newsom had taken me walking to show me the spring blossoming.

And I could drown myself. Maybe that was easier than being hanged. Negresses who killed their masters and mistresses, even by accident, everybody knew, would sooner or later get hanged. By the lynch posse or the court. It was all the same thing.

I lowered the little broke neck baby into my arms and put my head on its tiny chest to cry.

Under my sweating forehead, with my fingers on its back and chest, I felt little soft ribs stretched under my hands. The tiny half circles of its ribs got bigger, then wider apart and bigger, yet.

I raised my head to look at the baby's blood swollen face.

Its little lips were puckering, opening in a circle like it wanted that finger back to suck on. And then it squinted up its face into a bunch of thick wrinkles and spread its tiny toothless gums and yelled at me.

It sounded like a baby cat meowing.

It sounded so good.

And just like that, the baby was turning in the gathering darkness from twilight color to blazing sunset again, and then all the way to hopeful colors like early dawn, right at morning. I could see where my hands on it were dark like shadows. And its little chest was working like a bellows at the fire.

Suddenly, I heard chairs scraping and men hollering out and footsteps running.

I just had time to slap the baby to my chest and toss the cut gown over Miss Virginia's ripped body before the men tumbled into the kitchen through the quilt. I didn't have time to do anything with what, by now, I had figured out to be Miss Virginia's heart which I had pulled right out of her chest by her one gut.

This is what came of stupid young girls being sent to birth babies, I thought to myself. I should have cried to have one of that Master Lot's daughters.

But now the men were into the kitchen, swarming around us in the dark, stumbling and barking their shins on tables and chairs, calling out for lit lamps and firelight.

Even my eyes, getting used to the dark of the room as I waited and watched in it without light, could no longer see anything that wasn't right in front of my face. The flash of red light from the dining room as the quilt swung from the doorway three times, letting in Newsom and Masters Harvey and David, had blinded me. So I was the last to blink and see what the men were staring at, once Master David got Miss Mary to bring a lamp.

They were staring first at the baby, asking me was it a boy. I looked. It had the little worm thing like Newsom. But not so big. And not hairy. Kind of cute.

I said, "Is it a boy?"

And Master Harvey looked at his father and said, "She still can't tell?" and laughed.

And then Master David betrayed me by pointing at the floor where the heart globby thing lay on the edge of the quilt and the straw at Miss Virginia's still feet, and he said, "What the devil is that?"

Here it was.

I would be taken out and strung up right here and right now.

But Newsom laughed. He reached toward me, still laughing like a demon, and said, "Give me my boy, Celia."

I handed him up the baby. He patted it on his shoulder, bumping it up and down and listening to it hiccup and mewl. And he said, "That there thing, son, is the devil that comes out of women when they birth these babies. Dangedest thing I ever seen. Like to scared me to death, boys, the first time I seen one of these things sitting in a pan, after your mother spat Harvey out." Newsom chuckled and said, "This here boy I'll call Buddy after a good friend of mine never made it here from the old country. Virginia. Good friend of mine, was Buddy."

Then he looked at me, smiling almost kindly, and said, "Celia, see how well you can get that poor woman washed up and maybe slide a fresh nightgown onto her. The boys'll carry her into her bed when you're done. You done right well here tonight, girl."

He touched my cheek and was gone through the quilt with baby Buddy. Master Harvey followed after him, asking him to let me wash the baby and wrap it in diapers and bunting.

Master David had stayed behind. He'd knelt to put his ear over Miss Virginia's face. He looked up at me when his father was gone. "She's barely breathing," he said. "I don't know. But I got the feeling you might have saved somebody's life tonight, Celia. Either that, or you almost killed mother and baby both by running away from me. See what happens when you run from me?"

I got up to take a bucket for fresh well water.

Master David came up behind me and took the bucket from my hand.

Behind my back, close on my neck, he said, "Never mind, Celia. I won't tease. Just one thing. You still got that doll I carved for you?"

Still not saying anything, because we both knew I wasn't supposed to talk to him, I reached into my pocket and pulled out the doll with the red ribbon. Master David lifted up my hand to see her better.

He had that low chuckle, like his father. "I knew you were nothing but a child, like my sister Mary. You don't have to talk to me. Just keep what I give you, Celia, and I'll know how much it means to you."

And he was out of the door to the well.

I had plopped the heartbeat thing into a basin, waiting for Miss Virginia to tell me what to do with it, and started shoving armfuls of bloody straw into the fireplace, by the time Master David got back with the bucket of water.

He put it down near Miss Virginia and left without another word.

I was glad. I washed her gently, stripping down sweating parts and picking stuck fabric off bloody parts, until I got her as clean as I could on the straw and old blood from the birthing.

And then I went to find Newsom to ask him to get Miss Mary to get her sister a gown to sleep in.

And as Miss Virginia was still bleeding

133

between the legs, I tied clean rags there as tight as I could before I dressed her.

When the men lifted her, everything stayed where it should and no blood dripped. Newsom told his sons to put her in his bed, with her baby Buddy swaddled in sloppy diaper rags by Mary. Newsom said Miss Virginia's children, who slept in her bed, shouldn't disturb her during this first night after the birthing.

I was up hours cleaning that kitchen till my back ached, every step I took. I left the quilts in a corner, though, to wash the next morning. The whole time I worked, I thought back to Master David and how particular he was that I should like that doll he carved me.

I did like it. I had seen a bigger, softer one, looked like it had a real face on it too, sitting propped up on Miss Mary's bed when her door was open. Miss Mary's doll was full of ribbons and bows and ruffles made of fabric finer than even Miss Virginia got to wear. I knew I couldn't have a doll like that.

But my doll that Master David made for me was almost like that. Most especially with her pretty red ribbon.

I worried a little, though, what Master David would do or say to me if he thought I lost his doll or burned it, to hide it from Newsom. After all, even if I didn't talk to him, by now we had seen how his father didn't really want him following after me, either.

It was hard to tell what to do when Newsom wasn't around to make himself clear, I thought.

Because it seemed like everybody wanted something that wasn't quite what Newsom had said for me to do.

Look how many times I'd left Miss Virginia alone during the birthing. Even if she did tell me to leave her, what was Newsom going to say, if he found out, about me doing what Miss Virginia said instead of what he said?

Lucky for me she didn't haul off and die while I was up pouring her shots of that whiskey. That's all I could say.

Strange and blessed night. Because when I fell into my bed, Newsom wasn't there.

Chapter Four: Along the Shattered Surface

The next morning, I was out of my bed late.

Miss Mary had been a little relieved of seeing after Newsom, just enough to see after Miss Virginia's children and the breakfast alone. I woke because she was calling out to me from the kitchen to come clean and wash up and prepare the dinner. Even though Miss Mary was my same age, she couldn't do any really big cooking by herself.

And once I was up and dressed and looked in on Miss Virginia, I found out that Miss Mary wasn't going to change her sister's bleeding rags nor the baby's diapers, either. Miss Mary had helped her sister that morning to move out of Newsom's room and back into the room and bed she shared with her other children. But that was all Miss Mary did for her, besides bring her a cup of tea and a buttered biscuit.

As much as she didn't like having to look after her father's clothes and room, Miss Mary was in a hurry, this morning, to get back to those very chores. And Miss Mary wanted everything dry and dusty as usual. None of this stuff gushing out of the body, like Miss Virginia and her baby were both apt to do.

So I smiled at Miss Virginia while I brought a basin of warm water from the kitchen fireplace to wash first the baby and then her. She was bleeding something terrible. Bloody, smelly pee all in her chamber pot for me to take out and pour in the latrine. Truth be told, I was a little afraid Miss Virginia was still dying.

But the baby was strapping and fine and hungry as a pack of wild dogs for his mother's milk. Miss Virginia said her nipples were sore from the nursing and could I bring her buttermilk to rub into them. So I left a pitcher of it, with a cup, on the table by her bed. That way, she could drink it or rub it on, whichever she wished.

And then I got bread rising and bean and beef stew simmering so I could leave the dinner and see to washing those quilts.

Once, when Miss Virginia had seen the state of my bleeding rags, she had told me that fresh blood was best washed out with cool running water, not boiled and beaten out of clothes in a pot, like sweat and dirt. So this morning, I slung the birthing quilts over my shoulders to head to the creek out behind the house, down past the walnut and cherry tree groves.

It was nice out.

The air was a touch crisp and stung inside when you took a deep breath. Leaves were all colors and waved on every side, even the pine needles. Looking out towards the fields, which I only did in little snatches for fear of catching anybody's eye, you could see all the sunny colors of Newsom's crops just growing for him.

I got to the little dip of a hill where the creek ran, clogged with falling bright leaves, and made my way careful out onto the slippery stones.

The water was chilly and made my feet and

137

legs tingle.

I had my skirts hiked up and tucked into my apron at my waist. That way, I could get the quilts all the way into the stream and let them soak good.

And while they soaked, I listened to the calls of birds that hadn't left for fear of the gathering cold, and the chattering of squirrels that had got into a quarrel over nuts and berries to steal and store.

So I wasn't paying any attention.

I didn't hear the steps behind me.

But all of a sudden, a man's voice said, "Now, Celia. How was you planning to get them quilts back to the line at the house? Soaked like that, they got to be about as heavy as you."

I stood and turned to see who was talking to me. I was in a panic because I could tell, even with my back to the path from the house, that this wasn't Newsom nor his sons. And whoever it was, though he sounded friendly, he didn't sound none too sure that he should be talking to me.

It was one thing to have to stand still and listen when Newsom's children talked to me when they shouldn't. Miss Mary, Master David, and even Master Harvey. At least, Miss Mary and Master Harvey didn't want nothing but to tell me what to do, and I couldn't answer them back anyway. Because they had the right, as far as I could understand, to tell me what to do up to a point. As long as it wasn't too far from what their father wanted of me.

But somebody else?

By now I was facing who had spoke to me, and this was trouble for sure.

138

One of the negro hands.

I had seen them now and then. Outside the kitchen window when the shutters were thrown wide for air and light. Or when I was outside the kitchen door boiling my wash or on the way to the latrine, emptying my chamber pot.

Maybe they'd be going to fetch the slop pail for the pigs that Miss Virginia left outside the kitchen door, or fetching and carrying to and from the fields for Newsom's sons. Or even loading stores into the barn, or herding up stock that had strayed. I had seen them around.

Four men and a little boy.

But they didn't speak to me. And if our eyes almost met, they were as quick as me to look away.

So I didn't know the name of the man that was talking to me now. But I knew he was the youngest one. Near on almost Master David's age. Near on almost mine.

I didn't say anything. I would have looked away if I could. But I remembered those eyes, eyes like I never seen before and never thought to see again. Eyes of a slaved man looking into my soul.

I just stared. How had he got up his nerve to follow me here and speak? "I tote them quilts back to the house for you, if you like." He stood up a little taller. "Celia." Like he had practiced it. No "miss." He watched me, licking dry lips.

My face burned. My stomach went funny. I wanted to hear my name like that and see his lips move to say it again. But I just bent to drag one of the quilts out of the water, to hand it to him. The cleanest one, without any blood, because I knew it should be done soaking.

But when I tugged on it, it was heavier than I was ready for. And it was pulled by the flow of the creek. It wrapped around my hand and tugged me back. I slipped and fell on my rear in the stream.

The water was cold. The stones struck me hard and made me cry out. As soon as the sound was out of my mouth, I heard the young man splash into the stream and yank on my arm to get me to my feet.

I got snatched up and fell against him. We went down together onto the quilts and into the water.

Trying to get my skirts down out of my apron to cover my legs, where I felt one of his hands while we splashed around trying to stand, I only got the whole dress loose and soaked and tangled in the quilts. My legs got wrapped in all that heavy wetness and couldn't get free.

I clawed at the young man's shirt, trying to grab his hand and get my feet under me again. Instead, I kept pulling him down with me.

We rolled over, trying to get to our knees away from each other and get untangled from the quilts and my skirt, which was twisted like a wrung out dishrag. We both stopped laughing and looked up when we heard a shout from toward the house.

It was Master David, running down the little slope of the hill to the creek.

I was glad, at first, to see him. I thought he would know what to do about this tangle and the mess of these heavy soaked quilts that, by now, I knew I never could have got back to the clothes line without dragging them through the dirt and getting them caked with mud.

So I smiled up at Master David, though I couldn't say nothing.

But Master David was frowned up a sight to see. He shouted at me, "What the hell are you doing?" And when my mouth dropped open, "Wait till Father hears about this!"

Heard of what? I hadn't even spoke to the young man after he was so nice to offer to help me carry my wash load. What was there for Newsom to hear of?

And from Master David of all people.

But now Master David had splashed into the stream with us and shoved at the young man and grabbed at my elbow to haul me out of the water. I reached back to grab at the quilts, for fear they might float downstream without me.

Master David shouted about that too. "Get your hands off that boy, Celia! Wait till Father hears. He'll wear your hide out for this!"

I had heard Master David smart off to his brother and even a little to his father. I had heard him shout at Miss Mary for talking back to him.

But I had never heard him roar like this.

I heard shouts and the sound of men running toward us at the creek. I let go of the quilt I had my hand on and let Master David drag me to the creek bank, sobbing.

If I couldn't talk to him, I couldn't argue with him. Or even just explain to him that nothing wrong had been done.

Master Harvey and two of the other negro hands came over the hill slope. Master Harvey

141

yelled, "What's all this noise about? David, you all right?"

Master David waved his free hand so as to make me lose my footing on the stones. "Go call Father, Harry. I just caught this trollop down here making time with Joshua."

My heart went light. I pulled up short. So that was his name. Joshua. The first negro man whose eyes I'd ever looked into, that dreadful day in the wagon when I came to Newsom's farm.

I looked back at the young man who had offered to help me, between the curly lashes that made a dark ring around the bright whites and dark centers. There was something he called up in me from where it lay hid. I wished I could have said his name when he said mine.

"Celia."

Joshua.

Master Harvey snatched my free arm and yanked me from Master David and up the little hill. I wondered what they would tell their father if I said anything to them right now about my forgotten quilts.

I turned to see the quilts float away down the creek, snagging here and there on big flat stones. Good thing the hot summer had passed and left the creek a little dry.

I called out, stretching one hand. "The quilts!" I said, thinking to tell Newsom I had just said it out loud but not to anybody in particular.

Master Harvey shouted to the men. "Get those damn things and bring them back to the house."

Joshua had already gone for the quilts, as soon

142

as I spoke. Master David was at the edge of the water, watching his brother haul me. He turned to watch the quilts go but didn't move to stop them.

The other two men who had come with Master Harvey plunged on into the water. One of them, a big burly man whose looks were mean, I thought, walked up to Joshua and shoved him into the water. He snatched at the quilt Joshua had saved.

I didn't see any more because Master Harvey got me to the top of the little rise and on the path to the back of the house. But I heard shouts. Then Master David yelled about how niggers better break it up.

Bits of grass and clumps of mud were stuck to my skirt hem by the time I sat in a straight chair in the kitchen, shivering because the fire was low for simmering and not high enough for heating or boiling. I stared at the floor while I waited for Newsom to come and whip me like Master David said.

Lucky for me, Master Harvey didn't really seem to see any big deal about the quilts and about me falling in the creek with Joshua.

While I waited, I heard him chuckle with his father, who he had found somewhere probably out by the barn, coming in through the front door and making their way through the parlor and dining room.

"Myself," Master Harvey said, "I just think the girl's too little to carry two big wet quilts. But David seemed all het up about it, so I thought I'd better tell you his way."

I went warm inside when I heard Newsom

chuckle, too.

But I must have still been shivering. Because when Newsom came into the kitchen, he took my chin in his hand tender-like. "Girl, look at you. Go put on those old rags you brought with you here from your old plantation. You'll catch your death in these wet things. What made you try to wash the quilts in the stream, anyway?"

My teeth chattered. "Miss Virginia said cold running water is better for blood than boiling."

Newsom and Master Harvey both guffawed. Newsom said, "See there, Harry? I told you David takes way too much a interest in this girl's doings. If he ain't stumbled along, the quilts would have been out of the creek and up on the line, and dinner would be near on the table. Well, get your rags changed and get to your chores, Celia. And let it be a lesson to you."

A lesson about what?

I didn't ask. I ducked my head and dropped a curtsy to Newsom and Master Harvey on my way out of the kitchen.

But Newsom must have thought to himself what kind of lesson I needed because he followed me to my room and let himself in while I was stripped.

I had just been thinking it was good to have a change of clothes and not have to dry your clothes on the floor next to you while you slept. I was proud Miss Virginia decided I could keep my gown and apron I wore here from the old farm, and that meant I had enough clothes to hang on the peg on the wall.

144

I wasn't in a hurry to put on the old clothes, though. Just because of that old blood stain on the back of the skirt, and where it came from, and how looking at it made me feel.

It was good to see spare clothes hanging. Made you feel rich.

But how would it feel to know that everybody in the house was looking at the back of my skirt and thinking of me and Newsom in that covered wagon the day he went to fetch me?

Shameful.

And it made me wonder if they knew, anyway, that he came to my room every night and what we did in here.

Which is why I was still standing there stripped when Newsom let himself into my room and closed the door and locked it shut behind him.

He stood watching me. I saw he had brought his cane and was leaning on it.

"So," Newsom said, "you thought you'd go down by the creek and talk with Joshua? Away from the house where nobody could see you?"

My heart sank. "No, sir." I moved over to the clothes peg.

"Leave those." Newsom pointed with his cane. "Bend over that table there."

I bent. Maybe a caning was a lot better than what he had forgot to come and do with me last night, anyway. I would rather be caned.

It stung. It fell three times before I cried out.

He didn't cane my back, which was what I thought he would do. He caned my seat. It took two good lashes before I felt how deep it bit in the flesh and didn't want to let go and slide by.

When I cried out, Newsom dropped the cane and told me go lay down. So the second part of the whipping was getting what I thought I had got away from the night before.

The scratching and being shoved deep in the mattress. And the smells. Rot body smells and dry sweat and wool that needs to be changed. Cigar smoke and whiskey gone stale in his mouth and his belly.

Somehow, in the daylight like this, it felt again like everybody knew what he was in here doing. And everybody wanted him to do this to me.

I couldn't think why they would want it.

I would have rather got slapped, like Miss Mary and Miss Virginia got. Or even horsewhipped, like the men.

But not spanked, like the children.

Besides. He was getting too heavy on my belly these days and causing me deep pain when he pressed.

When he was done, I rolled up in a ball and held my belly and cried.

Newsom touched my shoulder. "Celia?" His voice was rough. He didn't like to show nothing like softness when you had done the wrong thing. "Celia, what is it?"

Well, he asked. All he could do was beat me some more if he didn't like my answer. "You make my belly hurt worse and worse every time." Maybe he didn't hear me. I could hardly hear myself.

He was quiet a while. His voice was softened up again when he spoke. "Well, you should have spoke up sooner. We can fix that. Now get up and get that dinner on the table."

There was a little stale wash water from that morning in my basin. None fresh in the pitcher. I slept so late, I hadn't wanted to take time to pour out the old and fetch some new.

So Newsom washed a little in the old water and got dressed while I rocked, holding my belly.

On his way out of the door, he said, "Now you do like I told you and don't talk to nobody but Miss Virginia and me."

I thought, watching him close the door, that someday I would get in his face and ask Newsom what I was supposed to do when people like his sons and Miss Mary talked to me.

Someday. But not today.

And no day soon after, either.

Because soon after baby Buddy's birthing, everyone had to start getting ready for Master Harvey's wedding.

Miss Mary was happy and edgy both all the time because, as she said, "Maybe now someone from Master Harvey's in-laws might come sparking me." And she could get out of her father's house, despite Miss Virginia's baby and how nobody could come calling on them anymore.

You would have thought folks would yell at her for speaking so open about wanting to get out and get married. Seeing as how they called her a child and treated her like one.

But no. They just ignored her and talked around her about land deals and prime farm land and how much money Master Harvey's bride would bring into the pot and how he ought best to invest it.

Miss Virginia had been moved, for a while, between her own bed in the daytime and her father's bed at night. Newsom argued loud and long that sleeping with Miss Virginia's "passel of illiterate brats and ragamuffins" would wake baby Buddy at night. So I had to spend a lot of time sewing them quilted pallets to sleep on the floor, so they could let their mother and the baby have the bed.

But that wasn't enough for Newsom. He still insisted the baby had to be with him at night because he didn't see the baby all day, being so taken up with business as he was. And just look how Miss Virginia's children were up off their pallets all hours of the night to ask for water and rush out to the outhouse.

In the end, Miss Virginia put up quite a fuss about having to sleep away from her children. Newsom yelled at her that she was nothing but a harlot ingrate, anyway, lusting after the husband she had abandoned. She didn't fool him and he didn't want to see her face sneaking in his room again, uninvited.

So before her heavy bleeding had even stopped, Miss Virginia was back in her own room and her own bed at night.

But Newsom at night kept baby Buddy.

It didn't make any sense, him always fussing and demanding to have people in his room at night. Because Newsom didn't stay in his room at night, his own self.

As soon as it got quiet with heavy breathing and dark with all the lamps dimmed and the fires banked, you could hear all over the house the sound of Newsom easing open his bedroom door and shutting it with a click and making his way down the hallway to my room.

I would lay still and listen to the sounds of him coming. The shuffles and the pauses where he had to feel his way around where a chair might not have been pushed back under the table in the dining area, or some such change in the dark.

There was a branch outside my outdoor wall that would wave and scrape with even the least little breeze. At first it scared me to hear it start up. Was that Newsom? But then it got so I liked to hear that scraping branch and even hoped every sound I heard in the house at night was it. Because that would mean that at least, for the moment, Newsom wasn't coming.

Silly to put so much stock in the minutes he didn't come.

Because every night, he would come some time. He would always come.

He told me what hurt me was the baby growing in my belly and, to fix that, I needed to get on my knees or on my side.

So I got to laying in bed with my back to my bedroom door every night, listening to the branch just inches away from my face outside through the wall, listening behind me to the sounds in the house of people asleep and people stirring. Guessing what everything was. A child sneaking into Miss Virginia's bed to cuddle. Someone might fuss at it in the morning, but it would be happy tonight. Master Harvey up sneaking a late extra sip of his

149

father's whiskey, to help him sleep. Miss Mary sneaking down the hallway to Miss Virginia's room, to whisper for hours about how to get someone to marry her and get her into a house of her own. A cat that sneaked in from the barn and was prowling the kitchen for scraps and mice.

And only after all the sounds but the branch outside had died, there would come the steady shuffle of Newsom.

I kept my back to the door while he made his way down the hall. I kept my back to the door while I heard a hand seize the latch. I kept my face to the outside wall while the hinges sighed the door open. I closed my eyes when the door shut.

And then the creak that was Newsom easing his weight across my floor shot my eyes open. So I saw his shadow that fell across me in the banked firelight, when he was halfway to the bed. I shuddered at the rustle like a whisper of his nightshirt pulled up and the bedclothes pulled apart so he could slide in behind me, his man part bare.

I kept my back to him because, anyway, that was how he took me when the baby inside me started getting big and it hurt to have him on top of me.

With my back to him, it was like I wasn't really there. Not all of me.

And the bleeding and throwing up eased down.

But, peculiar thing.

I got real afraid of the sight of my room in the dark.

I first found that out one night when Miss Virginia called me from the kitchen to go get some diapers I'd been hemming for the baby and left on the table in my room.

I was on my way down the hall in a hurry, not bothering to fetch a lamp because it wasn't really dark yet.

And it hit me.

I stood still in the hallway and stared down toward my room. And even though I knew nothing and nobody was in it, I was afraid.

I couldn't make myself go forward. I was ashamed to go back to the kitchen for a lamp, showing myself how scared I really was. And I was a little afraid to leave Miss Virginia waiting for those diapers. Baby Buddy had soaked all the done ones through today while we all sewed for Master Harvey's wedding and cooked for his in-laws, who still weren't allowed to come visit in the house.

I stood and the darkness of the room gathered in the hallway, spilling out of the door.

It was a seeping cloud at my feet, coming towards me.

And if I just stood there…if I just stood there.

I turned and ran for the kitchen.

I didn't think I ran all that hard or crashed all that loud against the kitchen doorframe. But Miss Virginia's oldest, Master Coffee, soon came in to find me. "What's with you, Celia? Mama said come find out what happened in here."

I had got an awful stitch in my side and a cramp in my belly from that little short run. I couldn't catch my breath right.

So I fell into a straight chair at the cutting table, holding my side and my belly, both. "Master

Coffee, be a good boy and carry a lamp to my room for me and see if you can't find those diapers. Tell Miss Virginia I was took with a pain and just need to sit a little minute."

Master Coffee, who was just turning eight, came to the table to get the lamp I lit for him with my shaking hands.

"Now," I said, trying to sound like his mother, who never let on she feared anything, even Newsom, "mind you don't try to carry this lamp along with that load of diapers. You might catch fire to something. You leave the lamp on my table, and take those diapers straight to your mother for me. Now, there's a good boy."

My breath had slowed. I must have sounded like I made sense. Because Master Coffee just took the lamp and left with a pout for running a free errand but not another word.

So I got up and found him some dried cherries, for a treat.

When I got to Miss Virginia's room, she was frowning but only out of concern for my pain. And the stitch was fading, though the cramp didn't want to ease.

She smiled when I slipped the handful of cherries into Master Coffee's fist, and his face lit up.

He ran out of the room so the other children couldn't catch him and make him share. And ever after that, he was willing to run errands for me because he always knew I'd pay him something.

And that gave me one more person, besides Miss Virginia and Newsom, that I could talk to.

Besides. I didn't really talk to Newsom.

Not unless I had to answer him. He'd come up behind me and want to know why I was gazing out the kitchen window with the shutters open so anybody could see me. Or what was I cooking for dinner that noon. Or had I seen Miss Mary, and did I know was she through mending that shirt for the wedding. And did I think Master Harvey was right and Newsom should have got the sisters to make him a new shirt for the occasion.

Stuff like that where I could answer the littlest bit possible. And always without looking at him.

Looking down at his feet maybe. Or the tip of his cane. And I guess I didn't always hear how he answered me back. Or even all of everything I'd say myself.

Because the next thing I'd know, Newsom would be gone and the chat would be over, and whatever it had been about, I really couldn't remember.

Brain fever. Miss Virginia said, "Sometimes you get that, carrying children."

It made sense. All of me was burning up. Why not my brain?

I took to staring out the kitchen window, hankering to be out in the chilling air. I took to listening for the gurgle of the creek, icing over. I would close my eyes and remember the cool shiver of rippling water pillowing under me and the heat of a hard lean body swimming on top of me, when I fell in the creek with Joshua. My whole body shuddered.

But I didn't see Joshua for a long time.

I suspected Newsom and his sons took care to send him on errands and chores that only took him away from the house.

But sometimes the other negro men would pass by when I was at the kitchen window or boiling wash or coming from the latrine.

And it was odd. But now that I had got in trouble for almost talking to one of them, they started nodding a little in my direction.

Well, two of the men and the little boy would nod to me.

But that last one—the one who had took the quilt from Joshua and knocked him in the water—that one would just catch my eye and stare.

He frightened me a little.

But as the baby in me grew and the brain fever got hotter every day, I thought less about who to talk to and who to stay away from and more about how to get a little cool.

The kitchen heat, when I was cooking, got unbearable.

And now that Master Harvey was getting married, there was more cooking going on than ever.

Newsom was peculiar in how he didn't like folks dropping round his place. So in order to be polite—and for a few other reasons, I expect—Miss Mary with Master Harvey would take some fresh baked treats like pies and fruit tarts I made real good and go calling on the future in-laws. Since these visits were a lot to Miss Mary's liking, my baked goods were always in demand.

And as soon as I baked something for the in-laws, Newsom would turn up. "Why you never cook none of that for me, Celia? You got your eye on impressing Master Harvey? Cause you can dang forget it. When Master Harvey gets his own farm, you're staying behind right here. Any other plans you think you're making, you can just forget them."

Couldn't he tell I mistrusted Master Harvey? Didn't want nothing to do with the man?

So I learned to bake twice whatever the treat was Miss Mary wanted to take to the in-laws. Once for them and once for Newsom's supper table, if I didn't have it ready in time for dinner.

Along with all that baking, Miss Virginia wasn't up and around to help with much of anything except washing her baby's diapers.

To be fair, I do have to say she did a fair lot of sewing right there in her bed. New dresses for her and Miss Mary to wear to their brother's wedding in the spring. New trousers for all the men and shirts for the brothers, too. Because all theirs were work-worn and didn't look too gentlemanly.

And if she got all those done in time, she meant to sew up a little something from the fabric leavings for her own three young ones.

But not the baby. It was understood that Buddy would not attend the wedding or the housewarming, but would stay behind here with me that day.

But that meant the cooking was all on me, except for Miss Mary's little help with her father's breakfast.

I couldn't get away from the heat.

It was like there was a fire in me burning to match the fire outside. And every time I left the shutters or the back door open on the first icy rain or drifts of snow on a soft breeze, somebody would be into the kitchen yelling about drafts and was I trying to die of the whooping cough like that neighbor up the road last winter.

And then the windows and door and the buttons at the neck of my dress would all get shut up tight. I'd be sweating and burning again in no time.

So, while the family ate dinner, I took to sneaking to the creek.

I took a basin, so people would think I had gone for washing up water. But nobody knew or asked where I had gone because I eased the kitchen door shut solid behind me, quick and quiet so as to cut down on a draft.

The creek was icing and the brittle water sang over the stones.

I would sit on the bank and shatter the ice along the edge and splash it in stinging drops with my fingers along my forehead and cheeks.

The burning inside would ease.

I would unbutton my bodice at the neck and let the little cold drops play on my throat and my nape. I could almost hear the hot skin sizzle and cool.

I would unbutton my cuffs and turn up the sleeves to the elbow and bathe the forearms. I would lift my skirt and ease onto my bare feet, my steps along the shattered surface of the ice shooting night-colored drops up to sting between my toes.

Surely, this was heaven on earth. Like Newsom's daughters sang about on Sundays in the parlor while the men took the horses to church in town.

156

As the baby grew and burned me up from the inside, I thought one day it might be good to sneak out to the creek after supper, as well. And it was there, listening to the ripple of the icy water over stones in the purpling dark, that I admitted to myself there was something wrong with what Miss Virginia said about new life.

I couldn't say she seemed to love baby Buddy.

She took care of him, all right. But she never looked at him. She never touched him more than to change his diaper or wash him or hand him up to Newsom to be took to bed.

But my baby.

Already it was like Miss Mary's doll, but kicking around inside me, snuggling down trying to get comfy while I worked or waited for Newsom to go away. Or lay in bed listening for my branch on the outside wall.

The baby inside me was like a doll, but it was like a call, too. A call to…to…well, I didn't know. Maybe to little pleasures like the creek, here. Maybe to something else besides Newsom's being with me, day in and day out. Feeding his family. Waiting for him with my back turned.

I thought of Miss Virginia. I didn't want to be like her with my baby, when it was born.

And I didn't think I would be.

I bathed my face and neck and arms with ice in the dark and sang to the baby that turned and fell asleep inside me.

And then a voice at the top of the rise behind me, between me and the house, said, "Who you sanging to?"

157

My heart sank and went cold between my chest and stomach.

I didn't know this voice. I turned slow and looked up to see who had spoke.

Sure enough. It was the hand who had took and shoved Joshua into the water.

He stood at the top of the rise, outlined by baring trees and faint stars. He had his fists on his hips. He sounded like I had made him angry.

I got up and buttoned my bodice and sleeves. I dropped my skirt and started up the hill to one side of this man.

"Can't speak?" he demanded. "Uppity, ain't you? The master's ho. Ain't got a kind word for a negro like me."

I kept walking, but I looked up to see that he hadn't moved over into my path.

He hadn't.

"Can't stand a black bitch like you," the man said. "Come around here getting everybody all worked up. A tease is what you be. I bet you don't even care what happened to Josh on account of you and your teasing."

I stopped, staring straight ahead. I wanted to turn and ask to hear about Joshua. I even wanted to ask him to hurry up and tell me.

And I had a dreadful feeling about how this man said "Josh." Like he knew Joshua, and I didn't. Never would. Always be a stranger.

While I waited and stared ahead, the man said, "Got horsewhipped good on account of you. What was you doing, out here splashing around in the water with that boy?"

He came up behind me so quiet I didn't know he was there until his hand slid around my stomach and yanked my back up against him. There was something hard on his body there behind me, and he ground it into my backside. I tried to twist away.

His restraining hand clawed into my stomach. I cried out. "What you doing throwing yourself at young boys and old men, anyway?" His voice came out of his gut hot and damp on the back of my neck. "You scared of a real man, bitch? Why you scared? How you ever going to find out what you missing?" And his free hand started to work its way into the damp thick cloth of my skirt.

I snatched my skirt from him in both hands, yanked free against his clutch on my middle, and ran ahead to the back of the house.

As I lay in bed that night with my face to the outside wall and my back to the door, listening to Master David argue with Master Harvey about how much land his work had earned him, and how much he was stealing from his brother and sisters, and listening for my branch on the wall and the crackle of my dying fire in the fireplace, I thought to myself it had been silly, anyway, to be going to the creek at twilight. I wouldn't miss it.

Fool that I was, I could have fell in and killed my baby.

Chapter Five: Shame

Miss Virginia was back up on her feet every morning, making her father's breakfast, by the time snow buried the house in quiet. I woke to find that, where I had swung the shutters open to let out Newsom's and my stink and damp heat and let in cool, dark air, the snow was drifting in on me like white spring butterflies.

I thought I'd best close the shutters before Miss Virginia sent Master Coffee to wake me to help start dinner, and I'd get in trouble again for freezing myself. I went to sit up and close the shutters, but I found I couldn't move my leg for pain.

First I thought Newsom must have buried his razor, or even a knife, in my leg the night before. Trying to punish me for giving him my back, even though I couldn't help it, with the baby.

But then I thought, no. There's no blood. With my other leg, I could feel that the bedclothes was all dry.

But only for a minute more. Because as soon as I thought, no, the bed's dry, my leg that was numb with pain seemed to cramp in on the bone and break off at the hip, and a sizzling streak of something shot out of my body, like I had wet myself, running.

I started crying for shame. This was too, too terrible.

And to make it worse, I couldn't even ease myself out of the bed to sneak and soak the sheets, at least, in the washbasin with the little water from my pitcher.

I couldn't move. That one leg didn't even feel like it was mine no more. Fell away, or something. I started to whimper, scared. I reached to grab hold on the edge of the bed frame and pull myself over to the floor, where I could crawl to the door and call out for help.

Something was wrong. This was no time to be shamed of wetting the bed or scared to be caught with the shutters open, letting in snow. I didn't want to be alone any more.

I was just getting the feeling back in that lost leg so as I could pull it up under me and push myself up to stand on the other leg, when that knife cut through the bottom of my spine again. I got pushed into the cooling wet that was pooled on my bed ticking. More wet leaked out of me. I couldn't stop it.

I was sure my back was broke and I would have to get carried out of here, or die here. I turned my face out of my pillow to look towards the door, so far away for a body that couldn't walk.

And then there was a tap.

Light. Rat a tat. Like Master Coffee did, most mornings Miss Virginia didn't want to toss the leftover mush and bottom coffee to the pigs, before she'd offered me some. I was that late getting up, most mornings these days.

Sure enough, Master Coffee piped through the shut door, "Celia, Mama want to know do you want her to water you some coffee and maybe butter you up some of that porridge before it go to the slop bucket?"

161

I said real weak, "Master Coffee," and my voice must have fell somewhere in the middle of the room. Because I heard him take off slapping his bare feet on the hallway floor, shouting, "Celia ain't answer, Mama. I don't know what she want. Can I have her butter on my biscuit?"

And the pain took me over and dragged me under with it till, when I opened my eyes again, I couldn't see but a blur.

But I could hear Miss Virginia at the door, calling, "Celia. What's going on in there?"

I could hear myself breathing rough on the sheets soaked damp with my breath and my sweat under my cheek. I couldn't make no other sound.

She took to banging on the door.

Soon, when I came up from the pain again, I heard Master David say, "The door ain't locked, is it? You want me to try it?"

And I thought, Oh no. I'm laying here soaked in pee and most likely got my nightgown hiked up over my butt, where his father always leaves it. Wish I could turn around and see. If Newsom hears about this, and the shutters open, too….

I heard the latch at the door working, and the pain fell on me again till there was nothing else I could think about but getting alive to the other side of it.

Next time I opened my eyes, Miss Virginia was moving around my head and my body on the bed. She clucked her tongue and spit out orders real sharp to her two boys. "Tommy, you see to Amelia and baby Buddy while Coffee, you run tell sister for me to get that kettle full and boiling. Celia's time has come. Then run find grandfather out in the barn and tell him the same."

"But, Mama, that last beat biscuit—"

Then I heard Master David and shut my eyes, hoping everybody would think I was still fainted. "James Coffee, you heard your mother. Nobody's thinking about that biscuit but you. If you don't get out of here, I'm a show you a beaten biscuit."

I heard stamping feet and Coffee was gone. I tried to feel if anything covered me, but without opening my eyes to see. Miss Virginia said, "David, help me lift her here. Let's get her off these wet sheets."

I stopped faking and opened my eyes. "No. Miss Virginia, don't let him touch me."

Miss Virginia put her face close to mine. "Celia. Can you move? Thank God you've recovered from that faint. You had us so scared."

I tried to reach for her, to hold her near me, but my arms had got limp like my legs. "Miss Virginia, don't let nobody see me or touch me like this. Your father will have my hide and yours too, if you do."

"Nonsense." Miss Virginia stood and backed away where I couldn't see her. "David, lift her for me until I can get those wet sheets on the floor."

Master David didn't pull back or shield himself in any way from all the wet ruined white of my nightgown as it flowed into his arms and against his body, trailing after me. "She's sweating and shaking, Virginia," he said. "Is she sick?"

Miss Virginia panted over the work of stripping my mattress. "Overcome, I guess, David," she said without turning to see the shape that had filled up the doorway.

"What the hell," I heard Newsom say just before I heard his cane whistle through the sharp, cold air.

Virginia still had not closed my shutters for me.

It must have been the flakes of snow that fluttered to the floor and melted into cold water that brought me around after my fall.

I lay for a stunned heartbeat with my cheek in the cool pool of melted snow, hearing David shout back at Newsom as the cane steady cut through the air, falling again and again.

And then, I don't know how, I got my hands on the legs of the chair at my table and pulled. The chair toppled over on my back. I ducked my head so it wouldn't get hit and got my left hand, which could still feel, on the table leg, which was sturdy enough to hold as I hauled myself up on it.

Miss Virginia was shouting now, too. But I couldn't understand nobody any more. It took all my thinking to work my body up to lay out and breathe across the top of the table, with the wood steady pressing the burden of my baby further down between the bones that had split apart at my hip.

If I lay there a second more, I'd pass poop right there on the floor. I had to get to the latrine. No way I could use my chamber pot with all these people standing around hollering.

I shoved myself away from the table hard enough to get a good start towards the door.

Newsom's face, red and pasty in patches, came closer. But he wasn't looking at me. He must have been, as usual, after David.

As I fell through the doorway, past him, I heard Miss Virginia. "Celia! You crazy wench. Father, go get her!"

I fell on down the hallway, banging one wall and then the other. I couldn't help it. My legs were pushed apart by everything trying to burst out of my body between my split hipbones. My right shoulder, where the chair had hit me, was no use. I couldn't feel a thing above the wrist. The hand throbbed every time I used it to feel up the wall and try to keep my balance.

And that's probably why, when I stopped at the end of the hallway because there wasn't no more wall to fall against, I couldn't think fast enough to get neither my throbbing right hand nor my left hand under me to gather the hem of my gown and catch the big, burning bundle that had slipped between the bones and was coming out of my scorched bottom parts.

I stood spraddle-leg and closed my eyes while my body had the runs right then and there in the dining room, squeezing first a giant hard lump of bowel stuff and then gushing out more wet that must have been pee, could I have stood to look at it.

My legs trembled. Soon as the bowel movement fell out of me, I fell into it on the floor.

And someone screamed, "She'll crush the baby."

I looked up to see Miss Mary, white as a boiled sheet on the line, standing above me and pointing at the pile of sticky mess where I sat. "Look what she's done." Miss Mary shrieked till her voice cracked and splintered like glass.

Hands grabbed hold under my armpits and hauled me up with my legs dangling. I slipped, trying to get my feet under me. Whoever was holding me up pulled me away, trailing blood and that one gut thing that had come out of Miss Virginia when she birthed baby Buddy.

Birthed.

Oh no.

Sure enough. There was a blue thing, curled in on itself, lying still on the floor, covered in bright blood.

I had birthed my baby, and stupid me.

I had sat on it.

I saw Miss Virginia step around my still baby to slap her sister firm in the face.

And then, like a good idea had just hit me, I took up screaming where Miss Mary had left off.

Next time I came to, I couldn't remember nothing for sure. Maybe there had been voices. Falling into each other, like rain in the creek where it was cool.

There had been heat. And sweat. I was still burning.

But I was dry now.

I remembered wanting to get away from the wet. So hot and sticky.

And something else. Little and blue.

Oh. My baby curled on the floor.

I jumped awake, crying out. I couldn't see nothing but a too bright light all around me. But I heard a chair scrape and someone beyond that called out, and soft hands were soon on me, and Miss Virginia's voice. "Celia. Celia. Stop that.

166

You're all right now."

All right? How was I ever going to be all right, after what I had done to my baby?

"What's she saying?" That was David's voice from behind her in the blinding lightness where I couldn't see.

My hands must have went up to cover my eyes. I felt the back of my fingers get pressed into the hollow between Miss Virginia's shoulder and chest, my fingertips digging into my eyes, and she said, "David, you know Father doesn't want you in here snooping around. Now get out, before there's more trouble. Please, brother."

"But has she come to? Hell, it's me will have to carry her coffin, I don't doubt, when Father beats her to death."

"If I don't beat you to death first." That was Newsom's voice. I'd know it, no matter what.

I sobbed once into Miss Virginia's shoulder.

Not Newsom. Not now. First thing after I'd murdered my baby.

"Father," she said. "Celia has wakened very distressed. Let me calm her, please."

"Go ahead on and calm her," he said. "How am I stopping you?" And chuckled. Of all things. Then his voice got stern, like usual, and he said, "Virginia, I do fear that you forget yourself more and more often, around here."

"Forgive me, Father," Miss Virginia mumbled, peeling me away from her soggy shirtwaist. My nose had begun to run on it.

David, silent, squeezed a dirty handkerchief between his sister's shirtsleeve and my face, to wipe

167

the rest of the run. His face was sad but smiling.

Miss Virginia took the handkerchief and began to scrub. "Celia, don't you want to see your baby?"

Through my mind lit and dimmed the little blue body, curled on the floor and sauced with my blood.

I jumped away from Miss Virginia, trembling and shaking my head.

Newsom face swam into my view behind his daughter's. "Look at her. What's wrong with her? Celia. What's wrong with you?"

Miss Virginia spat at him over her shoulder, "Father. I said let me calm her. You don't know how to take the time."

And though he raised his hand like to strike the back of her head, Newsom said nothing more about Miss Virginia forgetting herself.

She pulled my head into her neck. "There, there," she said. "Come back to us, Celia. It's all right. What are you so afraid of?"

I said, "Don't make me look at the baby," and started sobbing for real, now.

Newsom said, "Why ever not? It's as fine a gal as I've ever seen. I even named it after my wife's mother. Hannah. There. Ain't that a fine name to welcome your little pickaninny into the world?"

He was trying, you could tell, to imitate Miss Virginia's soothing tones. He probably thought it worked because I raised my face from Miss Virginia's shoulder to look at him.

"She's alive?" I said. "But I fell on her."

Newsom broke out laughing. "Damnedest thing I ever saw, too," he chuckled. "Damn fool nigger wench just went and sat smack on top of her

168

newborn brat. Blam. Just like that. No sooner spit it out than she squashed it."

David, it seemed, was still in the room. He chuckled along with his father. "I always heard them niggers was lazy," David said. "Ain't a job they can't sit down on."

Newsom slapped David on his back, the first sign of affection I had ever seen pass between them.

I mumbled to myself, "I thought I had broke its neck."

Miss Virginia said, "It's all right, Celia. The baby's fine, now. Just wants her mama, is all."

I looked around, searching for a swaddled bundle. There on the floor, between my cleaned bed, where Miss Virginia was holding me, and a bright fire in the fireplace, was a little wooden boat like a corncrib with a tiny roof.

And inside it, wrapped in boiled linens, was the tiny golden face of my sleeping baby.

Had to be mine. All Miss Virginia's children was much bigger than this.

I flowed to the floor to be near her. "Hannah," I said, kneeling and resting my good left hand on the cradle roof, "it's your mama here. Oh, how beautiful you are."

The room hushed. I heard the unusual quiet when I started wiping the tears off my face. Now what?

I looked up around at all of them. Newsom finally said, "Well, ain't that a sight."

David, unasked, left with his head down.

And Miss Virginia said she'd better see to supper. "You've been passed out all day, Celia.

169

Miss Mary helped me get your bed linens changed. You must remember to thank her. But we've gotten nothing into you all day. Father, don't you agree that a tray should be brought to Celia, so she can partake of our supper without taxing herself to sit up in the kitchen?"

And then I remembered what Miss Virginia had told me—how long ago?—about births giving a woman freedom from her man for a while.

How long a while?

Newsom said, "Fine. I'll take my supper on a tray in here with her." And he was gone, calling back into the room, "I'll just be a minute to check on that hay store. Can't have the livestock starving out on me, in this snowstorm. Like to become a blizzard as not."

The quiet fell around us in the room blanketed by snow.

I said, "Miss Virginia, it's like you said. That little baby," I nodded my head at the drowsing golden face, "will be my new life. I can feel it already. Can I pick her up, do you think?"

"She'll wake up." Miss Virginia rose from my bed. "I wouldn't, if I were you. You need your rest, Celia. Being passed out is not the same thing as sleeping and regaining your strength."

"No, ma'am, it isn't." I slipped my hands in between the tight swaddled sheets and felt my way around the little limp body. It went rigid. The face went red.

The mouth opened on shining pink gums and the tongue curled back to force out a little mew. "Ach."

170

There was my excuse. She was crying.

I freed her from the swaddling clothes and picked her up. Her diaper trailed away and she was glorious as the rising sun, streaking across the face of the dying fire.

I pulled her with me into bed, smiling and cooing and thinking up my very best lullaby song. Something someone used to sing, swinging a hoe, walking in from a field.

A woman's voice drifted through time to me.

"That's right pretty," Miss Virginia said, tucking the bedding in around me and Hannah, who had found my nipple and was tugging the wateriest milk out of it. "But I don't think you should keep her in there long without a diaper."

I smiled, drifting off to sleep. Let her wet the bed. Glorious, glorious. Tiny and pure. Innocent and needing me, this golden little being.

Better a bed wet from pee than from Newsom.

How long, now, had Virginia said I would be free of him? I would have to ask her. Maybe when she brought the tray. If she brought the tray.

Who cared about the tray? There would be time to ask her about all that tomorrow.

Newsom brought me my tray. He had put his food together with mine—a big bowl of fresh milk and risen bread to sop in it, thick with butter, "to spoil the new mama,"—and kicked the door shut behind him. "So as nobody will think we're agreeable to company."

He set the tray on the table, fumbled awhile, lighting the lamp, and then pulled the chair and tray over to the side of the bed. He sat with the tray on his lap, with the crotch of his breeches just inches from my face.

I was that sure I could smell his stink, barreling through the sweet cloud of my baby's milky breath and watery, skin-scented pee. I turned my head away.

"Now, now," Newsom said. "Ain't no way to greet a tired pappy. Let me get a look at the little mite. You done had her to yourself all day." He reached under the bedclothes and slid her out of my clutching hands.

"Hell," he bellowed. "Celia, I thought you knew all about diapers. Damn." He went to stand up and the tray of milk and buttered bread slid, crashing, to the floor. "Well, damnation," he shouted.

The baby's head flopped as she tried to force out a little mew.

Newsom stood, holding her dangling big-bellied skinny body. She curled up her legs and shot a golden stream over the food on the floor.

I tried to sit up and grab for her. "Give her to me, Master Newsom," I said in a voice I hadn't never heard, nor never thought to hear, come out of my heart. Out of my breast. Out of my mouth.

I think I feared that he would drop the baby among the broken chunks of the milk bowl on the floor. Else I never would have misspoke myself like that.

Miss Virginia was in the room just in time to see the baby settled back in my arms and her father's hand sail, backwards, across my mouth. I fell backwards, still clinging to Hannah, following the path Newsom's arm had took.

"Father."

"Enough," he yelled. "Have you forgot whose roof you are under, daughter?"

Silence.

I peeked past Hannah's mewling little body, curled against me, to see Miss Virginia standing with her head bowed, like in shame. "Pardon, Father. It was just my concern for Celia's condition—"

"No more, I said!" he thundered so his bare voice shook the fireplace mantel and the closed shutters.

Miss Virginia fell to the floor to pick up the broken bowl and ruined food. I heard the pieces clink on the wooden tray. Behind her, Miss Mary stood and watched until Miss Virginia called back, "Sister, go get me some rags to clean up this milk."

"And pee," Newsom growled. "Mind what you do with them rags after you sop up the pickaninny's pee with them. Ain't fit for nothing, negress women with their pickaninnies."

Newsom collapsed again into the chair by my side while his daughter reached around his legs and shoes to get up the last of the broken bits.

"How does a man stand it?" he asked me. "Now, Celia, how in hell is a grown man supposed to sleep in that bed full of pee? No diaper. You got that damn baby peeing all over everything. The bed. The supper. What's with you?"

When Miss Mary brought rags, Miss Virginia sent her for more diapers. Newsom took the baby from my hands and my breast for Miss Virginia to

173

swaddle it, mewing and kicking, and tuck it—too firmly—into the corncrib thing.

"Cradle," Newsom snapped at me when I asked when I could get the baby back out. "Morning. Now move on over. You take the damn wet spot, since it was your laziness put it there."

I said, "But Miss Virginia said doctors and"—whose wives? Somebody's wives—"wives don't let you do that"—I pointed at the crotch of his breeches—"when you just had a new baby."

Newsom slapped me again. Full-handed this time. "Don't make me wear myself out, teaching you to mind," he said. "It's been a hell of a day."

I took the wet spot and curled up in it, giving Newsom my back, as had become our habit.

I hoped he wouldn't remember to himself that, wait a minute, the baby was out now, and maybe he could make me turn around and do it face to face.

But just like Newsom. He was in too much of a hurry to think of much of anything.

After it was all over, the burn of his flopping and grabbing and grunting and the sharp, sloppy pain, with rushes of more blood, I lay listening to the whisper of snow on the shutters. So soft. So quiet.

Just like my baby's breath in my face when we was alone together, drowsing. We would have more times like that. Just the two of us.

She was so tiny. I could hear her, almost, breathing in her sleep and crying out, now and again, wanting milk and my warmth. I wished I could pick her up and give her my breast, but I was pretty sure that wasn't what Newsom had in mind. I pictured Hannah's soft face all scrunched with searching for the nipple and fussing and thought how, as soon as Newsom left in the morning, she'd be in my arms again. I hoped she could feel me thinking about her.

Somehow the heavy snow muffled the branch's scratching at the wall. Everything was so quiet, when I got up to use my chamber pot, that I thought my burning pee thundered loud enough to wake up both Newsom and the baby.

But they both slept through it.

Miss Virginia, I remembered, had had me wash her privates real well, over and over again, after she had Buddy. She said it was important to keep clean there. At the time, I had wondered. Was she trying to get rid, a little more, of Buddy?

But now, I just wanted to ease the burning and sponge off the running.

So I went to the pitcher and basin and tried, with my left hand, to slosh some water for washing.

It was tough going. But when the damp rag got pressed to my privates, I did feel much better.

I sank into my chair and held the rag there.

I was still there when Hannah woke me, crying in a little scratchy scream, now. I dropped the rag and threw myself across the floor to her.

I was still digging her out of the swaddling when Newsom hauled his grumbling self out of my bed, steady on about "bawling brats" and "a man's pleasure," and left my room with his shirttails hanging and his breeches dragging from his arm.

So I took Hannah to bed and put her where I had been laying. It was dry now, from my body

175

heat cooking and drying her tiny little bit of pee. And I put myself in Newsom's stinking, sticking spot. Because putting up with him was just the least I would have done for my pretty, weak, mewing little doll of a baby.

She nursed while I slept, till morning.

I didn't wake till Miss Virginia sent Coffee with some tiny little baby things. Shirts and gowns and a little knit cap for her head. Boot socks for her feet. Bitty things that Buddy and all Miss Virginia's children had long outgrew. And the diapers I had sewed for Buddy my own self, too busy baking and cooking to look out for my own, she was good enough to return to me.

I smiled and thanked Coffee and folded all the little clothes real careful, with my left arm.

My right arm didn't heal too quick. Neither did the rest of me.

Virginia said it was on account of women who just had a baby wasn't supposed to be right back knowing of a man so soon. I asked her to tell her father that, and she said, "Celia. Just…just…." and waved her hands and left my room.

I could bear anybody leaving my room these days but Hannah or me. Newsom had eased up, I didn't know why, and let Master Harvey and even David come and go in company of their sisters. Miss Virginia, who came too busy and tired to sit, or Miss Mary. I still dreaded Miss Mary.

She came and sat, bringing her sewing and knitting and sliding her eyes at me till she worried me she wanted to steal my baby, or something.

Till the night she opened up, turning all sorts of

176

unnatural colors, and said, "Celia, how is it? How do you learn to want it? Does it make them want you more, if they think you want them? That's what I need to know."

I was sitting up in bed, nursing Hannah. She was getting chunky and dimple as you please, and I loved how she kicked out her little booties. Dressed in Miss Virginia's baby things, Hannah looked sweeter than Miss Mary's doll.

"How is what, Miss Mary?" I asked, tickling at the new little line of cheesy fat under Hannah's chin. I should have washed her better, but her skin smelled so tasty with my day-old milk on her. I tried to nuzzle in the folds.

Miss Mary sighed and slapped down her sewing. Then she sucked at her finger where she must had stabbed it with her needle.

When she looked up at me, I could see red firelight shining too bright in her eyes.

I moved Hannah a little away from her.

Miss Mary said, "You know, Celia....I would ask my sister—I *have* asked my sister—but it's been too long or something since she first got married. I can't understand a thing she says. And *you*. You're younger than me. Everybody says we're the same age, but I'm almost a year older than you." She glared at me like I might have stole her rightful years from her. "And nobody's helping me find a beau at all these family visits with Harvey's new in-laws. And I know how it'll be when he's married. We'll never see his wife's family again. It was even that way with his first wife. She lived and died here in no time, and even when she was so ill

177

for so long, only the women from her family would come see her. And the day she died, her father. An old man. And not even a widower, so what good did that do? Of course, I was too young then to worry."

Miss Mary thumped her sewing into her lap again and fixed her eyes on the fire. "I don't want to be no old maid. And I don't want to be like my sister, neither. It must be something, something I don't understand. Everybody says I'm a child and it's shameful to think of these things." She looked at me again. "But you. You're as young as me. Younger. How did you get Father?"

At last. A question I could understand. I started shaking my head, smiling. "I didn't do nothing to get your father. He came one day and must have bought me because I was sent away with him, Miss Mary. That's all."

"But didn't you *meet* him first? Didn't you have to come serve him a meal, or something? How could he buy you, sight unseen, and take you for almost a *wife*, for heaven sake, Celia, and you didn't even *flirt* with him?"

She stood and balled her sewing in her hand. I winced at the thought of the needle. "And *me*," she went on, hunching her shoulders and leaning her face at me, "*me*, I dress in my finest clothes with lace and ribbons I had to *beg* Harvey to buy me, because Father wouldn't, and I've even done things Harvey wouldn't approve, if he wasn't always in a hurry to get off alone with his fiancée, but I've done them so *somebody* would want me and come get me *out* of this place before"--she started gasping like

178

for breath and turning darker red—"before"—spit foamed in the corners of her mouth. But thank goodness her red was breaking up into pale white and a case of the shakes.

"Before what, sister?" Master David said from the door.

Miss Mary slammed her balled up fist of sewing on my wood table. I knew those splinters. I winced again.

"Before I end up like Virginia," she hollered and threw my pitcher with her ball of sewing at David's head. "I won't," she screamed as the pitcher sailed, heavy and sloshing, through the air. "You all hear me? I won't."

David ducked away from the doorframe until the pitcher had struck there, broken in a spray of clear spring water, and slid to pieces across the threshold. "Crazy strumpet," he called after the ruffles and flounces of Miss Mary's dress had run past him into the hallway. "You will and you do. So I heard."

Her door slammed, and Master David looked in at me. His smile was weighted. "Guess I can't visit you, Celia, without my chaperone. I wondered why Mary sneaked off to see you without letting me know. Now I guess I know why." He winked at me.

Miss Virginia's voice came down the hallway ahead of her. "Then tell me why, David. What have you said to upset her?"

David shrugged and laughed. "Me, upset her? Celia, did you see me say anything to Mary before she got upset?"

179

I waited for Miss Virginia to come through the doorway, and then I said straight to her, because I still couldn't answer David, "Miss Mary was worked up before Mister David came along, ma'am. But if I did it, I don't know what I did."

"Never mind," Miss Virginia said. "David, go away."

David made what Miss Virginia called uncouth noises and left them in the air between us. Miss Virginia shut the door behind him.

"Celia," she said, "I'll talk to Mary. She shouldn't bring her questions to you. Don't pass whatever she says on to Father. It wouldn't go well. She simply—what I mean to explain is, she's only-- that is, she's hardly, really, more than a child. She needs a woman to talk with her. But she doesn't have patience with my views. Seeing as how—" Miss Virginia bowed her head "—I've lost my own marriage. She doubts my advice is worth her while."

"I don't see what I can say to her," I said. "I'll never be married."

Miss Virginia looked at me like in surprise. "Well, you're as close as a slave woman gets. You have Father. He's devoted to you."

I didn't say nothing more.

Hannah had drifted asleep. The booties and cap in the heat from the fire had her sweating. I fumbled at all the little ties, trying to get them off. I hoped Miss Virginia couldn't see my face. It must have been a study, but of what, I don't know.

Married? Me, to Master Newsom?

I must know nothing about marriage because

none of this was like what I thought marriage was supposed to be.

How about choosing? Wasn't that what Miss Mary was all worked up about? Choosing somebody, and him choosing her?

Without looking up, because the heat in my face didn't bear a close look from Newsom's own daughter, I said, "But Miss Virginia, didn't you *want* to be with your husband? Didn't you *love* him?" More quiet, I said, knowing this must be wrong to say out loud, but I wanted to know, "Didn't Mistress Newsom love your father? Want to be with him? At least sometimes?"

I waited. I didn't dare look up at her.

So I didn't see how she took it, that I brought up her husband, after I had been told not to—but maybe she didn't remember about that, I thought— and that I brought up her mother.

Like I had a right.

And see. That just proved my point.

Didn't nobody really think what Newsom did with me was nothing like marriage. That I was nothing like another wife to him. Because Miss Virginia said, "If you ever mention my mother again with your *filthy* lips, Celia, I'll tell Father. And Heaven help you."

I had got Hannah's booties and cap untied. I took them off, holding her with my strong left arm and folding the little things with the fingers of my right hand.

I wished that knot in my right shoulder would ease. Odd how it tensed and hurt me, ever since that knock from the chair that toppled when I was

181

birthing Hannah.

Miss Virginia was still there. Still waiting.

I couldn't unsay what I had said. So I started easing myself and my sleeping baby down under the bedclothes, hoping Miss Virginia would take the hint and go.

She said, and her voice was tight, "After I've welcomed you. Stood up for you. *Cared* for you and took care *of* you!"

I said soft, "I'm sorry, ma'am. I didn't mean no disrespect. Like you and Miss Mary say, I'm going on a year younger than her." Now I looked up at Miss Virginia, who stood straight as a board, glaring at me. "She was just asking questions, and I guess that brought questions to my mind, too."

Miss Virginia looked like she almost softened up. But then she said, "Celia, Miss Mary is still a child. Her questions are not like yours. You. . . ." But it was too much for her. Miss Virginia turned and left. I could hear her knocking down the hallway on Miss Mary's door.

And I lay with my questions, holding my baby and dreaming to myself. If I could have married anybody, could have picked somebody, who would it be?

Joshua.

I pictured him picking up the baby, blue and naked from the floor, and she turned golden in his hands and he said, "Celia."

So when Newsom came in and took me from behind, I woke in the dark with the fire gone out and my mind still on Joshua and I shamed myself, crying out and clutching Newsom's hands on my breasts till he whispered in my ear, "Ain't I told you not to make all that noise in this house?"

And then I cried for real.

Chapter Six: You Give Things Up

We moved in the dark and listened, being quiet as we could.

Newsom, who couldn't breathe right once he got worked up until he was satisfied, gasped like a drowned man in my ear and still held tight to my breasts. Which, I could feel now, were hurt, not tingling like I thought before, when I thought he was Joshua.

And I wept.

The noise we made seemed loud in a house as quiet as this had been when Newsom sneaked down the hallway to my room.

But our noise was nothing, now, to the noise that started up around us.

First was the bang of Miss Mary's door and the sound of her running down the hallway, like as not to Miss Virginia's room. Then was the sound of the two sisters' voices raised, Miss Mary's upset and Miss Virginia's trying to talk her down and soothe her. Sounded like Miss Virginia's girl, Amelia, woke and started to cry to get in her mother's bed. Or stay there, if Miss Mary was trying to throw her out and sleep there, herself.

"Now see what you've started," Newsom grunted on the back of my neck and kept on grunting, till he was finished with me.

Then he rolled out of the bed and pulled on his breeches in the dark, a bent shape fumbling with the buttons in the lantern light somebody was now carrying down the hallway.

I wished I had left some of that broken pitcher scattered across the threshold for Newsom's bare feet.

But I had forced myself out of the room, away from Hannah, to get a broom and dustpan and rags to clean up the crockery and the spilled water. Only, not being able to find Coffee, late as it was, I had to haul in an empty bucket and lean it mostly in my left hand, to replace the pitcher, and then fill the bucket halfway, trip by trip, with dips from the kitchen water supply.

I noticed that my old fear of the dark in my room had got more grabby. Now, with a nice fire lighting my room, I was fearful of the dark in the hallway, like it was coming to get between me and my baby Hannah.

Every time I got to the bucket in my room with another dipper of water, I had to wipe the sweat off my brow and out of my eyes and sit to calm the wild hammering in my chest.

I felt my ribs would break out from being pounded by my heart. The hallway looked so long. And my baby was alone in there.

And everybody locked in every one of these rooms along the way meant us no good.

I quit after only three trips. Plenty of water to wash myself and the baby in the morning, if old Newsom didn't help himself to it first.

How could Hannah not have waked all that time that I was gone from her, cleaning up the pitcher shards and hauling water?

I felt I'd been gone from her near on to dying, I'd been gone so long. She snuggled against my

185

breast and kept right on sleeping, not even thinking about the nipple.

But later, when Newsom got up in the pitch dark to fumble on his breeches and go out to put his family in order, it seemed the hall was no distance at all.

I couldn't understand it.

Hearing Newsom down the hall, shouting at Miss Virginia and slapping somebody, maybe Miss Mary, for a change, it seemed that him and all his family was just right outside me and my baby's door. About to break in and bring their shouting and hating with them.

I felt like I could see the lamps that must be burning in Miss Virginia's room, and probably getting lit by now in Master Harvey and Master David's room, too. I felt like I could hear all their voices right up close in my ear, like Newsom's breathing.

In my ear. Down my neck.

I put my hand over my ears and tried not to listen. Maybe I could go get Hannah from her cradle.

Maybe I should wash first, so she wouldn't smell Newsom on me and come to think maybe him and me was one person together.

I looked across the room to where I thought the basin on the table should be. But it was too dark to see anything, even shapes.

And then I had the worst feeling that maybe even Hannah wasn't really there no more.

And then I knew she wasn't. Listen. I couldn't even hear her breathe. She wasn't there.

I had fell on her, remember, and must have killed her.

All this was just, I don't know, something like a dream, maybe. And now I was waking up to find I'd had my baby and killed her and passed out.

Suddenly noise stopped.

That's when I thought to myself, Hey, the men must have all been yelling at once, and Miss Mary too, because now it really is quiet. What happened?

And just like that, Newsom was banging on the door. "What's going on in there, Celia? What are you yelling about?"

He shoved my door open. Lantern light raced across the floor and showed me Hannah's crib and her tight little face, shut to sleep in it.

I let out a breath. My heart was working so hard and fast it hurt. I pressed my hand between my breasts.

"Yelling?" I said. "I didn't hear no yelling but maybe Miss Mary calling out to Miss Virginia, down the hall. They all right now?"

Newsom turned to somebody behind him. Shape of Master Harvey. "See?" Newsom said. "I told you. Cries out in her sleep for nightmares. Surprised you all ain't heard her before."

"Nightmares?" I heard Mister David pipe up. "Well why—"

"Shut up, David," Master Harvey said, backing away. "Come away. Father told you what to make of it. Now go tell Mary to get her mind out the mud and go back to her own bed. Let decent folks sleep in peace."

"Please," I called out as Newsom reached to

187

shut the door. "Don't leave me without a light, sir. Your lantern. Please." I started climbing out from under the bedcovers. "Or just wait

while I blow on the embers, sir."

"Stay still, Celia," he barked at me. "You want everyone to see you?"

I had on Miss Mary's own nightgown, the one she had sent me the first night I came there. Why "everyone" could see Miss Mary running down the hall to Miss Virginia's room in a nightgown, but not me, getting up in my own room to light the fire, I couldn't tell.

But I was that glad no one had caught me braving the dark hallway to clean up my broken pitcher and fetch me and my baby some more water for the morning.

And too, I was glad I'd started pouring my chamber pot pee out of my window, like I knew Harvey and David must have done with theirs. Spared me a lot of dressing up to try to make it to the latrine just to empty a too-full chamber pot.

But it was a shame how, when the spring came, under my window might not grow any grass or flowers, same as none grew under Master Harvey and David's window. Not that they seemed to mind. They didn't mind nothing but the stink when their sisters threw open the window to air the room in warm weather, if I recalled correctly.

You give things up sometimes.

Comfort for beauty. What you want for what you have to settle for. That's what happened to me, after Hannah was born. I started having to settle and give up hoping for anything I wanted, but my babies.

It started with that night, when I hollered out. It went on because, as Miss Virginia put it, I was "long abed." Nobody told me to get up sooner and see to nothing. In fact, that right arm and shoulder of mine got so gimpy that I couldn't count on them, and when I did get up, I got to be somewhat left-handed.

But that wasn't all. It was dead heavy winter outside, all around. Snow high as a child's leg, so I couldn't even send Master Coffee to run the simplest errand without having to wait for him at the back door, afraid maybe he was too simple-minded to slip his feet into even some wooden shoes, protect himself from the cold, and was out there somewhere, stuck and freezing.

And all the time I was at the door, Hannah was alone.

And that was the biggest reason I stayed abed.

I couldn't bear to leave Hannah alone in that room, down that hall, shut out from me by all that darkness that gathered every evening, like it was squatting and waiting, patient, between us.

Much as it scared me to be in the dark room with her, hearing her breathe and feeling her nurse at my breast, but not seeing her, and thinking, Oh now it's happened, I've been fooled and she ain't really here, I'm holding--I don't know--Newsom or something, as much as I hated those scary moments and hours that got to happening almost every night, till I got in trouble for burning so much good wood to keep a banked fire, enough to see by, or burning oil, to keep my lamp low, or burning tallow candles, bought in town because Miss Virginia and Miss Mary was too prissy to learn to make good fat candles like the old days and the old ways back in the old home state, as much as I hated all that...

I hated knowing the blindness and the darkness sat like a shadow and a living thing between me and my Hannah, even more.

So, even as the talk gathered around me and against me till I ran, rubbing my hands clean of beef fat and salt from cooking dinner, not even taking time to wash them proper so they wouldn't peel and burn, I kept going back to my room and my baby and my bed, where I could lay and hold her, and anyway, who could say anything because my shoulder ached and wasn't nobody visiting Harvey's in-laws in the snow and everybody knew, when you got right down to it, I wasn't here but for Newsom to have somebody he could put his parts into.

There came a time, though, and I think it was only weeks after Hannah was born, that I did start getting up and dressed and into the kitchen every single day, to cook a good dinner.

I had more than one reason for doing this. One, it gave me a chance in broadest daylight to get my chamber pot emptied, to get fresh snow to melt in a bowl in my room, making the cleanest-smelling wash water for me and my baby, and to see to it that I would get good victuals to eat, no matter what Miss Mary thought of me being so "lazy," as she put it, of all people.

When you're nursing, you need good food and plenty of it.

And getting up to the kitchen in time to start bread rising and meat roasting reminded everybody that I did something very important around here, while they were gossiping and talking me down, which I couldn't stop, anyway.

And it made me get dressed while I did all that. I was mighty tempted to live in that blood-stained, loose, white gown I had off Miss Mary. I had got used to it, and it felt so warm in the cold mornings and smelled so like hugging Hannah close to me and the shared smell of her skin and my milk.

Washing didn't get rid of that sweet smell.

Hannah was all I had that was good, anymore. After crying out like that for Joshua, I came to see right away how foolish I had been, dreaming or wishing for anything more than my own baby.

That was just not going to be my lot in life, and I had better face it. Just that one dream of Joshua was getting me kicked out of the big house and into a cabin out alone.

I couldn't tell how I felt about that.

On the one hand, I thought it might be good to get away from the hallway and the room that I was always afraid were somehow swallowing my baby away from me.

On the other hand, I heard Master David arguing, and his words scared me, "Are you kidding? Celia, out there alone in a cabin in the woods, trying to take care of a baby? You all heard her crying out that night. Ain't you seen she's afraid of the dark?"

People around the dinner table grumbled at him.

I stood struck dumb and still.

Afraid of the dark? Was I?

And how did he know it?

My mind flew back to all those evenings, more frequent now, that I raced to my room so fast I had to hold up my skirts to keep from tripping myself up, only to find a fire already blazing away in my fireplace, lighting and warming the room for me and Hannah.

Evenings?

No. Somebody was laying and lighting those fires so early, that I could swear, come to think of it, it was getting done right after the family's dinner. As the men were on their way back out to the barn, to see to feeding the livestock, or back out to the site to build my new cabin.

They weren't working on Master Harvey's cabin, anymore. Because Newsom was very particular about how they were to work on mine.

He called it mine.

But I didn't have a thing to say about it. Not even if I would live in it or not. I wasn't sure I wanted to.

Something about being out there, in the dark among the trees, just me trying to take care of my baby, put me in mind of something I couldn't quite put my finger on.

It made me shudder. But I had no one to talk to about it.

Miss Mary had been on and on about me screaming that one night, and how indecent it was, and no wonder no one could come calling, with a "negress harlot parading" right through decent

192

people's home instead of being confined to the kitchen, "pretending to work." For a while, Mister David answered all this by reminding her their father had said I had nightmares.

But one day Miss Mary shouted at him across the table, "And the baby? Living right in our house? Like she was my sister or something?"

And I heard chairs fall back, so I knew people must be rising from the table to go after each other.

But then I heard Master Harvey, firmer than usual. "Father, let Mary go. What good will it do to hit her? She's right. It isn't decent."

I stood stock still in the kitchen at the doorway to the dining room, where I had stopped when I heard the turn the dinner talk was taking.

Newsom said, "You're right, son. I should be building Celia and her baby a place of their own. We'll have to get right to it, I reckon. Being such a gentleman, you'll understand that this necessarily holds up our work some more on that house for you and your new bride."

And I wondered, as silence fell again, if Master Harvey regretted siding with Miss Mary against my presence in the house.

He didn't take it back, however. And only Master David spoke up to say the plan was crazy. My fear of the dark made it so.

But was there something else made it so?

I always felt there was something Master David and the rest weren't saying quite outright, when it came to them arguing about me and Hannah. Things had changed with Hannah's birth.

Not just that everybody made it clear nobody

193

expected me to get to the kitchen and do any work. Also, how I was treated.

Nobody tried to be kind to me anymore but Master David. And, of course, Master Coffee, who would smile at anybody to get a treat from the larder.

Miss Virginia positively wouldn't look at me these days when we worked together.

She got to keeping her hands and eyes strictly on her task, usually something simple like peeling potatoes or churning butter her sister had left to sour in the milk. Tasks that used to be good for chatting, even if it was always about herself and her feelings and ideas that I couldn't rightly understand.

Now that I had Hannah and nobody else but that Master David I didn't trust to turn to, I tried hard to remember what it was Miss Virginia used to say to me. Especially that first day. All about the first man who claims you and how blessed and good, or something like that, you are.

Couldn't remember a word of it.

And hadn't there been, not too long before, another woman who advised me about something?

I couldn't even begin to remember who that other woman might have been.

But I felt I sorely needed these women's advice now, if only I could remember any of it. Because along with the loss of all friends in the family but David, came Newsom's peculiar new easing up on the rule that neither of his sons could go in my room.

From what I heard from the dinner table, I was probably the last to figure out that Master David was in my room every afternoon to lay and light a fire. I wasn't there to see him do it, and it had never crossed my mind he would be so bold.

But I was certainly there, most evenings, when he trailed in, dragging one of his sisters, just to inquire after me and the baby. Did we want for anything? I would drop my eyes and answer instead to one of his sisters, like I thought she had inquired, "No, ma'am. Thank you."

Master Harvey didn't seem to want to take advantage of his father's new permission—if it was permission—to come around me. But now and again he might just stop in the doorway to ask about Newsom or Miss Virginia, putting his questions in such a way that I could just shake my head no or nod yes, if he guessed right where he might find them.

Because nothing had changed, clearly, about how I wasn't to speak to anybody but Newsom and Virginia.

I didn't understand the changes. And they most certain and sure did not extend to the negro hands.

One afternoon, right when I had finished washing up the dinner dishes and was on my way to my and Hannah's rooms with a hearty serving of the leavings, the little boy that lived in the barn with the men came running past the back door, holding his hand and crying.

I sent Master Coffee after him because I thought I saw blood running.

I ran out to look at the tracks in the snow, and sure enough. Hot drops of blood had sizzled a little path behind the boy.

195

Master Coffee dragged the boy back to me by the scruff of his dirty little shirt, like he had done something wrong.

I took him inside and washed his cut. It was ugly. I got Coffee to talk to him and find out what had happened.

He'd been out helping the men work on the new "negro cabin," as Master Harvey was styling it, and went to hand one of the men a saw.

"Which man?" Mister Coffee interrupted.

The boy, who was very young, likely short and skinny for his age, sniffled. "Mister George," he said with his tongue all caught up between his teeth, shushing the sounds till I wasn't sure what he'd said.

"Who?" I asked Master Coffee, getting those chills inside that I had felt that time, breaking the ice at the creek.

Coffee shook his head. "George," he said, looking like his grandfather, Newsom. "Mean old ornery cuss. Grandfather likes the work George can get done, big as he is and strong as a ox. But it's some of us think as George ain't worth the trouble he cause. Crazy coon. Ought to drive him off the place. Ain't saving a copper penny keeping him. What George do this time, Boo?"

Boo, if that was his name, took a long slow time explaining, while his tongue kept tripping him up. When George asked Boo to hand him a saw, George took the opportunity to drag the saw across the boy's fingers.

The child's fingers would probably be all right, not be lost or nothing, if I could get them cleaned and wrapped up tight in a bandage it would be too much bother for anybody to cut or unwind off him in the next week or so. I had nothing but soap and water, or maybe a little witch hazel soaking in a stash of gin and water, to clean the ragged cuts with.

Either would burn. But a child might not scream if he had his mouth full of something he didn't want to have fall out of it.

I couldn't bear to hear that little boy scream.

So I promised him if he could keep a slice of candied lemon peel in his mouth the whole time I was cleaning and wrapping his fingers, he could chew it up and swallow it down when I got through.

Of course, Master Coffee was going to tell terrible tales about me to his mother and grandfather if he didn't get the same treat. So, to teach him who was still in charge about deciding what errands would be run and how much I would pay for the running of them, I told him he didn't have to threaten. It wasn't becoming of a gentleman. He was going to get the same treat all along, just for chasing out in the snow after the boy.

He didn't believe me.

But he shut it. They sucked on their lemon rinds together while the tears and blood ran off of Boo.

And when the knot was tied in the bandage, they chewed their candy down together.

I was set to send them out happy except, I guess, for my worry about Boo's bare little cracked-heel feet. But Master Coffee assured me that wasn't nothing because all you had to do was hop and run everywhere you went and sit every chance you got.

But when I got to the door, to let them out, I opened it to see Joshua.

I guess any one of the men might have been sent after Boo. But Joshua? Who could have forgotten how I felt about him and sent him back to me? Was the whole household blind? Didn't they see how I felt? After that fall in the creek, didn't everybody know?

I stared at Joshua in the opened doorway. He stared back at me. I marveled that so many people with so many eyes could be so blind to how the thought of Joshua, to say nothing of the sight of him, made me quake.

I hadn't seen him in so long it had been like going without water or sunlight. Without air to breathe. Missing something you need so bad you get used to walking like the living dead, without it.

But seeing him now, waiting at the back door in the full light reflected off the snow, I could see how faithful my memory had been, and at the same time, what a cheat.

Nothing I could have thought back together would ever give the warmth, the glow, the tenderness, of just the light in Joshua's black eyes, still and poised in the whites, staring out at me between the dark curled lashes.

To say nothing of the all of him.

To say nothing of the chest, burnished like a polished copper pan, rising and falling with a low breath, spreading away the frayed soft threads of his faded shirt.

Where I had dreamed that he held me when I made that noise in the night.

And gotten banished from the house. A cry escaped my throat even now.

Joshua frowned and held out his hands. "I didn't mean to startle you. *Celia.*" He almost touched me. "I only came for the boy. And…."

And? And what else? Who else? Why, why, why else?

Words, unsaid, hung between us in the frozen air. Where was I in all this that he was doing and the very little about it that he was saying? Did he have nothing to say about me? To me? About us?

"We're going," Mister Coffee shouted and shoved us apart to make a way for himself and the little boy to run through.

The distance between Joshua and me was all of a sudden enough to shut the door.

I didn't.

Instead, we swayed back together. But he wouldn't raise his hands again. His mouth was still there in that open way, like he might have wanted to ask a question but didn't dare. To say something. To feed my heart and my hopes. But wouldn't.

I raised my hands like to touch him.

"Celia." It was Master David, crunching snow on the run towards me. "Get back in that house."

I didn't have time to obey, even if I had a mind to.

It seemed that in one heartbeat David was across the back yard, coming from the pear and cherry orchards where "my" cabin was being laid out and built.

And then he was pinch-faced from the cold right between us. Shoving me backwards into the kitchen.

I jumped away from his hand on my chest.

He slammed the door behind him, shutting out Joshua. "Oh, I can't touch you. No, you're too good for that. But you can have your hands all over every grubbing negro my father whips around this place."

He was still coming at me. I backed into the cutting table and turned to run.

"No, you don't." He had me by a handful of buttons down the back of my bodice and the knot that held my apron strings tied in a bow. I turned and reached around to beat his hands away with my fists. But he caught at them and used them to pin me backwards against the fireplace mantel.

He put his lips not an inch from mine. I felt the heat of his breath in puffs as he spoke and his body trembled up against me. "You little fool. Don't you know what I can give you? It's plenty of families, respectable families, where the fathers share negresses with their own sons. Damn you. I *am* my father. You can't betray him with me."

Sweat popped and ran down my forehead and cheeks. I was too close to the fire, and I hadn't even banked it yet. I thought I smelled my skirt singeing. "Miss Virginia," I yelled. "You've got to come, Miss Virginia."

Mister David slapped me.

My face spun around towards the floor and my body followed it, helpless. As I sat there and held my cheek with one hand and propped myself up with the other. I tried to figure out what had just happened to me.

Somehow, it was like that slap knocked it clear out of my mind. I couldn't think.

I heard David shout, "I caught her, I'm telling you. You just ask her. She was going after that damned hand, trying to get him to come in the kitchen so they could finish it off."

"Watch your words around my daughters." That was Newsom. When had he got here?

"Then don't listen to me," David bellowed. "Put her out there in that damn cabin where the darkies can get to her at all hours when you can't even *see* them if they shut their eyes. Maybe you'll believe me when she starts dropping charcoal black little brats."

Slaps. Screams.

I turned away, twisting myself till it pained me on my shaking right arm, when I heard the cane whistle.

My face got caught between fingers that hurt like splintered wood and wrenched around to stare into the bulging, veined eyes of Newsom. "Tell me," he said so spittle flew in my face, on my lip. "What the hell was you doing with Joshua this time?"

I said, "Nothing. About to ask Mister Coffee to find out what he came to the door for. But he said he came to get the boy whose fingers I bandaged. Ask Master Coffee."

Newsom let me go. "Cof*fee*," he hollered, like as if he hated the child.

Doors and windows slung open all over the house, and voices rang out, "James Coffee."

Meanwhile, I spied a lump of snow that seemed

201

to have fell from someone's boot.

I reached in between all the trouser legs and skirts around me and worked up the snow between my fingers into a little cold compress for my cheek. It was very soothing while we waited.

Coffee appeared, loud, somehow, even when he wasn't talking yet. "Yes, sir, grandfather?" he panted. "You sent for me, sir?"

"Sure as hell did," Newsom said, and that was another change since I had given birth to Hannah. Newsom swore a lot more at everybody, but especially to me and about me. "Tell me what you seen, boy, when this here nigger gal had the door open on my field hand."

"Seen?" Mister Coffee looked critically down at me, wondering what he was missing. I looked back up at him with the snow melting between my fingers and my face.

How well I knew what he was feeling.

"Well, sir," Mister Coffee began, still studying me. "I can't say I seen nothing. You see," now he was excited, "Celia had bandaged Boo's fingers and gave us both a piece of—" here he stopped, worried that he might be betraying a secret it was better we kept on keeping. "Well, anyway, it was just to shut Boo up so he wouldn't cry. Even I could tell that."

Miss Virginia, not meaning to help me, but wanting to keep her boy out of trouble, prompted, "A piece of biscuit, or something like that?"

Coffee, relieved and still in a hurry, said, "Yes, ma'am. Something like that. So anyways, it was sure good, and then Celia went to open the door and send us back to work on the cabin, or send Boo,

202

anyways, only she got worried about his feet, and I had to tell her, never mind, niggers is always sitting down on the job," a throwback, I didn't doubt, to all the jokes about me falling down on top of my newborn baby, but Coffee didn't get the laughs he was hoping for. "So, like I was saying, she opened the door, and this hand was there, name a Joshua, I recollect, and he said he come for Boo, and I said, 'We're going,' just like that, and I myself took and run Boo on back to work."

Mister Coffee stopped, so pleased with himself he had his little chest stuck out.

Newsom stirred, reset his cane on the floor, and cleared his throat. Everybody waited.

Finally, Master Harvey, who I didn't even know was there, said, "And that's it, Coffee? You ain't left nothing out we might need to hear?"

Master Coffee sagged a bit and frowned again. "Left something out, Uncle Harry? No, I don't rightly see what."

Master Harvey murmured low to his father, "See. It's like I told you. Anything to hold up this work on the cabin."

"That is *not* what this is all about," Mister David bellowed again.

"Enough," Newsom hollered.

Now Mister David took on Miss Mary's whine. "Coffee was gone, Father. He wasn't even there when I got to the door."

"Did you see Coffee leave out the door?" Newsom wanted to know.

David faltered. "Well, yes, Father."

"And what *exactly* did you see happen next that

203

Coffee might have missed?"

Coffee, ready to defend his story for fear, probably, of getting caned for all the treats he got out of me, stared like a bully full in the face of his anxious Uncle David, always in trouble.

David said much softer, "Father, you have to picture it. Celia was leaning in on Joshua like…like she wanted to touch him."

Newsom roared. "*Wanted* to touch him? 'Like she *wanted* to touch him?' But *didn't* touch him, am I right?"

Newsom grabbed David by the scruff of his neck and yanked him so close their foreheads knocked like hollow bowls. "Fool, let me tell you something. Niggers ain't nothing but animals out the jungle. The *jungle*, boy. If I, or any white man, for that matter, worried my head about what niggers *wanted*, I wouldn't get a Christian day's work done."

Master Harvey chuckled hearty.

Newsom slung David away. David caught himself backwards upside the mantel where he had pinned me just minutes ago.

Newsom raged on. "Niggers *want* to fuck everybody. And everything. Niggers *want* to slice a good white man's throat."

Harvey shouted, "That's right."

Newsom swayed with the force of his argument. "Niggers *want* to lay around naked and eat fruit dropping out the trees. Who *cares* what niggers want?"

Harvey roared with laughter. This was their signal that, once again, the old man would be all right. Newsom was primed again to take me and all the problems David brought him about me in something like his stride.

I was learning.

So was David.

He dropped his head and mumbled about excuse him. He had bricks to carry out to the cabin site.

Master Harvey, wanting to shut David up once and for all, I suspected, jumped in again. "Not so fast, little brother. Father, with your permission. I think it's time to remind David that a good hand got laid up, nursing whip wounds, useless as a old woman for two weeks, on account of David's tale-carrying about that creek incident."

Was Master Harvey reminding David, I wondered, or his father? Because if it was his father, I hoped he would not stop there but remind him that my cooking had suffered from the whipping I got, too.

At least, I hoped my cooking had suffered.

I promised myself that if I got whipped again for just wanting Joshua, my cooking would for sure suffer this time.

"You are a irresponsible fool." Newsom glared at his youngest son. "You think with your—"

"Father," Master Harvey interrupted again. "I think the ladies have already heard too much of this talk."

Newsom looked around, startled and bleary-eyed, like he had just found out for the first time that his daughters had followed everyone else into the room.

"Yes," he said, mistaking Harvey's intent. "You snooping chits. Get on out of here and see to your children and your chores. You want husbands? Get your mind out of whorehouses, you worthless--"

"Father." Master Harvey sighed.

"Yes, yes, Harry. David. Pull yourself together and come with me."

Misses Mary and Virginia disappeared before the shuffling train of the father and his sons.

I was left alone. I pulled myself to my feet, favoring my now-limp right arm. Had I leaned on it too long?

I would have to go to Hannah soon, as the sun was dying in a wash like faded blood, outside the opened shutters. I didn't want to be afraid to go to Hannah. But surely there would be no friendly fire waiting for me in our room, this evening.

Far away, I heard Newsom's cane falling. He wouldn't be deprived of his need to beat somebody, every time he heard that some other man or boy wanted me. Whatever made Newsom rage so, I suspected it probably had very little to do with David's tattling.

That rage was always waiting. Cold and clingy, like fear of slipping in the creek that night. What had happened, that long ago night before Hannah was born? A shadow waiting for me at the creek. An angry man, threatening me. Wanting me.

Ever since then, I was afraid to be outside this house at night, wasn't I? How strange. Wasn't nothing outside this house as liable to cut loose and hurt me as the people inside it. If I had any sense,

I'd rather be outside at night with mountain lions than in this house.

I shook my head like to clear it. Enough of that. David was silently getting caned for trying to tell on my need to touch Joshua, and I would have to hurry before the dark crept around and settled over Hannah and in between all the spaces of our room.

I couldn't pity David. He should have left us alone.

I stared out through the unshuttered window at the spill of sunset and wondered where Joshua had gone, what he had done, when David shut the door in his face.

And right there, lying still on the windowsill, I saw something that shouldn't be there.

I reached out and picked it up.

Cold. Hard. But warming in my hand. It was a carving, very carefully done.

A woman with full skirts and a ruffled apron held in her arms a baby bundled in ruffled blankets. The woman's tiny face was finely cut and smoothed so that even her cheeks rounded with the softness of her parted-lip smile.

I wondered if she was meant to look like me. I gazed around but saw no trace of Joshua. Could he have left this for me? Seen me with my tiny red-ribbon doll, maybe, and carved me this even better one? I shut the shutters, dropped the carving into my apron pocket, and hurried with my tray of dinner leavings to my darkening, cold room.

After I had a nice fire blazing and the lantern wick turned to a steady, low flame, I searched under my mattress ticking and found the doll with the red ribbon that Master David had gave me. I stood and turned and quick, threw it in the fire and watched how the flames leaped and snapped, hungry for it.

I took Joshua's carving—it *must* be Joshua's carving—out of my apron pocket and slid it under Hannah, in her cradle.

She woke and made her bubbly noises to be fed.

I didn't have to worry about Joshua's carving, there. Nobody never picked up Hannah from her cradle but me. Especially not Newsom.

I worked my left hand over my shoulder to unbutton the back of my bodice and slide it free of my breasts for nursing Hannah. I wondered why Master Harvey was always in a rush to calm his father about me.

Did he just hate to see his brother get whipped all the time? Or did he not want his father upset?

I felt I was, as always, missing something about these people.

Chapter Seven: Walk It Again

When spring came, neither "my" cabin nor Master Harvey's house had got built, and would-be brides were crying everywhere.

That is, to hear Miss Mary tell it. She herself was certainly cutting loose a storm. At the dinner table. At the supper table. Probably at the breakfast table, too, only I wasn't awake to hear it.

I slept till way after the spring birds in the trees had started twittering and calling—day birds only, none of those who are up singing at dawn—and even then only rose to fetch Hannah from her cradle and take her back to bed with me.

She was pudgy, happy, and healthy. The price I paid every night, just to keep her with me, I could keep on paying, I thought.

I wasn't going to be one of those mothers whose children got sold away so they could work better. Somebody, some time must have been long ago, had told me about such mothers.

And somebody else had told me it was wise for women with children to count themselves blessed. Maybe Miss Virginia.

Odd, if it was her. Well, maybe she gave advice better than she took it. I, however, would wisely take her advice.

But somebody else had said, and it seemed not too long ago, that girls my age weren't even women yet.

Now who would say such a stupid thing? Look at me. Look at my fine healthy baby.

Miss Mary?

Put that out of my mind. Laying abed too long in the morning will give you idle thoughts. Seemed to me that was another wise thing Miss Virginia must have said.

After a while of nursing and playing with Hannah, I would bathe her and rock her back to sleep in her cradle.

Nobody was particular happy to see me show up at the kitchen anymore. But after a while, Master David broke down and went back to trying to talk to me.

I wished he wouldn't.

"Celia," it always went, "you remember what I said. Fathers and sons are one and the same man." And on and on.

But at least he started back building my fires and even waiting quietly in my room for me, evenings.

Once, the old man went in there, looking for me in the kitchen when I was out taking down diapers from the line where I had hung them to get the sunshine to burn out the pee smell. Nothing happened but Newsom asked David why I wasn't there, and David said he didn't know. He was waiting, too.

And I walked in with my armload of stiff sun-dried diapers just as Newsom offered his son a cheroot.

"Where's your supper tray?" Newsom asked me and sent David to the kitchen to fetch it.

As soon as we were alone, he pulled me close by my arm. "He's in here every night?" Newsom asked.

"David? Most every evening, lately. He lays me a fire."

"You scared of the dark, like he says?"

"I don't know."

"He stay in here?"

"No. He leaves after I pick up Hannah."

"Why?"

I stared mutely at Newsom.

David came whistling in with my tray of the family's nibbled pork chops, the scraped bottom of the gravy, and some cold mashed potatoes. "Hell, Celia," he said. "You eat better than I do. Where do you put it, little bit? Well, there's your fire. I'm a go out and enjoy me this smoke before it gets too cold and dark on the front porch."

"He's a good boy," Newsom said. "Still follows all his mama's rules, even after she's cold in her grave. Won't smoke in the house."

He closed and locked my door and began to unbutton his breeches. He didn't seem to know, or care, that this was early for our nightly get together.

Sometimes I wondered where Newsom's mind was.

Like about Master Harvey's house. It was the strangest thing, but it seemed that Newsom himself was the reason that Mister Harvey's land couldn't get bought up and his house couldn't get built in time for him to get married before another winter.

Why would Newsom want to keep another mouth around to feed?

I heard Miss Mary, from my place in the kitchen while they ate, accuse her father of not

211

wanting another house for her to go and visit, or maybe stay. "Harry will lose his bride to another man." Her voice bit at her father like as if she was talking about herself. "Waiting on you to give the go-ahead to build their house."

Newsom snarled back like a dog. "Ain't a damn thing stopping the bride's family from sending over the manpower to build that house. I got me a farm to run and ain't got but two lazy sons and four lazy field hands to run it. I ain't thinking about that house till my crops is in and Celia's cabin is built."

"Celia's cabin?" Miss Mary shrieked. "Father, surely you're not going to put Celia's cabin ahead of the building of Harry's house? His wife's family helped buy the land that house is sitting on."

"And ain't laid finger to brick to help build the damn thing."

Master Harvey's voice said quietly, "*Helped*, Mary. The word you used yourself is that they 'helped' buy the land. I don't need you speaking up for me. If you are speaking up for me."

I heard Miss Mary say, "Everything is Celia. Ever since she got here, everything is tainted with her. What she did, what she didn't do, what she wanted to do. Beating and depriving people, all because of Celia."

Newsom said, "That's enough," just as Mister David said, "I haven't heard Celia ask for none of that," and Miss Virginia offered, "I wonder if my boys might not help with the farming a bit, so the men could be freed up now and again to keep working on Harvey's house?"

212

But the spring spun away into hot summer storms, and I sagged in the kitchen, sweating and baking fruit tarts again for Sunday visits. I wondered how I had fooled myself into thinking I only cooked when and what I wanted to and gazed out between the wide-spread shutters, braving mosquitoes for a glimpse of Joshua.

I never saw him all that spring and summer.

Hannah got big and began to crawl out of her cradle and around our room, while I was gone in the kitchen.

So in the fall, I started keeping her with me in the kitchen while I cooked. She and I would sit at the cutting table and eat together, her smearing mashed bits of food onto my breast, wanting to nurse, while the family ate.

Still, through the cooling autumn with Hannah in the kitchen at my breast, I gazed through the open kitchen shutters and caught no sight of Joshua.

Miss Virginia explained, "The crops are coming in. Soon the men will be gone every day, working late on Harvey's house."

And I began to spend my days packing and cloth-wrapping large hot meals for the men to take over to Master Harvey's new site with them.

It was peaceful, with the men gone all day. I suspected the hands went, too. So I began to close the shutters against the gathering evening chill.

No point giving Hannah the croup. Joshua, for sure, wouldn't be out there.

When winter fell again, I was expected to help with the sewing Miss Virginia and Miss Mary had abandoned the year before. Finishing dresses and trousers for the wedding. And yes, after all, the men had been persuaded to have new shirts, instead of wearing old ones mended.

I stood straight in Miss Virginia's face and told her, "I don't know how to sew."

It was true. Nobody had ever taught me. I had been taught to cook.

But what I hoped she heard in my tone was, *Make me learn.*

She'd been steamed at me for asking about her mother for a solid year. She wouldn't look at me. She didn't have a good word for me. I was her father's whore.

And now she was going to let on like she believed his stories that I was some kind of regular household help?

I waited a polite little bit for her to suggest something, like maybe she would teach me something simple that would help free her up for finer sewing. But she didn't.

So I turned my back and finished my day's baking. She couldn't stop me. The men would need their hot meal.

The men had kept up their work on Master Harvey's new house, even in the snow. What I didn't know was, someone had been left behind to finish up the work, alone, on "my" cabin, too.

I learned later that one man had been left behind because he couldn't come along and work well with the others. He was a troublemaker. He was a danger.

But I didn't know he was even alone here with me and Newsom's daughters and grandbabies, until,

214

one day when the heavy snow sat low and grey over our heads and I went outside with a bowl to gather chipped ice from the creek, he was there.

I was breaking up the ice at the edge of the creek with a sharp stone and dropping chunks of it in my bowl. I would carry it back to help me get through my work in the kitchen. Sliding lumps of ice and snow down my back and between my breasts had become one of my chief joys of the hot, close day.

How I was tired of all the baking.

The day hadn't got dark. It had started dark, and stayed dark, and simply had never got light.

But it felt like something had gone away. The sun. The path to the house. I looked up and around to make sure the house was just right over that little hill there, where I had left it.

And there he stood with his fists on his hips. George.

He didn't move aside when I stood up.

I gathered up my bowl, clutched it to my chest, and thought I would throw chunks of ice in his face if I had to. I wondered why he frightened me so. Just standing and staring.

I should walk on by. I had done it before.

I moved. Kept coming. Reached him.

"Ho," George said as I went to pass. "Still can't speak."

He grabbed my arm just as I almost slipped by. The bowl with its ice clattered and crunched to the snow and slush at our feet.

With his free hand, George slapped my face backhanded. Only his grip on my arm kept me from

215

falling. I sagged from his fist and then righted myself, weaving a little.

"Take that to your white man," George said. "Tell him it's from me." He shoved me a little up the path, and I stumbled on to the house without the wooden bowl.

I slammed the kitchen door and latched it tight behind me and thought, pulling at my hair and screaming out her name, about my baby. I should never have left her alone to go to the creek for ice. What a fool's errand. Anything could have happened to her. To me. To me, and I would never return to take care of her. Where was she? Not here. Not in the kitchen. "Hannah."

I faced my room, down that long dark hall, and knew she was in there alone with that feeling and I would never make it to her. "*Hannah*."

Then I whispered, "Please come to mama, baby. Please come."

Above my whisper, I heard Miss Virginia call from her room. "Celia? In here. Come on in here. You'll wake the dead with all that racket." I stumbled toward her voice like toward light and salvation.

Miss Virginia smiled, sitting at her table with all her sewing, when I came in. Her children tumbled on her bed and across their pallets on the floor. Hannah squealed and tumbled with them.

I fell on my knees and snatched her up in both arms.

"Celia?" I looked up to find Miss Virginia studying me. "Mercy sakes, girl. What happened to you? Where've you been?"

216

"Outside to get some ice. I must have been gone too long. I couldn't find Hannah."

"Well, that part I know. You weren't gone long. But Hannah gets bored crawling around that hot kitchen by herself, and this time, she just lit out and made it all the way to my room. Walked."

Miss Virginia beamed. And then I understood. My baby had walked, all by herself, for long distances. And I had missed it.

Cowering at the creek from that man.

Miss Virginia's smile faded away. "Celia, I don't mean to trouble you, but you don't look none too good. I thought, this time, wasn't anything bothering you but the heat. This minute, though, I'd say you look as sick as the first time. Sicker."

"What first time?"

Miss Virginia stared at me as though she feared I'd lost my mind. "Hannah," she said. "*That* first time."

I sat back on my heels. "Not again."

She smiled, maybe a little sadly. "It's to be expected, Celia. The nursing won't keep it off forever."

"The nursing?'

"Yes. Didn't you notice when your bleeding stopped again?"

"Stopped? Again? After Hannah was born? Miss Virginia, it never started again."

She went whiter and then pink. "Oh," she said. "Well, it starts up again for most women, well before now. After all, Hannah's going on a year-and-a-half." Her voice got gentle. "You mustn't fret. It will be easier this time. The second time is

217

almost always easier."

"Yes." I looked around at the children, who looked back at me with no interest at all, seeing as how I hadn't carried them any food.

Except Hannah. She had waddled to me, falling and crawling and pushing herself to her feet again. She really was walking.

All of a sudden, all in one day.

I rose and picked her up with my left arm. "Better go finish that bread for the men's bacon sandwiches tomorrow," I said. "I've promised your father. He enjoys them so."

Without raising her eyes from her work, Miss Virginia said, "Remember, Celia. If you tire of the heat and standing on your feet to cook, I'll be happy to teach you to sew."

"Thank you, Miss Virginia. I'll consider that." As I turned, I only regretted that she hadn't said it more kindly. I wished she hadn't sounded--and looked--like she was tricking me.

Because now I knew why I was running out to the yard for snow and the creek for ice, I could see this would only get worse. And if there was any real danger out there. . . .

Any real danger.

I turned back to Miss Virginia's bright-lit, noisy room. "Master Coffee," I said sweetly, "I seem to have left my bowl of ice down by the creek somewhere. Hurrying to get back, worrying about Hannah. Could you be kind enough, maybe, to go fetch it for me?"

Coffee looked up with that mean shine in his eye.

218

"I'll be most grateful," I assured him.

"Coffee, go on," his mother said, and pricked her finger and stopped to suck it. Then she looked up at me, and the look of trickery was gone. "Celia, may I trouble you for a nice cup of tea?" she asked, and her heart was in it. "I do so hate all these cold meals and eating the biggest meals so late in the day, with the men gone. I wish they'd finish Mister Harvey's house."

I licked my lips, glad for the brief peace between us. "Miss Virginia, is there any reason they might have left one of the men behind? Here? Instead of taking all the men to work on Master Harvey's house?"

Miss Virginia frowned and thought. "Oh." Her voice was flat. "You must mean George. They left him here to furnish your house." Suddenly her face went slack, like with a new thought. "He hasn't troubled you none, has he? Celia?"

"No, no." Now, why did I say that? *Tell her*, I yelled at myself. *Tell her what he says.*

And who knows where the cane will fall this time? I answered myself back. She *did* give you another way out. "Miss Virginia, maybe I'd best take you up on that offer of sewing. If what you guess is the problem, I can't make it another two weeks, with all this baking and cooking late into the day. Will your father mind much, do you think?"

Miss Virginia laughed. "Celia, I have long suspected that the only reason those men are working so diligent on that house every day is because they want your good food to keep coming." We both laughed at that. "Think about it. All those dried fruit and nut tarts, and prime bacon sandwiches, and all that butter and cream on everything, and they don't even have to share? I'd get out there and build that house my own self, if I thought I'd eat like that. Wouldn't you?"

I had to agree.

And when Coffee brought my bowl of ice--with no scary tales about a man on the darkening trail—I celebrated the end of sending the men out every day to work on Harvey's house by handing Coffee one whole tart for himself, and serving up the rest with Miss Virginia's tea.

Miss Virginia invited me to take tea with her while she taught me to sew. Miss Mary even joined us. She always did like my tarts.

And we never told anyone about the evening we all three ate and sewed together, talking about who likes to do that marriage thing better, men or women.

The only time the laughing stopped was when Miss Mary said, "Sister, you're doing all the talking. I'd like to hear from Celia. She's got experience. Celia, who do you think likes it better? The man or the woman?"

I didn't even have to think about it. "I don't think either one of them likes it. They just do it because he thinks he's suppose to."

When the laughing stopped, I was right sorry Miss Mary had asked me. It wasn't a question worth ruining our tea party and our truce. Who knew how long the peace would last?

Especially with the men coming back home to stay.

They took it well when they heard I couldn't stand around the kitchen baking and cooking any more, sending them food to feast on at Harvey's house site. In fact, they took it so well Miss Virginia got suspicious.

"Hell, that house is damn near done, anyway." Newsom laughed, blushing to hear about the coming baby. "We can send one of the hands up that way every day to put the final touches on things. Plenty of time to finish up for a spring wedding. Am I right, son?"

A slap on Master Harvey's back.

Miss Virginia said, "So, you all were thinking to quit hauling the whole wagonload of you over there every day anyway? Is that it?"

The men slid their eyes at each other. There was a lot of shrugging shoulders and making those sounds men make when they're not saying anything.

It seemed Miss Virginia might get mad.

"No harm done," Master David announced out of the blue. "The gang's all home and glad to be here, and Celia can get off her feet and help sew for the wedding. Sounds fine. What's for supper?"

Late though it was, as the family gathered at the table for a milk and porridge supper, I found a fire blazing in my fireplace.

I sank into a chair, holding Hannah, and wondered what to feel. The light. The warmth. The sense of being safe and snug. Inside.

All of them passed so quickly. Every day was a new trial. You walk down a hallway, down a path, and turn and find that the path you've already

221

walked is not familiar, now. To walk it again is to face your biggest challenge.

"I'm afraid," I told Hannah, fallen asleep with her few little white teeth clenched on my nipple.

"Afraid of what?" Mister David asked from the doorway. He came in and got down on one knee by my chair.

I looked him in his eye. "I don't think you should be in here."

He said, "You spoke to me, Celia," and kissed my mouth.

I got up, struggling to hold onto Hannah with my left arm and push Mister David away with the right. It didn't work. He clung to me all the way to my bed.

"I only came," he said, struggling to keep a gentle grip against my prying with my elbow, "to see what happened to you. Virginia is worried that something happened to you today, out there by the creek. Celia, stop pushing me away. What happened? I can help."

"What do you mean what happened?"

Of course, it was Newsom. In the doorway. How long had he been there?

David whipped around to face his father.

"Father, Virginia was only worried that something unpleasant may have happened to Celia today, and that with everyone working away at Harvey's house, Celia might not want to come forward and tell."

"Well, what're you asking her for? She can't talk to you, no way."

David said, "I hope she'll tell you. None of us

want her hurt."

"Well," Newsom opined, "*some* of you sure don't want her hurt." Then he chuckled, just like that, and sent David off to "rest up. You'll be up early," Newsom told him, "to drive that fool nigger George can't nobody get along with out to Harvey's house to finish the windows. Don't need all these men off the farm just to finish some windows. It's careful work, but it's one man's work."

"Yes, sir." Without another look at me, Mister David was gone.

Newsom said, "What happened to you, Celia? You going to tell me?"

"I was frightened in the dark by the creek, sir."

"Did you fall?"

I looked up at him. "Why do you say that, sir?"

Newsom touched my cheek. "This. How'd you get this? Something hit you?"

I thought a long, careful minute. If I told, what would happen? What to me, what to George, what to Joshua? What to Hannah? What to my chances of ever being alone with Joshua? What, what, what to say? What to do?

What was I really afraid of around here? Everyone? Everything? Even the dark?

If I was afraid of everything, what did I fear most?

Newsom.

I said, "I got frightened in the dark. Maybe a tree branch hit me when I started running, sir." Best to keep him out of my concerns. After all, what had George actually done?

When I was laying quiet in the dark, waiting for

223

Newsom to snore himself awake and leave to go back to his own room and sleep with little Buddy, the answer came to me, unwanted. *He hit me for no reason and will always get away with it. No one will ever protect me.*

I put the thought away, over and over again, until I fell asleep.

In the morning, Newsom told me that, for real, I had started crying out in my sleep. "Should we give you maybe a little of my whiskey, to help you sleep at night?"

Miss Virginia, newly my friend again, came into the kitchen where Newsom had found me cooking dinner. "Now, Father," she said. "We've agreed that spirits aren't good for nursing or making babies."

Miss Virginia was smiling. So was Newsom. I couldn't think why they were so happy.

In fact, everybody seemed to be getting awfully happy.

Even Master Harvey.

And as the winter soon melted and flowed into creek beds and fed the earliest flowers and grasses of spring, even I wanted to be—not just hope to be, but really *be*—happy.

The wedding dresses flowed with enough ribbons and lace to make it clear that Harvey's wife was marrying into a family that could hold its head up in town. Buy what it wanted, not just what it needed.

And the men's new trousers and shirts looked truly fine. No one thought of new shoes until it was too late to order any.

But, "a penny saved," Newsom decided, "is a penny more paid on the land mortgage."

Miss Virginia's children had never looked so clean. And shod.

Their feet must have been killing them. Amelia kept peeling her pretty little shoes clean off during the wedding.

She came home from the festivities without them.

I regretted that. I would have loved to have Hannah wear those shoes out, thumping around the kitchen in them just for every day. Pretty as a living doll.

After the wedding, the house fell into a pleasant noisiness, without Harvey. Like as if he used to make folks quieter than was good for them.

"Everybody was always afraid Uncle Harry would tell on them to grandfather," Mister Coffee explained, back from the creek with a fresh bowl of water to cool my neck.

I handed him a few perfect cherries and held out a peach from Harvey's in-laws. "Was everybody afraid of Mister Harvey? I mean like Uncle David is afraid?"

Mister Coffee studied the peach. "Uncle Harry ran the farm for grandfather. Uncle Harry could make grandfather mad at anybody. Even you know that." He took the peach and then doubled back for the cherries.

I lifted them away. "Who'll run the farm now, Mister Coffee?" I said. "Sometimes I worry."

He waved me away. "Ah. You worry all the time, Celia. Uncle Harry said women always worry. Give me the cherries."

True, I was worried. I worried more as "my" cabin neared finishing.

"Do I have to live in it before the baby is born, sir?" I asked Newsom one night as he dragged on his breeches to leave my room.

"What? Live where? This another bad dream of yours?"

"The cabin. Your negro cabin, sir."

"Oh. *Your* cabin, Celia. Don't you want to have your new baby born there?"

"No, sir. I don't want to be alone."

"Well, we'll see."

But without Mister Harvey to go to, decisions seemed to get noisier.

I heard them yell about when I should move to the cabin over breakfast. I used to never wake in time to hear them talk over breakfast.

"We'll miss visiting season," Miss Mary snapped without Mister Harvey to reprimand her. "It's like I said. Everything depends on what that negro woman wants."

"What sister means, Father, is that Celia's baby won't be born until near the end of summer," Miss Virginia cut in to pacify. "All the spring parties and summer soirées will be done. People will be worried about harvest."

"Seems there are plenty of harvest get-togethers."

"Certainly."

David added, "And don't forget Christmas. Won't it be nice to be married into a family that gives Christmas parties?"

"Of course."

Miss Mary shouted, "But harvest barn dances and Christmas parties are when people announce the engagements they made in the spring and summer."

"Now, Mary," Miss Virginia started, and I heard a chair topple.

I sighed. Now, I could not go back to sleep. I worked my way out from under Hannah and swung open the shutters.

Early morning birdsong and sunshine rippled into my room. "You see how it is," a voice said outside my window. I pulled myself up to the ledge, heart hammering, to see who had spoken in to me.

Mister David. He said again, "Celia, you see how it is. If you're afraid to move out to that cabin--and mark me, I know you have good reason to be afraid—you're going to have to come clean and tell Father. He won't push all these other arguments. He doesn't understand them. He doesn't care about them. You say you don't want to birth the baby alone. But he knows you won't be alone. He knows Miss Virginia would be checking up on you every day, ready to help you through it." He laughed. "Miss Virginia sure don't want nothing bad to happen to *you*."

I stared at Mister David, not wanting him to go. Not without telling me, first, what *he* thought I had to be afraid of, out in that negro cabin.

He couldn't read my thoughts. He stared back at me and only said, "What is it? Do you want me to kiss you again? I will."

I backed away from the window ledge.

227

David frowned. "You remember what I said about fathers and sons sharing negro women. It's an honorable thing. All the best families do it. Come close here. Come on. I won't try to kiss you. Just listen to me."

I came back to the ledge.

Mister David put a hand on the ledge near me. "Listen. Whatever you're afraid of out there in that cabin, I won't let it hurt you. I'll be there. I'll take care of you. And someday you'll be thankful to me."

Now his hand touched mine. I stared, wondering if he knew what I feared. If *I* could even be sure what it was I feared. Nameless as it was. Darkness. A dirty word spoken by a man along a path.

After all, what had George done to me that Mister David himself hadn't already done? And I didn't fear Mister David. Much.

Mister David said, "Who do you think talked Father into making sure it was George who got sent every day to finish up Harvey's house? Harvey? Not on your life. He couldn't care. As long as the old man doesn't keel over before Harvey's taken him for every pretty penny."

David reached in and slipped his hand behind my head to hold me still. He caught my lips in a quick suck with his. "Me, Celia," David said as I pulled back from his kiss. "I got rid of George for you. You didn't even have to tell me what he did. You can't tell on George to Father without getting blamed and beat."

He leaned in further to catch me by my

shoulders and pulled me to him into the most sucking, biting, chewing sharing of mouths that I had ever tried to breathe through. When he let me go, my head reeled like it was too light to rest on my shoulders. "You should trust me, Celia. You know you should."

Did no one see all this happening at my window?

Well, it was certainly early in the morning. Anybody seeing David under the tree outside my window might have simply thought he was stopping to pee, as he seemed to prefer to do under windows, anyway.

But this was two kisses, maybe three, that David had gotten away with right under Newsom's nose. It made me wonder about the old man's rules and whippings.

Was I only wrong when caught? No. Only wrong when Newsom said I was wrong. And where was his protection from George? Why couldn't I figure out how to get it?

The same evening of the window kisses, Mister David left a lantern burning in my room, it being too warm for a fire that day. He came back, like to check on it or me, after I started nursing Hannah.

"Why do you still nurse her?" he demanded, shoving open the door against me. I backed away to keep Hannah from getting crushed between the door and me.

David came into the room with his eyes on my breast. I put Hannah down and she toddled to my bed. I tried to pull up the bodice as quick as I could.

"Leave it." Mister David grabbed both

229

shoulders of the bodice and tried to jerk them down at once. They stopped at the top of my arms and wouldn't budge. He yanked again. I could hear button threads pop. Little buttons clicked onto the floor. The bodice gave way.

David threw himself at me with his hands cupping my breasts. He squeezed the nipples, bringing his body up against me as I backed away. I couldn't back fast, and he was up against me in no time, his hands between our chests, his hips at mine, working, reaching.

He was moaning. I knew those sounds.

He ground my breasts in both his hands. Milk squeezed painfully through the nipples. I cried out. Swallowed the rest of the sound. Said, "Mister David." Had he shut the door? Could anybody come to the end of the hallway and see? What would happen to me?

We had backed against the bed. I resisted falling over by twisting away.

He let go of my breasts and grabbed at my waist, baring it with both hands. "Why do you nurse a baby?" he mumbled as he bent his head to my aching breasts. "I can do this. Let me do this. Let me, let me…" He snatched me forward against his chest, against his hot crotch, the rhythm, the movement, the words out of his mouth, the nipple into his mouth.

I went slack with the first shock of his wet lips and tongue taking the tip and the head and the full of my nipple. All those times with Hannah and Newsom, it had never felt like this.

But when the sucking began, and the sharp

thrill of that tugging deep inside, so painful when the baby was new, so drawing when done gently--had Newsom ever done this gently?--I hit at his head and neck and shoved his face away.

I came away with one nipple bleeding. I hadn't thought he was *hurting* me. I pressed my hands to the blood. He reached for me again. I broke from him and ran to the door.

Hannah watched me speed by her and cried, reaching for me.

"I'm sorry," Mister David began. "Don't open the door. Not yet. I can't go out like this." He cupped his hands between his legs. "Let me catch my breath."

A fist pounded on the door. Again.

I pulled down my bodice as far as I could and threw myself on the bed, grabbing up Hannah to nurse. When David opened the door to his father, Newsom saw me first, tugging the bedclothes up over my breasts and Hannah's head as she gulped down tears and my milk.

He looked over at his son, who swept his hand in a gesture to invite his father to take the only chair.

Newsom said, "What are you doing in here with the door shut when she's got her titties hanging out? I think I may need to cane you."

But he looked unsure. Mister David raised his hands like in surrender.

"Just keeping her company, Father, till you could come," Mister David said, backing out. "It was too hot for a fire, and the lamp was low. I shut the door so people wouldn't peek at her—you know—nursing her little one. Now you're here, I can go."

Newsom watched his son leave, and it was peculiar how I felt almost sad for the confusion I saw on his face. He wanted to be angry, but he didn't know what to think. He wondered if he was missing something.

"Why you let him all up in here when I'm not here?" Newsom finally demanded of me.

I said in my most level voice, "Give me your leave to talk to him, and I can tell him to go, sir."

Newsom shook his head and blinked at me. "Girl, you sassing me to my face?" he said, still unsure. Unsure about everything, now.

"No, sir," I answered, dropping my gaze. What was the use? I didn't even know anymore who my worst enemy was.

Newsom wasn't bothered by the blood on my breast. "That baby getting teeth?" he asked and turned me away from him. It struck me, as he fumbled open his breeches and tried to jerk his worm against my bare bottom until it was enough of a razor to slide between my shut legs, that he might prefer taking me from behind. That way, he didn't have to try to be gentle, nor did he have to see how much I hated him.

Chapter Eight: Rocking Like You Do a Baby

Buddy was my last try.

I waited at the kitchen door for Newsom to come in from the barn for dinner. He sometimes came in through the front door, but this time, he took the shortcut.

Newsom wanted to wash by the warmth of the fireplace. I waited until his shirtfront was open and the sleeves hung down around his breeches.

"What about Buddy?" I said.

Newsom frowned over at me, blinking through the dripping wash water. His skin was flushed with the water's cold and the fire's heat. "What about him?" He didn't much like anybody to talk about Buddy.

I plowed on. "What good will it do to send me out to the cabin so Miss Mary can have her callers, if you don't want people snooping around the house asking questions about Buddy? Buddy will still be here when I'm gone." My voice died at the end.

Newsom slapped water on his face with such vigor that it splashed me. "You got that right," he growled into his hands. "Buddy will still be here when you're gone. Don't put your mouth on his name again."

I moved back as fast as the bulge over my hipbones and the ache in that one leg would let me. I had heard of this kind of problem. People getting tired of you, all of a sudden. Where had I heard?

Well, it didn't matter now. All that mattered was getting wherever I had to go with both of my babies at my side.

Why was I so afraid of that cabin? Mister David must have filled my head full of nonsense.

Newsom said as much, rubbing his face dry with the end of my apron. "Don't want to hear no more about it. Ain't never seen a cabin for niggers built so solid and pretty as that one. Ungrateful, wretched, whoring gal. Ain't never heard of niggers afraid of the dark." He dropped my apron and raised his face to glare at me with red-veined eyes. "Niggers afraid of the dark would have to be afraid of themselves, now wouldn't they?" he demanded.

And I thought, odd how his eyes and his breath always look and smell as if he just drank his nightly whiskey. No matter what time of day.

And he was having trouble doing what he wanted to with me in bed for several weeks now. Months, maybe. But every night. Not just nights he admitted he'd drunk too much to get what he wanted.

Not that that stopped him from scratching and clawing and grinding till it hurt worse than nights when he got what he wanted.

He snatched his shirt up and made little ripping sounds as he shoved his arms into the sleeves. "Damn. Got to get Mary to mend these things better." And he pushed through the door to the dining room.

After grace, I heard him order Mister David to get me set up in the negro cabin as soon as the meal was done.

David said, "Why all of a su—"

And Miss Virginia said, "Should I go with him, Father?"

Miss Mary said, "About time. That new cousin-in-law of Harry's has been catching all the beaux since the June boating party."

I hid in my room, holding Hannah between my itching breasts and the twisting bulge that the whole front of my body had become. If I didn't go, if I wouldn't go, maybe they couldn't make me go.

And then Hannah wiggled out of my sore arms and got down on the floor to fish her "mama doll," as she called it, out of her cradle to play with.

And I lay watching her, curled in on myself as far as I could and not so burning hot, for a change, and thinking, I've made too much of this. What's so scary about a cabin? Nothing more scary than a room. Maybe, if Newsom will let me talk to David, I can ask him to keep coming out and lighting the lantern or the fire for me in the evening. Maybe I just won't stay in here, after dinner's on the table. I'll get right out to the cabin and start a light burning, myself. No one will want Hannah bumping around in the house all day, anyway. And I can't leave her alone—the thought gave me a quick shudder—alone out there in the cabin.

Dinner must have ended quicker than usual. It seemed no time before Mister David and Miss Virginia were at my door, knocking and smiling and picking up my things.

Halfway through expecting Hannah, Miss Virginia had given me one of her "fat lady" dresses, to see me through. And when Hannah was born, she didn't want it back. So now, on the peg on the wall, I had two dresses hanging, as well as a spare apron.

And there were all those baby clothes she hadn't took back from Hannah, though Hannah had got too big now for anything but a loose shirt. So she was down to the one piece of clothes every day that most pickaninnies wear, to hear Newsom tell it. All these had become clothes for the new baby.

Miss Virginia carried mine and the baby's things. Mister David took my wash bucket and basin, and promised to come back for the cradle and lantern.

I had been so distressed, I hadn't thought to put away Hannah's mama doll.

Mister David waited until Miss Virginia left the room ahead of us to fetch a laundry basket to carry all the diapers.

"That's not the doll I carved you," Mister David said, his voice flat. "Who made that?"

"I don't know," I said truthfully, whispering. As long as I was breaking the rules to talk to him anyway, I might as well break them all. I enjoyed not calling David "sir." "I found it on the kitchen window ledge. You didn't carve it?"

"No, Celia. When did you find it?" Suspicion.

"Round the time I had to burn the other one you made me. You didn't make me a new one?"

"No." Jealousy. Finality. Anger, low and rising.

It was hard telling the truth so it sounded like a lie. But I was learning. I was almost in a hurry to

236

get out of my room and start trudging to the cabin, I so bad, so much, so urgent didn't want to hang around and answer any more of David's questions about that burned doll.

Miss Mary was in the kitchen, getting started washing up the dinner things, when we went through. But I didn't see Newsom nowhere around.

The walk to the cabin seemed long. It had a door facing us. You could see it from way away.

When I said, "No windows," Mister David said, "Sure there is. Round back. A pretty one with shutters," just as if he thought I had suddenly got permission to start chatting with him.

When we got near up on the little porch at the door, Miss Virginia said, "Isn't it the sweetest thing? You missed the flowers that were blooming out here all spring and summer. Iris and pansies, was it, brother? And, oh, hollyhocks and such. Real sweet, Celia."

I was touched. Newsom couldn't get a flower to grow. Who had planted them?

"Flowers where, Miss Virginia?" I said.

Miss Virginia smiled, so pleased I had taken an interest. "Oh, all around the porch and windows. All around the cabin. To say nothing of the cherry and pear trees in bloom, as soon as you looked out your cabin door. It's just the loveliest place, Celia."

"Who planted the flowers, Miss Virginia?" I went ahead and asked. Joshua, I thought. It had to be Joshua. If God was merciful, let it be Joshua.

Mister David snapped at me, "Who the hell needs flowers blooming? Ain't nothing but weeds to make you sneeze."

237

And after he had passed ahead of us into the cabin, Miss Virginia hung back and whispered to me, "He would say that, you know. We can't get a flower to bloom around our place, he and Harry have marked it so like wild dogs."

I didn't realize, till her face fell, that I was suppose to laugh.

Hannah ran into the cabin behind Mister David. I came in and the shadows swallowed me.

Miss Virginia stood in the center of the room, glaring, still, and with no house smells, like it was watching me, and she turned around saying, "Look, Celia. A wooden floor."

And I thought, Your father don't want mud and dirt on his feet.

"And see? A nice bed. Feel this mattress."

And I thought, Your father don't want to grind on me on the hard floor. He's getting old and his bones ache near on bad as mine.

Miss Virginia got tired of my sullenness. She put the basket of diapers and clothes on the floor, slid it under the one table in the room, and dusted her hands. "Celia, you can bring back that basket when you come to make dinner tomorrow morning. Come on, David. It's work to be done."

"You go on. I'll be right there, Virginia," Mister David said with a tone like Master Harvey might have used.

Miss Virginia started. "Well," she said, "didn't you say you'd go back for the cradle and lamp, brother?"

"You want to bring them for me, sister?" Mister David said. It sounded like a challenge. What had

238

gotten into him?

Miss Virginia turned to the door, saying, "I'll just let Father know we've got Celia just about moved in over here. Maybe he'll come and see to things, himself."

Mister David turned his back on her as she left. He stood a minute as if thinking. Then he moved and knelt at the black fireplace. His hands, pale in the darkness, reached out. I watched as he laid a fire and lit it, saying, "Place don't smell like a home yet. You wait till you've cooked a supper or two in here. Then it'll smell like home, Celia."

I turned from him and pushed open the shutters at the back of the cabin. They let out on a view of another little footpath that led to the creek.

The smell of fruit that had fallen and rotted, and saplings that had sprouted up and died in the shade of the taller trees, drifted into the house. The smell of raked and burning leaves. The sound of the negro hands over by the barn, shouting orders to each other and laughing.

How could anybody be happy today?

David was at my back now. "Don't be sad, Celia," he said. "This'll work out. You'll see. It'll be better for you here. I can take care of you out here. Listen to me."

I turned to look at him, frowning with the weight of worry I was feeling. He put his lips to the frown between my brows and said, "After this baby is born, you'll be through with Father, Celia. I'll see to it, if you're ready for me to. And then this place could be like ours."

I moved away from him. What madness was

239

he talking?

I would never be through with Master Newsom until the day he died. And who ever would see to that day for me? Not his own son.

What was I thinking? Death. Newsom. His own son.

Such thoughts. Sometimes I scared myself. Senseless, crazy thoughts coming out of nowhere.

I went and lay myself, real slow and careful, on the new bed and put my head in my arms. I could smell the dust and feel the dirt that had settled on the bed quilt while it waited, all these months, in the unwanted cabin. Even little dead fall leaves had blown in through the window or the opened door and were crackling under my weight. I remembered my ride here--how long ago?--in Newsom's wagon.

David came near and I felt his weight as he sat on the bed behind me. When I didn't move away, he lifted his feet from the floor and stretched himself out all along my back.

Hannah chirped without looking up, "Time to night-night? I don't want to night-night," and moved under the table to make the laundry basket a cabin for her mama doll.

David pressed his body closer up against me. He fitted his chest and stomach and legs around the bend of my back and rear end. His arms went around me. The warmth surrounded me, lulled me. He started moving, slow and very slight at first, like he wasn't sure he wanted me to feel what he was doing.

But when I still didn't move away, he slipped his hands down my thighs to grab and press me

240

back against him. He slid his hands to my knees. Up again, opening my legs. My backside dug into his lap, and he moved tighter and harder against it until I felt the heat build in his crotch through my dampening skirt. He let go of my legs and bunched away my skirt from between us.

David was breathing hard. This was the first thing that came through my haze, almost like not caring, and worried me.

But at the same time, I thought how David moved so much smoother than his father. All Newsom's jerky stabs and grinds. The pain. I shoved those out of my mind. Flowed backward into David. He surged forward. Up. Fitted against me. Moaned. Pressed and lifted harder. Fit better. Grew against me. Said my name, "Celia." Flowed away again, like he couldn't take it. I couldn't take it. But we reached for each other again.

This was almost soothing, rocking like you do a baby. But hotter. Making you want to ease down, ease more into it, build on that small, greedy, good feeling, somewhere deep inside you and yet far away. "Celia, Celia." He lips nipped soft and moist up and down the back of my neck.

"You all in there?"

David leaped up from the bed, dropping my hips and untangling himself from my skirt all in one bound.

Newsom's shaky voice rasped on. "David? Celia. Come unlatch this door." Had we left the door latched? I didn't remember latching it after Miss Virginia left.

Maybe it wasn't latched. Maybe he was faking.

241

Maybe he had gone around to look in through the shutters. For sure, I didn't remember hearing Mister David close them.

"Sshh," David hissed through the closed door at his father. "Celia's wore out, sleep. I was watching till you could get here."

I heard the door open. Sure enough, no sound of it being unlatched. I went cold inside. Why hadn't Newsom come on in? Was my skirt down and proper?

"Watching?" Newsom challenged. "Boy, you hang around that pregnant heifer entirely too much. Why don't you get on out and marry you some pussy of your own, like your brother did? Treating niggers like a lady. You shame me."

Newsom came over to the bed and leaned into my face. "Flushed," he said. "Damn if it don't look like she got a fever."

Hannah, from under the table, piped up, "No night-night!"

Newsom dismissed David. "Go on and get your sister. See can she figure out what to do for this black sow, now. You don't never stop causing good white folks worry, do you, Celia?" David glanced straight and sure at me behind his father's back as he slipped out the door and into the gloaming.

My voice was husky. "Can I ask you for some water, sir?"

He looked into the bucket Mister David had carried from the house. "This water don't look none too fresh. And where's your dipper? Gal, you ain't even moved nothing out here, yet. You need to get on up out of that bed and quit your pining and get this cabin fixed up. It's a right nice little place. Wish I could a had something this nice when me and my wife was first married."

Miss Virginia came through the door now, clearly not wanting to be further bothered with me and the cabin, and said, "Yes, Father?" Then she shot across the room, closing the shutters and announcing draft, and said she'd send Coffee down with a kettle of supper broth, as soon as it was ready. Hannah could sop it with some of the bread I'd baked at dinner, and that should get us through.

Then I thought I heard her mumble to her father about the cost of letting me and Hannah eat the Newsom family's food. "Now that they have their own cabin, and a splendid one, I might add, shouldn't Celia get her rations, like the other negroes, and do for herself? Cooking for your negroes is beyond me, Father."

Newsom was silent. I watched him stare at Miss Virginia, frowning, for sure, but clearly stumped by her question. He couldn't seem to figure out a thing without Master Harvey.

"We'll see," he said at last. He waved his hand backwards at her face, like for her to go away. He did that a lot at people, lately. Miss Virginia swept out of the door without a further word. Was she upset again, now?

Mister David passed Miss Virginia on the path to the cabin door, carrying the cradle and a lantern. I could hear them spit words at each other as they passed, crunching pebbles and leaves into the moist dirt and trampled grass.

When David got up on the porch to work the cradle through the door, Newsom said, "Take that on back to the house. Your brother Harry already got a baby baking in the oven. Says he wants it."

"Then light the lamp for her," David said, switching and handing the lantern inside. Then he was gone.

Again, I wondered why his father didn't explode at Mister David's tone. It made me feel like I didn't know which one of them was in charge, for sure. I felt uneasy.

I thought about what I had let David do. How close we'd come to being found out by Newsom.

Maybe we had been found out by Newsom. I watched the red light flare on his face as he lit the lantern on the table. Why wasn't he saying anything, if he saw? If he knew.

He fell into the chair and pulled out his whiskey flask. Just like I thought. He wasn't saving it for after supper, anymore.

Again, I almost pitied him. My stomach clenched.

The wind whipped down out of the sky and wrapped the three of us, me, Hannah, and Newsom, into the cabin that evening.

When Mister Coffee brought the kettle of broth and bundle of bread, Newsom sent him for a bucket of fresh water and a ladle. Coffee slammed it onto the cabin floor, sloshing water over the sides. "Mama said Celia got to bring the ladle back tomorrow."

Newsom thought to say, "Tell your mama the ladle's mine, boy," before Coffee was out of the door and running to escape the coming storm.

The storm was a mild one.

It darkened the world around us and made me glad that even Newsom was in the cabin. I wondered why he stayed.

Maybe it was because here he could drink down his flask of whiskey without answering to anybody. Miss Virginia loved to remind everybody that her father only "took a shot of whiskey to help him sleep at night."

As the storm blew around us, I held the resting bundle of my unborn baby and watched Newsom dip bread into the broth and hand it under the table, sopping, into Hannah's mouth.

When she refused to eat anymore, he seemed not to notice. He swiped the soggy pieces around her mouth and left running broth and sticking crumbs before he let it drop to the floor.

I reached under the table to shove the laundry basket of clothes gently out of harm's way.

"Hannah's had enough," I told Newsom softly.

He looked puzzled and slipped the last piece into his own mouth. He made a face and forced himself to swallow.

When he shoved the kettle away, I retrieved the dipper from the water bucket and used it to scoop and drink a little of the broth. I was, truly, glad not to be alone.

Maybe this cabin would change how I felt about Newsom. If anything could. Why had I feared it so?

How pleasant not to hear the endless bickering of Master David and his sisters, fast being learned

245

by Coffee and his younger siblings, too. I really had nothing to be afraid of. Mister David had filled my head with confusion.

"Master Newsom," I said respectfully, "who planted the flowers?"

He looked up at me. But his eyes were so red and quivery that, for a moment, I was afraid of him.

He dropped his head to his chest and began to snore. Hannah, too, I found, had fallen asleep where she played.

I brought her, slowly and with painful tugging, into the bed. Newsom's feet I unshod and propped up on the bed, ankles crossed, hoping he'd think in the morning that he'd wanted to sleep in the chair.

I couldn't bear, not tonight, to have him grabbing at me. I went to the bed and gathered Hannah to me and slept.

Newsom was gone when I woke in the morning, so I never knew what he thought.

He became more and more peculiar.

I was right down in my heart, so I may have missed things. But it seemed to me that Mister David was just about as good as his word, about taking care of me. Carrying me stores of flour and meal, and even meat and molasses and dairy from Miss Virginia's kitchen so I could cook breakfasts and good suppers in "our" cabin. David's word. Hauling in fresh water in the bucket and laying fires even before he went in to dinner, so that when I came back from cooking, I wouldn't have to leave again for the creek or the woods, to gather kindling.

Come to think of it, Mister David pranced right around in public like his father had handed me over

246

to him.

For a while, this had me on edge. It had been a long time since his father caned or whipped me. And I didn't relish the thought of having it start up again.

And it surely would, to say nothing of even worse, if Newsom came face to face with what had become of me and David.

I still didn't talk to David. But that was the only rule of Newsom's that we still followed. It was the only rule I felt was all the way up to me.

The other, the lying down together, I'm not sure why I didn't fight it anymore.

Sometimes I thought it was that worth it to me not to be alone with my Hannah, listening to the noises outside the cabin. Looking over from Miss Virginia's kitchen windows, hoping Hannah was all right, in the cabin alone. Dreading, while the family ate the dinner I'd made, having to walk back to the cabin through the shadows and smells of the damp woods.

With David's stores, I always had a nice stew brewing for me and Hannah's supper, even before I went over to cook for the family. And because of David, I never had to strain my back, trying to haul my own water and wood. Because of David, I never lit a lantern in the dark.

It was worth it to me.

The lying down. It wasn't even bad. Not like with Newsom.

And funny thing. Newsom left me clean alone for the longest, once me and David got started.

I didn't think it would happen. It had gotten to

247

be every day, I'd lay down to rest my back after cooking for Miss Virginia. The fire would be burning low, not so hot I couldn't take it and might do something foolish like open the shutters, but not so low it couldn't simmer the stew.

And Mister David, instead of riding back out to the fields or the barns, or whatever he'd been "overseeing" that day--his new word for getting promoted to a horse, so he could get around better-- would come from the dinner to lie down behind me.

It was the pressing and holding and rocking. The heat and the rising and the wanting, wanting. Something I had never felt. But he felt it, and it came to be like I felt it through him, with him.

And then, when the snow fell, it was under the covers, me in my nightgown from Miss Mary, and him in nothing at all.

Because all of a sudden, one afternoon, it wasn't just the pressing and rocking and lifting and letting go just to reach again and again until that sharp cry I always wished he wouldn't make quite so loud that it startled Hannah and made quick noises outside start up and die down.

That day, that afternoon, when I finally felt his man part, bare skin and smooth, slip between my thighs and slide right up inside me, I didn't even think of betrayal anymore.

It was like David had said all along. Like maybe he was Newsom, younger. Or like Newsom had let David have me. Take care of me if he wanted me.

Or like maybe it really didn't matter. David kept me safe here. And so I was his as much as

248

Newsom's. Like the land. Like the woods. Like the trees in the orchard.

I raised up behind a little, leaning forward away from him, so he could move all the way in. And he grabbed my knees and pulled them apart and down over his thighs and shoved till it hurt. Till we both screamed and clutched at each other.

David was there in the cabin, kissing all over my body, when the baby started to come. He washed and dressed and rode to get Miss Virginia, and kept riding.

I didn't think he went to get his father.

The baby came faster this time. I was alone with nobody but Hannah to wipe her little warm fingers across my forehead when it came.

Miss Virginia had stayed just long enough to get rags up under me on the floor, so I wouldn't ruin the bed. And she had come back just long enough to put a steaming basin of water and some more rags, clean I hoped, at my side.

I wondered, laying on my side and then getting on my knees to help work the baby out, when and why Miss Virginia went back to being hostile to me. I hadn't noticed it.

When I came to the cabin?

Could she know about me and Mister David?

Surely everybody knew.

Not that there was nothing to know. Odd thing, too. Newsom still came over every night.

But he had stopped trying, till the baby was born, to put anything in me.

The baby was born. Hannah sat by me, playing in the firelight with a bunch of pinecones and tattered ribbons off some old rags, making them babies, I guessed for her mama doll.

When the birthing was over and that thing Miss Virginia called the "afterbirth" on its long gut had slid out, I told her don't be afraid. I wasn't dying.

When I could sit up, Hannah watched me bathe her brother. She played with his little fists and asked about that long gut hanging out of his belly.

She hid her eyes when I pulled my knife off the mantel and cut it. I had to hold her, next to him, and show her it didn't bleed.

I washed us all three as well as I could, and we got in bed together. That's where Newsom found us when he came in that night. He poured the basin of bloody water out of the window.

"Don't," I called out. "I want flowers to grow there in the spring."

"Fool," he said, but his voice was low, not rough. "This water won't hurt nothing. Probably make flowers grow better."

Newsom sopped a chunk of bread in my bucket of buttermilk for him and Hannah's supper. Then he had me lay Hannah and the baby together on a quilt by the fire to sleep.

He tried again that night. And that night, he got it to do what he wanted. I wondered if he liked the blood all over his lap.

But then came the tugging inside, from nursing the baby, and my body shrunk, like it had before, and it seemed in no time I was smaller and tireder than I had ever been.

David liked to feel how my insides tightened around his part, if he had it in me while I nursed the baby.

But better, he liked holding me face to face.

His father didn't. His father almost never looked in my face these days. I didn't mind. I didn't miss the sight of those red-veined, bleary eyes.

The hardest thing, after the birth, was going back to the house to cook and leaving my babies.

"They'll be all right," Miss Virginia said, catching me with the shutters open, letting rain in her kitchen in the early spring. "Hannah's big enough to run for help, Celia."

Run for help? And who would be with the baby, while Hannah ran for help?

The baby alone in that cabin.

No. Better not to think about that.

Think of the fire crackling and the stew bubbling, sending soft hearty smells around the room. "This cabin always smells like home," Mister David would say. "More home than the big house."

My children would not feel alone.

By late spring, I still had not named the baby. Newsom did not approve.

"Only wild animals drop a litter and don't nothing get named," he would say. "Didn't I have to name your first one, too? Don't you have any sense of Christian ways, girl?"

I continued to call my newborn "the baby." The fact that Newsom didn't push me any harder for a name made me wonder if he hoped I'd name it after him.

I was right. By summer, he'd started everyone

calling my newborn Bobby. Newsom's own baby name.

As summer harvests of fruit and vegetables began, I saw less and less of Mister David up on his horse. He'd said his father was promising him some prime land, if he could increase the crop yield over Harvey's best. "I could be a rich man in another year. Get married. Start a farm of my own and buy out some of what the old man's willing to Harvey."

I didn't mind that Mister David was gone. The long hours of summer daylight had burned away my fear that I had to rush to the cabin after dinner.

I left not only the shutters but the cabin door open. Hannah and her brother spilled in and out of the door, her running and him crawling, raising butterflies from the grass and eating fallen fruit.

I would lean out of Miss Virginia's kitchen window, catching a little summer breeze and watching them play. If they scampered and crawled out of sight, I could usually call one of Miss Virginia's children to find them.

Miss Mary didn't like me hollering around the house for her niece and nephews, though. She was always in practice to be courted by a beau, though none ever came.

But she drifted more dainty around the house in layers of ruffled and ribboned gowns that were always being newly retucked and reshaped on account of some picture she had seen at some shop or some—more fortunate—girl's house.

Mary didn't go in for hollering any more. For the rest of us, this was a blessing. We was most on

252

fed up with hearing Miss Mary's bellow.

For her own part, however, I misdoubted that Miss Mary wouldn't soon take up hollering again.

Without it, her father had near on taken over her life.

She had to make his bed. His breakfast. Darn his clothes. Sew buttons on his breeches. I didn't doubt she'd have to bathe him, if she didn't speak up for herself soon.

The only chore, however, I ever heard Miss Mary lament was washing her father's bedclothes after Buddy wet the bed. Which was near on every night. Buddy, it seemed clear, didn't care to sleep alone in Newsom's big room, even if Newsom did leave him a light burning.

But no way was Newsom going to miss a night coming over to my cabin. Not now that he'd managed to get it back in me and keep it there, till he was satisfied.

The only thing that unsettled me anymore was that someone had started prowling around the cabin, when the summer sun finally set.

I could hear someone out there, crushing the stalks of flowers that had, indeed, grown all around the cabin, prowling outside the shutters open for a cool night breeze, while Newsom slept.

I hoped it was just Mister David, up to more of his old tricks. Maybe missing our after dinner lie-downs and sorry he was spending all his time on that horse, out to the fields. Snooping and sniffing up the smell of me and his father.

Yes, it was just like David. Still, I wished I could ask him and be sure.

It would have made me sleep better.

Chapter Nine: The Cold and the Dark

In the nights I was uneasy, but the long, sunlit days of that summer put me into a mood like almost happiness. It was so long, from cooking the family's dinner till fearing the gathering of blind dark around my cabin and my children, dark trapped under the trees with their full leaves.

It was almost like I lived in two places or in two of me. The one who had day, hours and hours of it, sweet or storm. The one who played with two smiling babies and watched them from the wide open window of another family's kitchen and thought, Soon now. Soon I'll have this on the table and these people can do their own washing up while I sit on my little porch with my children.

And then, on the porch as blue got swept up into the hands of grey, there was that other me who got herself ready to listen in bed to whoever was bending the stalks of my flowers, coming to listen at the windows in the dark.

It was that first me, the one who had been held and rocked and left quietly to take back up with Newsom, that met Miss Mary in her and her sister's kitchen one day.

She came in sighing and tying on a apron while I was putting the last of the bread to bake in the oven. She couldn't get her strings tied behind her back. She let her arms fall.

Miss Mary came to lean on the window ledge

and look out toward my cabin.

Were her eyes shining at my children?

She caught me watching her watching them. She let her head drop. Her hair, "hung loose like a slattern," as I had heard her father say sometimes, fell forward and covered her face from me. The sun combed in between the strands. I had never thought of why was Mary's hair so black, when Miss Virginia's was so wood brown. It made her cheeks look all the more uncommon pale for summer.

Still looking out the window, Miss Mary called back over her shoulder to me, "I've had a sad letter, Celia. Sometimes I wonder. Why?"

I began wiping the flour and dough off my hands with a damp rag.

She whipped her head around to look at me. "Must you stay in this kitchen, Celia? Can't you, maybe, take some work with you to the creek? I want to go there." She looked out the window again. "I wouldn't take work to the creek," she said. "I would wear an old dress and splash right in the water with your children. Could I borrow your children? Babies is so much easier than sister's big, bad boys. Amelia's nothing but another boy, if you ask me."

I had heard of letters. They were gossip that people could get to say right on the paper, and send it past other people to get right to the ear of the only person they wanted to hear the news. Strange, awful things, letters. Making people laugh and cry and run waving paper and shouting. I had seen it.

If I had ever received a letter, I would have burned it before taking a chance.

I went to the cabin and came back with my laundry bundle and my babies stripped bare. Miss Mary squealed like when that group of young people came in a wagon to ask if she could go picnic—she couldn't—and flung off her untied apron, running to us through the door.

She had forgot to put on an old dress. She hiked up the ribboned and laced one that she had on with her bare hands and splashed through the creek, kicking water at my babies, anyway. Hannah and Mary got soaked through till they were wrinkled and laughing and grabbing at each other.

The Baby wasn't none too sure about all this running water. He crawled around me, splashing in the shallow water and raising one chubby hand at a time to look at where the pebbles punched him and the water drops rolled off him.

I told him, "You'll get used to it, Baby," and untied my bundle. I washed the diapers and my nightgown, slapping them lazy against a rough, flat rock. Tearing and wearing good cloth, for no reason. All this dirt and sweat and pee wouldn't come out as good in the icy run of the creek as it would have in a boiling kettle.

But I agreed with Mary. It was good to a go a distance from the house.

When my washing was finished and stretched on rocks and hanging from trees to gather more dirt and dry, Miss Mary scooped up The Baby and said, "You take a turn, Celia. Go on in the water. You gave me a good excuse to come out here, in case Father asks. Let me see my end of the bargain all the way through."

I had been dying just for that. The feel of running water on my skin.

I don't know why. I didn't know how to swim or anything. And a good scrub with fire-heated water and a handful of rags kept me and my children clean enough.

But to hear the stream lapping past the cabin window, to know it was there, so cool, and never go to it. That was a shame.

I pulled up my skirt, like Miss Mary had done, and walked out into the creek as deep as I could go.

It was at my knees for the longest. Then at my belly. And all of a sudden, for no reason, the rocks and running water dropped away under my feet till, when I found my balance again, the water was at my chest.

I should have been afraid. Me, afraid of so many nothings. But I wasn't. I only thought, if the water went any deeper, I would go into it. This would be the way and the time to die. I would welcome it.

When I heard in my mind what I was thinking, I turned and hurried against the current back to the wet land where The Baby was reaching for me from Miss Mary's muddy lap. What had I been thinking? It put me in mind of thinking of Newsom's own sons killing him. Thoughts of death, of welcoming it, inviting it. Wanting it. What had got into me?

Miss Mary held The Baby, trying to keep him a little clean off the ground, while I reached into the trees and gathered up my stiff laundry.

"That was a rare delight," she said, carrying The Baby on her hip back up to the house. "I don't care what Father or brother may say, if they hear we were out there. I'm glad we went."

The bread had burned on the bottom, much to my surprise.

I broke the worst of it, steaming, into chunks for Miss Mary and the babies to melt butter on and eat together. The rest I crumbled fine and stirred with more butter, and even honey and cream and eggs and bits of dried apples, to make a rich bread pudding.

What would Newsom say, with bread pudding on the dinner table, instead of bread?

Maybe I wasn't that happy, that I wanted to find out. I whipped up a quick batch of pan-fried cornbread.

Still gathering up the cooking things for Miss Virginia and Miss Mary to wash, I was yet in the kitchen when Newsom finished his first serving. He came through the doorway already saying, "Gal, what's got into you? If I didn't know better, I'd think you was sparking me. That was some meal. Dessert on the table, and ain't nobody finished the meat yet."

He was smiling. He said it again. "What's got into you?"

I hoped I smiled back. "Nothing, sir," I said quiet. The children napped on the chair where I'd sat them to eat. I wanted to gather some of these good leftovers as soon as I could and get my babies back to the yard in front of the cabin.

Newsom went back to the table.

He had never said such a thing to me. It was an odd day. It had been happy for those few long hours in the wet sunshine.

But something else was laying over it. It fell on me, as soon as I got in the cabin and set the food on the table for the children's supper.

"You like them flowers I planted?"

It was a voice at the window.

The window was open, letting air run through the house all day, if it didn't rain. I didn't think to close it until the grey started creeping in from the woods and the creek toward the cabin.

This was high summer, soon after dinner. It was still light out. Would be for hours. But I wouldn't feel it.

It was George at the window.

He had his face so far in it felt like he was sitting in the room with me. The room was too small.

I wouldn't have known his voice, purring like that. Like the barn cat before it scratches your child's hand ragged.

I backed from the table towards the door. I bumped into it, standing open, and spilled, twisting, backwards, running out. I leaped down the little porch and headed for the Newsom house, to keep my children from leaving that kitchen.

I kept them there till it was dark.

Nobody seemed bothered but Hannah, when I was afraid to take her out back to the latrine and we didn't have a chamber pot just down the hall from the kitchen no more. So I took her outside the kitchen door and made her squat in the wet dirt. I didn't know she needed to poop. I had to quick bury the little droppings in the damp earth with a stick.

Hannah was offended by it all. She liked her clean little chamber pot and didn't never pee in the grass if she could help it, unlike Miss Virginia's boys.

I hurried and got her back in the kitchen to wash up, just in time to catch The Baby crawling out from the brace of dining room chairs I had set around him to keep him away from the supper fire.

Miss Mary, who had looked up from washing the dinner things when I came running in from the cabin, had her little frown on. "Celia," she said then. "What has got into you?"

I hollered out, "Miss Virginia, may I stay and help getting supper?" Which I never did no more.

Miss Virginia looked into the kitchen with her little worried frown she always had these days. "You want to get supper, Celia? Well, I'm sure sister and I won't say no to that." And, shaking her head, she was gone.

Miss Mary studied on this. "Does it show that bad I'm behind on Father's mending? Well, thank you, Celia. I guess I'd better get to it."

When the two sisters came in to see how supper was getting on and found my babies tucked under the cutting table, eating baked yams and playing with pots and spoons, they carried out the supper and brought back Newsom. He was in his usual foul evening temper. "What's this I hear about you hanging around and won't go home? What's with you now, Celia?"

Miss Mary went to interrupt. Newsom put up a hand. "I already heard from you, daughter. Now

261

I'd kindly like to hear from the gal."

So I said, "Master Newsom, misses, I had no idea me staying to cook supper might cause such a uproar. Master Newsom, you know how my arm pains me, and The Baby is getting so big. Would you help me carry him back to the cabin now? I need to bed the babies down, and you're right, sir. I've overstayed my helpfulness today."

Couldn't nothing bad happen if Newsom was there, could it? And foul as his mood was, maybe he'd get to thinking he could pull out his flask and sip a little, instead of putting up with his daughters at the table.

David came in the kitchen to wash just as we were going out the door. I thought I saw him studying us peculiar. As I turned back for one last glance, the lamplight caught his eyes fixed not on me but on his father. It wasn't a loving look. He didn't even try to meet my eye.

I couldn't afford to worry about one more man. So I didn't think of David again, just yet.

Newsom did, after all, get to the cabin, with the dinner remains cooled on the table, and decide to sit and sip his whiskey while I lit the wick on the lamp and shut the shutters. "Why you keep the damn things wide open, gal?" he asked. "If it rains, you'll come back to a flooded cabin."

"Just so the children aren't stuck in the close air all day," I said. "Maybe I could bring them to the kitchen with me, sir, when I come to cook your dinner. It would so relieve my mind to have them nearby."

"And relieve you of cooking, I don't doubt.

262

Don't Bobby spend all the time he can sucking at your tits?"

"Not if I can hand him some food. He's getting a tooth and likes to chew."

Newsom grumbled. I lay beside the children on their pallets on the floor and mumbled them my lullaby. I hadn't never rightly recalled the words, only most of the tune. But they didn't care. It had got to be the little signal between us that all was well and they could sleep now.

They slept.

The only thing with having Newsom there to drive George away was, after all, I had to put up with having Newsom there.

Once I heard Miss Virginia say, "Better the devil you know than the devil you don't." That night, I figured I finally knew what she meant. But by morning, I wasn't sure she was right.

Newsom hadn't barely dragged himself to breakfast at the big house, and I was still struggling to wash The Baby, who was full on breast milk and should have been ready to play and splash, but wasn't, when here came Mister David knocking at the door.

He was down off his horse, which he must have tethered to a tree behind the cabin, because I didn't see it. He must have meant to stay a while.

I wasn't sure what to make of this.

Being with him had eased a space in my life when I was afraid and alone with my babies here at the edge of the orchards and the woods. He had shown me what was wrong with the way his father treated my body and my feelings, too. Made me feel, without saying so, that I had a right to be so twisted up with dread and hate when his father got through with me.

But did I miss the secrets and the fear of being caught? Did I even miss David? The sneaking and the kissing and the other way that being in a man's arms could feel?

Odd to say it, but no, I didn't. In some way I couldn't explain, he brought too much of his father with him to me here, and no, I didn't want him back.

Mister David came in and sat in the chair still warm from his father. I shut the door without looking around to see who might have seen him.

"So, you and Father are on better terms, Celia?" was the first thing out of his mouth.

I went back to washing The Baby in his basin before the fireplace. The morning's gruel spattered out of the kettle in the fireplace at him and he squealed. I checked him close. It hadn't got him.

I loved the feel of his smooth, gold arm. I kissed it where a burn might have been but wasn't.

Mister David said, "Because, you know, it ain't like I stopped coming around because I gave up on you, or anything. I wasn't just, you know, sowing oats or nothing. I thought, maybe, you didn't understand that."

I tried to coax The Baby to crawl out of the basin onto my lap, so I wouldn't have to lift him. He loved to crawl, wet, into my lap. "Hannah," I said, "hand me something to dry him a little. How's he doing on diapers? Do I have any clean?"

Hannah brought his shirt and a clean diaper.

She was too little to ever remember to bring me a drying rag.

Never mind. It was still summer, and The Baby's shirt would soak up the water and get him dry in no time. He'd be wet in the heat by dinner, anyway. I laughed at the thought.

Mister David said, "What's so funny? Aren't you listening, Celia? I'm not doing all this just for me. Someday, I'll set you up as cook at my place. Father can't live forever. And white women, you know, they know what's going on. My wife'll be right happy to have the help, anyway."

I had little idea what he was on about. I sat after The Baby had toddled off my lap and Hannah had settled into the wash water, splashing herself instead of waiting. "Hey," she said, rousing from her daydreams to snatch her doll from The Baby's mouth. "Mama, he already left a tooth mark on it." Hurt and furious, she showed me the little dent in the wood of the mama doll's head. "He can't play with it," she said firmly.

The Baby had found my cooking spoon and was chewing it, instead. Probably tasted the gruel on it.

The gruel. I couldn't go on listening to David's nonsense getting nowhere. I needed to feed my babies before their breakfast burned.

But what about this evening?

I rinsed Hannah's little sunburned body and thought. Maybe it would be a good thing if Mister David wanted to hang around a little again. I looked over at the shutters. For all he thought I should close them while I was gone, I noticed

Newsom had been in a hurry to open them for fresh air this morning.

"Has something happened between you and my father, Celia?" David insisted again. "I always thought you might want to come to my place, when I can get one and pay for you. It'll look like I'm setting up house. Plenty young men do it that way. First the house and the help, and only later the wife, when everything's in place. I might not even need a wife before I send for you. Father might decide he's getting old." His voice took on a wheedling note. "Do you think you might want to come, as soon as I can buy some land and build me something? A cabin like this. Or when…when Father passes on?" This last whispered in a rush. I finally looked at David.

When his father passed on, would I still be here? That day, if it ever dawned, looked so far away. What and where would I be by then?

For a moment, I thought I saw what David saw in me. He thought he saw me a little bit happy, relieved that me and my babies were still all right and the sunshine lasted so long in the summer days, and he wondered if he had been forgotten.

I smiled at him, so if he felt an urge to drop by in the afternoons when the harvest was in and the days were getting shorter, he might feel willing to risk it. It was a bold thing. He looked a little taken aback.

He went on whispering, rising to come to me, "It's just that you had the baby, and it kind of twisted me up inside, and I thought it was better not to come. He is my father. I shouldn't feel…. It's not natural, Celia, all the things I feel about him. About you and him." He had reached me and didn't seem decided on what to do. He watched me, staring into my eyes, and waited for something I must not have done. For he leaned close, closer, and his hand came up and hovered over my covered breast like he would touch it but didn't dare. He leaned over me without letting his body touch me anywhere and put his lips near my ear and said, "What if the next baby was mine? Would he know? Could he tell? Can he still…. Do you still let him? Celia?"

He let his hands come to rest, light like maybe he wasn't doing this at all, on both my breasts.

Then he pulled them sharp off me and turned and went back to his seat. Looking at the floor, he said, "It seemed better to do this another way. I get out of here and send for you. If I have to get a wife to make it work, she'll just have to understand. Seems simple, most of the time. Do you understand, Celia?" He looked back over at me.

I was wondering, *Do it matter if I understand or not?* Truth was, I didn't. He was thinking of leaving, was all I understood. He would be gone. And what would I feel then?

I couldn't tell. I said nothing, and David said, "So you're back to not talking to me. Father's rules serve you well, don't they?" He stood like he was angry and would go. But he got to the door and turned back and stared.

I turned my back at that and went to spoon up the gruel. Then I fed my children and didn't look up when the cabin door closed on David's visit.

Who was I to hope? Talk of getting out. Of leaving. It almost sounded like running away.

Strength left me fast, after that.

It wasn't that George came back. Or at least, he didn't stick his head in the cabin and talk to me.

He couldn't. David took to swinging by on his horse, on his way to and from the field. And I began to close the cabin shutters when I left to cook, taking the children with me to play outside Miss Virginia's kitchen.

They drew Boo, when he could get free from field chores without getting caught.

His hand had healed just fine. Only a scar that was a beige line and some numbness where he couldn't feel anything. So I had a big child to keep a little bit of an eye on my babies.

But as the days shortened, I began to worry.

I couldn't help it.

My right arm, in the cooling air, wasn't content to just be weak. It had to ache. And facing that dark cabin at the end of the path, as afternoons started rushing into darkness, especially on cloudy days. Braving that quiet, sullen cabin, holding The Baby on my left hip and guiding Hannah with the other hand, balancing a bundle from the family's dinner on my head, hearing the leaves crunch under my feet and wondering who else—somebody back behind the cabin easing a crack between the shutters?—heard them, too, all that began to take a lot out of me.

As summer faded to a grey, low fall where it felt like the sky was glowering down my back, I felt like I'd left my happy time behind.

And I didn't even know, still, what had made it happen at all.

The ache in my arm took a slow spread up my neck to my head and down my throat to my stomach. Newsom said I was getting littler than ever. "Get too skinny, it'll give you wrinkles. Make you look like an old hag," he said one morning, drinking down the water I had poured for him to wash. "David ain't carrying you those supplies any more?"

It wasn't that. It was just worry. It was just— what was that word Miss Virginia used sometimes?—foreboding.

When the harvest was in and the snow had made its first dustings, Newsom took up the old heavy drinking again. His nightly scratchings began to leave me bruised again. Sore.

Washing soon wasn't enough to relieve the itching and pain. I started showing him the tender, pus-filled swelling. Hadn't he noticed the peculiar smell?

Nothing a little washing wouldn't take care of, filthy niggers, he said.

He took me by the hair and dragged me all the way down the path behind the cabin to the creek, a way I had never been, where he shoved me in and, as I slipped on the rocks and sat, shuddering from the pain in my tailbone, he told me to wash.

I did wash, crying. Wondering who was watching.

The creek never dried up all the way. After that night, I began to sneak out, sometimes, down the path behind my house, to wash there after Newsom fell asleep.

The icy rippling water eased the pain. The scabs began to heal and not form again.

And by full winter, when the crops was all in and Mister David was back to coming around my cabin before or after dinner, Newsom had given up trying again.

Mister David was engaged. His bride's family was helping with a down payment on some prime property. They was using their own men to build the house. The whole county had heard of how Harvey's house took forever to get built. Mister David would be gone by, oh, maybe the end of this upcoming summer. At the latest, the following spring. Mister David just walked with me, these days, sat a while, and talked up a storm. He didn't touch me.

But Newsom began to beat me something awful.

He didn't make excuses. He didn't look for reasons.

His beatings could last any time and get however awful. He would grab my hair and get to pounding and swearing and kicking. My babies would hide under the bed. He seemed to take near on as much pleasure in these beatings as he could no longer take in the other thing. I had never taken pleasure in either.

Sometimes I would sit in Miss Virginia's kitchen and find a knife in my hand, and wonder how it got there, and say, "Oh, of course. I was peeling potatoes. But this knife is too big. It's a cleaver."

270

The ache stayed in my head and my arm, and sometimes, even though my private parts had healed, tender but clean-smelling, I would double over a pain low in my gut.

Miss Virginia began to speak to me again in a kindly way. When I worked up the nerve to tell her about the scratches and swellings I'd been treating, she advised me on compresses I might try. The first one, she even put together herself.

It helped. But I had the feeling that all this healing on the outside couldn't follow in and heal the sickness taking hold on the inside.

I felt strange. The fear of going to the cabin after cooking supper had burst in my mind, one day, till I collapsed crying at Miss Virginia's cutting table. "Why, whatever is it?" she wanted to know.

And I told her about the dark and the cold waiting in the cabin for me and my children, and how hard it was to carry them or get the lamp and fire lit fast enough.

She said she had long thought all this fear was foolishness. I should simply leave the children there with a nice low fire going.

I suspected she wasn't nothing but fed up with my children crowding the kitchen, always underfoot. And her Coffee was accusing them of stealing treats from the larder.

The first day I was to leave the children back home, there was a big snow. I remembered Boo running through snow just that deep with his fingers dropping blood, and after I'd bathed my children, I crawled back into bed and curled my body around the pain in my gut.

271

No one came to find me until after the family sat down to a skimpy dinner.

It was Newsom.

"What is it this time?" he wanted to know. "Damn. They sold you for pretty and being a virgin, charged me good, but hell if you can't stay on your feet as long as a white woman. You people are supposed to be hearty."

"Last summer, I was happy," I said for some strange reason. I caught myself and shut that kind of talk up just as Newsom bent to peer into my eyes.

"Some kind of fever," he mumbled to himself. "Better tell that worthless daughter of mine to get one of the hands to bring you soup and such till you get better. Can't have the whole household coming down. People dying every winter from these fevers."

When I opened my eyes again, it was to see Joshua struggling to make it through the doorway with a kettle and a cloth-wrapped loaf of bread with curls of steam rising above it.

Joshua was brisk and wouldn't look at me. I struggled to sit up, to smooth my hair and twist it back behind my head, catch the springy tufts that wanted to get away from my fingers.

All the while I was working to sit up and ask Joshua to sit down, he was clapping the food on the table and wrenching a chunk from the bread without so much as a glance at me.

He held the bread out toward my children, walking over to them bent and cooing, "So, little bits, what you got to say for yourselves?"

Dared I ask him to stay?

I had no time to figure it out. Joshua was already at the door, calling back to Hannah and The Baby, who stood and sat staring and munching, "Now, Miss Virginia said you leave some of that soup and bread for your poor mother. You hear?"

A gust of cold, damp air hit me after the door closed. I closed my eyes and was ashamed to find that the weight of the lids had forced out a tear.

Fever made you weepy. Probably Newsom was right. I had a fever, after all.

Joshua came once a day for three days. The first day, he only brought the soup and bread. The next two days, he brought more bread and soup in a covered pot, took the bucket to fetch water, and brought in the diapers he'd found scattered outside the windows in the snow. I'd been throwing them out there, since I took sick, by way of soaking them. And ridding the house of stink. He sloshed water in a basin and left the diapers there to soak.

I watched him from the bed, not saying a word, as I was not suppose to. When he left again, I crawled over to the basin to wring out the diapers and stretch them on the floor before the fire.

The children were happy because I was always home with them. I was happy because my shutters were closed tight and didn't Newsom nor nobody but Joshua seem to want to come to the cabin.

I had been a fool to think I needed Newsom here. Miss Virginia was right. All I needed was to close and lock my shutters.

Feeling much better the night of the third day, I woke, finding the children asleep in the bed beside me and a low fire still burning. *Who was keeping it*

273

lit? I wondered. *Joshua?* It was a shame if he was coming in right when I was asleep, and I couldn't enjoy the sight of him.

But I didn't give it too much thought. Must have been the tiredness from the fever. Too tired to think. Too tired to worry.

When I woke again, gritty from sweat, and sleep, and stink, I stood in front of the fire to strip off my nightgown and wash the sickness away. As the water ran down my skin, tingling, the cabin door flew open. I turned, my mouth open with surprise.

Joshua stood there with his mouth open, too.

Snow flew behind him. Moonlight outlined him. He was a black shape cut fine against the flying white world, and he shut it out with his body and his eyes on mine and made all things right. Fever feelings. I reached toward him, then pulled my hand back to cover myself.

Joshua came to himself and seemed to remember where my eyes went and turned to close the door. With it closed, he looked at me again. I held the rag I'd been washing with in front of my breasts. The rest of me was bare.

I thought I should bend down and pull up the nightgown, sweat and sickness caught all up in the fabric, and all. But I didn't. I watched Joshua and wondered what to say to him at last. Maybe thank him for the care he was taking of me and my babies while I was ill? Even if somebody else was making him. I shaped my mouth for words to empty my heart.

Joshua jerked toward the door, snatched it open, and went back out.

When I came to myself, I stooped in the water, washed out the filthy nightgown, and laid it out before the fireplace to dry. Then I got back into bed naked and pulled the bedclothes up under my chin.

I woke again when Joshua came back into the cabin.

He came right up on the bed. I heard him say, "It's only me, Celia. Joshua. I just came to tell you, it's someone out there who would kill for you. Will kill me over you. Everybody knows how I feel. He'll kill me. He'll kill anybody. He be crazy, Celia. I can't fight him. I can't fight for you, and I can't have you. And that be all there is to it."

I went cold inside. Blank. Frozen. Someone. Kill. Me. I sat up to see Joshua better in the dark. But once I was close enough to make out his face, the smooth dip and flow of his dark brown cheeks in the glowing blackness of the cabin, I didn't move any more. I stayed so close I

felt his breath on my lips. My heart and thoughts stood still.

Joshua didn't move, either. Maybe he was waiting for me to say something. "I'm not talking about Master David," he whispered. His voice was low, frightened. Quick fear ran through me. How did Joshua know about Mister David? And if he knew, who else knew? And how could he be so bold, coming right out to mention Mister David to me like that? Wasn't he worried about getting caught or told on?

Or had someone sent him?

And was Joshua more afraid of *that* person than of Mister David? "Someone out there," he had said.

"Kill for you." Now Joshua said, "He told me be sure to tell you. It only be a matter of time."

"Before what, Joshua?" were the first words I ever said to the only man I had ever loved. "Who told you to tell me all this? And what's going to happen in a matter of time?"

Joshua ducked his head. He was half sitting, half squatting on one leg beside the bed, leaning in close to me. When his head went down, I slipped my hand under his chin to lift his face again. Cold pooled in my palm. Tears. Joshua was crying, like a woman, with no sound.

"I can't," he said. "No more. No more, Celia." Joshua rose, threw open the heavy door to the cold, and was gone.

Chapter Ten: The Water and the Woods

The next day, Joshua did not come again.

Toward evening, I put together a stew of bits of deer jerky with slices of onion and yam from my store of supplies. I was uneasy because I had to go fetch water from the creek, both for washing up and the stew. So I ended by burning the onion and yam skins in the fire, instead of hunting up more kindling than I could find along the walk back to the cabin. I was fast getting well enough, but I was that ill at ease leaving my babies.

I couldn't think why. Must be fever thinking.

The onion skins snapped among the burning logs and gave the little corn meal patties I roasted for bread a sharp, nice taste. We had a good meal.

I fell asleep in more dark than I liked, trying to save on the firewood in case Joshua still didn't come the next day. I held my babies close in the bed and stared at the red glowing embers, ready to rouse and puff them back to life, if they got too grey.

I should have been content, with Newsom gone for so many days and nights. I tried to be.

But I couldn't be.

The next few days that Joshua didn't come, we still ate well, me and my little ones. Every day I found things I could put together from my stores that tasted all right and kept tummies full. The children laughed more than I'd ever seen them, and we got to playing the silliest games together, seeing shapes in the fire and telling stories, and hiding from each other under the bed and table, and seeing who could eat the fastest, once we got down to no stores left but corn meal, for making gruel, and it got watery and tasted none too good.

How I came to hate that trip to the creek for water. I was right glad when the afternoon rains came. I set my bucket out to catch it, and didn't have to go no further than one step down off my little porch, and I set out the wash basin, and brought it straight in to heat on the embers for bathing everybody, and set out the chamber pot to get rinsed. Life got easier when it rained.

I tried to shrug off the sadness that Joshua wasn't coming back. I had no reason to be sad, I told myself many times every day. He wasn't nothing but a hand that tried to help me out one or two times. I used to be a foolish girl looking for a beau, like Miss Mary. Fever burns your childhood away.

And I tried to shrug off the worry Joshua's last visit left behind. But there was a waiting feeling around the place. The farm seemed uncommon quiet, off in the close distance from the cabin, with the animals calling out under the low grey sky.

When it snowed a little again, and I could see that my babies were shivering, even with their tummies full of that watery mush, I put aside my nonsense—for surely nonsense it was—and went up to the big house to cook dinner and get more supplies.

I didn't feel as well as I ought. The sickness,

though, didn't seem to be shining so much out of my eyes any more. Only, I could feel it in my lowest gut, eating away at me, it seemed. Burning, like I'd swallowed a live coal, one of those nights we were down to gruel and not too careful what we ate.

The door to Miss Virginia's kitchen was locked. I had to bang on it.

She opened the shutters, though I for sure had not banged there. She peered out at me.

Her face went all bright with surprise. "Celia. Are you better? Well, George never said a word."

And my stomach went cold and balled up on a pain like she'd hit me in it.

George? Why should she expect to hear about me from George?

And then I thought of him leaning into the cabin through the back window. Had he told Miss Virginia I had *let* him in? How dared I find out, without saying something she would feel she had to pass on to Newsom?

I didn't want to be in trouble for George, nor in trouble with George.

Miss Virginia opened the kitchen door and snatched me inside. She said "against the cold," but her eyes searched all around the yard behind me, clear down towards the cabin, till I wondered who she might be fearing to see.

It looked so personal, that fear in her face. Had her husband come around, after all these years, bothering her to come back to him?

Odd how I thought, now, that it might be a bother to go back to one's husband. Hadn't I felt a

279

little sorry for Miss Virginia, at one time, and wished she could go back?

I couldn't remember any more. So many things I couldn't remember.

Miss Virginia was saying, close in my face and anxious, hunched over, tucking her shawl around her like a much older woman, "What brings you up here, Celia?"

What brought me up there? Hadn't her father said he'd have her sending me soup and such by Joshua? Had she forgot, or had she figured I had stores to last until spring, once the fever passed?

And who told her it had passed? I my own self wasn't too sure the fever had left me, yet.

I said, "I came up here to cook your dinner, if I must, and maybe get your leave to carry some supplies down to the cabin. That gruel I've been cooking my babies the last four days is just about pure water, now. In fact, if you've a mind, maybe I can get a bowl or two of meal to carry down there now so it can start thickening up, and I can feed them after I cook for you. It can't be good in this cold for them to go so hungry, Miss Virginia."

This was quite a talk for me, but I got angrier as I went along. Why didn't she even send a message to me through that no account Joshua that after three days of soup and bread we were on our own? And that soup almost all broth, as it was. No warning.

I thought of myself, creeping down the porch with a bucket for water, peeking around like a rabbit before running to the creek, feeling so hurt that Joshua didn't want to return.

All because of Miss Virginia here. Surely she

was the one that told him to stop coming, and I'd been eating my heart alive and still beating out of my chest.

Miss Virginia had not once stopped looking at me with that blank, pale face, more wrinkled and tired and surprised than I had ever seen it before. Starting to resemble after her father, I wouldn't doubt.

She said, "Gruel? Celia, what are you talking about? Why haven't you been eating that soup and bread I've been sending you?"

"Soup and bread, Miss Virginia?" I said. "We did eat it. And I was right grateful, too, ma'am, seeing as how I couldn't have got out of the bed even to boil gruel, them first three days of fever." What was this all about? Was she saying I couldn't get any supplies, even if I did come cook her and her family their dinner?

I asked.

Miss Virginia shook her head at me. My heart, my hopes, were sinking. Were my children and me to starve, now? What had I done wrong? Got ill? How could I have helped it?

All those questions fell out of my mouth. I waved my hands and looked around, hungry and hopeless, at all the stacks and stores of vegetables and grain sacks all over Miss Virginia's kitchen. More in the pantry, most like. How could she listen to this and shake her head at me?

I ended by asking where was her father. Surely, cruel as he could be, Newsom did not want my children--*his* children—to starve alone in the cabin in the gathering cold.

Miss Virginia said, "Celia, get hold of yourself. Father is over to David's place with all the hands, trying to clear and score the fields in time for spring planting. It's near on time, and we were looking very slack, what with the bride's family having finished the house and stocked it down to the last dinner napkin, and we hadn't put in a thing except half the down payment on the mortgage. Father will be back this evening, as usual, and you know he always asks about you. He's devoted to you, I've told you. It's just that I didn't have any sign from George that you were over your fever, so I thought you were still in bed."

"And you left me and my children to *starve*, Miss Virginia?"

It seemed she finally saw what I'd been asking her all along. Her face folded in on a fearsome frown. "Starve? You ungrateful wench! Why, I've cooked you and your passel of brats that kettle of soup, every morning, before I've even set on dinner for my own children. *You* get the first kettle and the first loaf. I've put it right out here on this window ledge, rain, snow, or shine, every morning now for—what?—near on three weeks."

She went to the window and opened the shutters so that I might see that the ledge was empty.

"On the window ledge?" I said. "Joshua never told me I was to come get the soup and bread from the window ledge."

"You to come get it?" Miss Virginia snapped. "Well, I'll be. You just don't quit, do you, Celia? No such thing. No such a thing, I'm telling you.

282

Father might leave *me* and *my children* to fend for and feed ourselves as best we might, but *never* you and yours. No, miss. He didn't set foot out of this house the first day to drive the hands over to David's without making sure George knew he was to search at the window for your food and carry it to you, and gather you wood and leave it all at your door. And then bring back the empty kettle and the bread cloth, as he's done, I can assure you, and collect your empty water bucket, if you left it out with the kettle, and leave it at your door, full. Nobody's tending me and mine but me, but *you're* to be waited on at your doorstep."

I staggered backward into a chair at the cutting table and sat. The fall onto the hard seat jarred that painful place deep inside me. I clutched it and cried out for breath. I leaned over, gasping for air with my mouth open.

Over my head and far away, like at the dining room door, I heard Miss Mary say, "Sister, I think something's been going wrong. You know Celia wasn't never good at listening to shouting. Why don't you tell her, calm and easy like, about the arrangements you and Father made to see to her and her children?"

Miss Virginia whirled to face her sister so that her skirts scraped my face. "*You* tell her. I think she's lying and trying to get Father worked up again. Trying to get back in this house and who knows what all," Miss Virginia hollered and went to the pantry, slamming open the door and slapping things into burlap sacks, ranting all the while about working her fingers to the bone for a worthless negress whore.

Miss Mary said from her distance, "Well, I guess you've heard, Celia. Father took the men with him and David to get David's farm ready for the wedding. David can't bring his bride home to such a beautiful house, full of her own things, and fallow fields. And there's not enough money for David and his bride to live off Father until next year's harvest. They had to get out there and get to work clearing the land, so David could plant on time. David and the hands don't even come back at night. Only Father, to check on us and hear about you. He's only left that one hand, George, to see to the livestock and you and get our own fields cleared so we can plant on time this spring, too."

All the time she talked, Miss Mary had not come near. I pulled myself out of the chair, holding onto the cutting table, fighting the cramp and the pain and the spin in my head that had taken over my body.

"George is out there, miss?" I said. "George has been here, all along?"

"Yes, Celia," Miss Mary said, and Miss Virginia turned from her furious snatching of things out of the pantry, the edge of her burlap sack sagging from her hand.

"Oh, my God," I said, digging gripping fingers into my stomach with the one hand and scrabbling at the door latch to get outside, with the other. I had trouble with the latch.

"Oh, my God," I started yelling with each slipped twist of the handle. "My God! My God! My children are all alone!"

Somehow, Miss Mary must have got to me because she pushed the door from behind me, and suddenly it wasn't in the way any more. I spilled into the dark grey, and the damp and the cold of the frosted earth rose up to meet me, stumbling down the pathway to the cabin.

I ran as well as I could. But there was a tight cord bound between my womb and the joints between my hips and thighs that snatched back at every step I took, ripping my insides with fresh quick bursts of pain. I breathed with my mouth open, calling out, "Hannah! Hannah! Baby! Mama's here."

But I wasn't sure they could hear me, as all my force was in making my legs go forward to the still, lonely cabin.

I broke in through the door, and it banged open on nothing.

Nothing. No fire. No embers. No lantern lit against the dark. No bubbling in the pot of watered mush.

No children. Everything was still and quiet and cold.

I could almost hear their voices, the room remembered them to me so much as if they were still there.

I started searching.

Under the bed, the table, between the chair legs. Into the cold black kettle where thin spiky grains of gruel stuck out, dried and stubbornly glued to the kettle's insides.

I began to forget. I went to search Miss Virginia's laundry basket, as a good place to hide, forgetting that it hadn't been here since the day after Newsom moved me and Hannah in here. That was way back more than two years ago, before The Baby was born. What was I thinking?

I opened the shutters and shouted out back behind the cabin, calling the children to come in now, it would get dark. Forgetting that it was dead winter and cold out, and Hannah never would have taken The Baby to play in this weather, not on those aching empty stomachs, and with me leaving the door closed on them, like I had, when I went to Miss Virginia's kitchen.

Forgetting I had closed them in the cabin, and cursing myself for leaving the door open, inviting them to wander among the orchards and to the woods, searching for something to eat.

Forgetting I had already searched under the bed and chair and table so that I was running around the room, scrambling on my hands and knees, my face in the swept dust of the floorboards, screaming at them to come out, and then cursing myself for screaming like Newsom and scaring them. They would never come out that way.

I went around the room some more, crawling and calling more gently, until I snagged my skirt on a brick at the fireplace and cut my knee and had to sit and suck up the running blood.

Then I put my face on my knees and cried. George was out there. And my children were gone. What I had always feared. Something wrong with being out here in this cabin.

I should have known. I had known. It made no sense. It couldn't have happened.

286

I could have taken the children with me to the big house. It wouldn't have been that hard. Carrying The Baby and leading Hannah by my weak right hand. Why hadn't I?

I could have kept the shutters and doors open in the evenings, knowing Newsom would miss me and keeping an eye out for the day he came to look in on me again. Why hadn't I?

I could have stood on my little square front porch, calling out toward the big house to Miss Virginia, begging for help. Why hadn't I done even that? She knew I was sick. What could she say but shut up that noise, what did I want?

And for not doing none of those, my children were gone off, maybe to George, and George had…. How could I know what George might do?

I cried until my lap was soaked, and then I scrubbed my face dry with my torn skirt.

What, after all, had George done? Said things to me I didn't like. Struck me once, when Newsom and David and Miss Virginia and I didn't know how many people before them had struck me I didn't know how many times.

Maybe George was with my children.

Like Boo? Like he was with Boo, and then Boo was running through the snow with blood running from his fingers?

Maybe they had gotten frightened, I was gone so long, and they had started to cry, and George had come to them.

Like he came to me at the creek?

Maybe he wanted to be helpful and take care of them.

287

Like he's been taking care of us the past—how many?—weeks.

"No," I told myself, pushing off my knees to get back to my feet. "There must be something I can do." My voice had a quaver that scared me. I closed my mouth on it.

I made my way back to Miss Virginia's kitchen door. All along the way, I craned and turned all the way around, searching for a sight of my babies' little shirt ends ducking behind trees, maybe still playing, or their faces scrunched up bawling, coming to me to say, "Mama, where you been? We was scared, all alone."

The trees was still and stark and stripped bare for the winter, scratchy from peeling in the cold.

My children could not have hid behind them from my voice, even this shaky, calling to them. "Hannah? Baby? It's Mama. Come out, now."

My children wasn't nowhere they would have gone on their own. That much was clear to me.

I had to bang on Miss Virginia's kitchen door once more. She would not open it to me again. Miss Mary opened the shutters. She had her sad look.

"Miss Mary, I can't find my children." I started crying again. I turned around, to look again toward the cabin, and back around, to look again at Miss Mary. "I don't know where else to look, ma'am."

"Where have you looked, Celia?"

"The cabin. Along the path between here and the cabin."

"Well, they're not in here. Maybe you'd best check the woods."

288

The woods. I turned to face the solid weave of shadow and earth and sprawl-root trees that made up the edge of the woods. I could do it. I would have to do it.

As I started down the path, I heard Miss Mary call, "I'll have Coffee check the barn. Maybe they went in there to see would George give them some milk."

I went through the orchard of bare pear and cherry trees and had to cross the creek to get to the woods. The chilly water plucked at my toes while I balanced on the slippery stones that formed a wandering bridge.

I searched the water rippling and rushing below for little bodies, bloated and face down and still.

I got to the other side without finding any bodies face down in the water.

The woods fronted me. There were little animal sounds inside it. I stopped, staring in at the wall of bark and nightfall calls.

I went inside. The dark of brown and cold and winter's stillness closed around me and followed as I made my way deeper in.

"I thought you'd come here."

I stopped. Turned around. No one. I must not have heard anything. I must have been losing my mind. Fevered. Crazy in the head.

"Looking for your babies, Celia? Why you out here in the woods, looking for your babies?"

As the voice went on, I knew it was not in my head. George was out here, nearby, somewhere.

I turned quickly, to find him out, and heard a sound now behind me. I turned back to find George inches from my face, bending down to see my fear, to smell it on me.

"Stupid bitch," he said. "Stupid, lazy, bitch of a black cunt. Leaving your babies. Shame on you. Guess I better tell the master."

He started off, walking fast back toward the creek, like he knew where Newsom was.

I followed after him, running. I caught up and grabbed his arm.

He turned and swung the arm so I skidded backwards across the mulch and sat hard on the forest floor.

He said, smiling and spitting, he was enjoying the words so, "Leaving your babies to starve and to freeze. No food in the cabin. No wood. No fire. I seen it all. And you up stuffing your face and warming your ass with the white ladies at the big house."

Risking everything, for surely this huge, angry, scary man would report to Newsom that I had spoken to him, a negro and a field hand and a man, but I must and I would, if it got me my babies back, I said, "Where are they, George?"

His face spread out in the joy of a real smile. "So the master's ho can talk to a nigger like me?"

He came close and held down his hand. I didn't want to, but I took it, hoping now he would lead me to wherever he must have put my children.

He pulled me to my feet with the one hand and hit me across my jaw with the other elbow. "That's for leaving your babies, bitch."

I heard my neck snap even as I felt myself fall again to the damp ground. When I came to, George was bent over me with his head turned away, bellowing, "I found her. She right over here. Look like she hit her head or something." He reached down toward the ache that was my private parts and my thighs and my back, and I went to scream and cover myself with my hand.

But he was only pulling down my skirt over my stomach, my butt, my knees, my legs.

He went down on one knee to scoop me up and throw me over his shoulder. The blow to my stomach knocked the wind out of me. I gagged over his back, bouncing on the wound that was my gut and my raked womb, as he rose and started to jog toward the creek.

Even now, something was running from the soreness in my body. Somebody had used me. Somebody had fucked me. So hard that it was still hurting on top of that other, lingering, aching hurt.

I gagged some more over George's back as he started across the creek, dizzy and afraid that we were both falling. Still, in a fuzzy part of my mind, looking for little brown bloated bodies face down in the clear running water.

Voices rose up from the other side of the creek. Miss Virginia's. Coffee's. Coffee saying, "Damn. That Celia? What happened to her, mama?"

And Miss Virginia echoed him. "What happened to her, George? Oh, get her in her cabin, quick, before Father sees this. He'll have a hissy."

The dark was fast falling and George was swift on his feet, gliding up the hill from the creek to the cabin without a missed or stumbled step, like he didn't even have anything on his back. I was that light in weight. Nothing to him.

I felt his voice against the sore pressed hollow of my chest and stomach and lowest belly. "Don't you worry none, Miss Virginia. I'll see to her. Get her cleaned up and all before Master Newsom come check on her. She be all right, ma'am. Don't you worry."

Miss Virginia, following behind, "What could have possessed her? Oh, George, when I think what Father will...."

Coffee piped up, "Will grandfather be mad, mama? He going to whip Celia, now?"

As George turned and ran me into the cabin, ducking to clear a way for his head through the door, I thought I heard Miss Virginia chuckle to Coffee, probably relieved, "Well, Coffee, we'll just have to see. The important thing is she's safe."

I was thrown on my bed so it jarred that bad right shoulder. I curled in on the many pains, blinking to make myself open my eyes, turning to look toward where I felt fire, warmth.

And did I feel fingers?

Yes. Little fingers.

Hannah and The Baby touched me, my arms, my face, saying, "Mama? Mama?"

I let out my last cry, for a long, long time, and threw my weak arms around them.

George made a lot of noise bringing heated water from the fire in the basin to the table, telling my children I had been out to the woods, nobody knew why, but it would be all right now. He was there. Master Newsom was coming. They didn't have to be afraid any more.

"You eat that good soup Miss Virginia cooked you up?" he asked my children. "Miss Virginia good to you, ain't she?"

"Yes, sir, Mister George." My children both said the answer I had taught them to this question they were bound to get from Newsom's family members at any time. Hannah, old enough, finished up for both of them. "Miss Virginia is good to us, Mister George."

"Yes, ma'am, she is that," George said, sitting me up now and stripping down my unbuttoned bodice. I tried to resist, to hold it up over my breasts. He yanked it free and snatched the bodice down, in little jerks, even lower around my waist. "No more of your foolishness," he said to me sharply. "Don't make me have to discipline you in front of your own babies, Miss Celia."

My children started to back away, afraid and ready to duck under the bed. I had to smile at them. I said, as sweetly as I could, "It's all right, Baby. It's all right, Hannah. Mama's here now. I was searching for you."

"Now, just shut that up. I told you, bitch," George snapped and struck me with the heel of his hand on my head. Then he wrung out a rag from the steaming water and began to wash me.

He started with my back and neck, and just as the heat made me let go of my shivering and sit a little lower, a little softer, he jerked my dress up and ran his hand with the rag between my legs.

I jumped away, hurt and startled. His other hand shoved me down, to sit still on the bed. "Sit still, bitch," he mumbled. "Don't make me have to

293

beat you like your white man do. You like that, don't you? Getting beat. I'll have to keep that in mind, when it come to you."

Not knowing what to do with how they felt about seeing this man handle me so, my children had backed away from the bed, away from me. Away from how George ran his hands and his wet rag all over me.

When he was done, he threw the rag into the water so it splashed. "Dress yourself, ho. The master's coming."

As I struggled to kneel on the bed and get at the tiny buttons behind me with stiff arms, George sat just where he could block out my sight of my children, hesitant at some little tapping, tagging game as they lay before the fire.

George leaned in at me. "You going tell him, bitch? About you and me?"

I stared stupidly.

Now George frowned. I couldn't help thinking he looked like he was pretending to be mad. "Don't tell me you going let on you didn't like it."

Like what? I thought of the pain in my thighs, between my thighs, all the way through my lower back when I woke up at the feet of the woods. No, I thought.

But even as I thought it, another thought said, *What difference does it make? I've been hurt worse by Newsom. I've betrayed Newsom with David. None of this makes any difference.*

At least I got my children back.

Newsom pounded and shouted to be let in at the door. George hesitated, like he wasn't ready yet, but the door flew open anyway. Unused to latches, he must have forgot to latch it shut.

Newsom came in, pale, flushed, and glaring at me. "What's all this I hear, gal?" he shouted.

George leaped to his feet and went to Newsom with his hands up, patting at the air like Newsom was an angry dog or something. "It's all right, it's all right, sir," George said. "You know, master, she probably still sick, is what it is, and she passed out from fever out there."

"She had no business out there. George, don't take up for her foolishness. Celia," whirling on me, "what were you doing in those damned woods?"

My children had scuttled beneath the bed now, bumping and grabbing at each other for comfort.

"I was looking for my babies, sir."

Newsom hollered, "Looking for your babies? Well, whore, why didn't you just come on home and look for them in your own cabin?"

George, still patting at the air, backed up all bent over like he didn't want to seem taller than Newsom and smiled into Newsom's face. "Now, see, master, likely it was me stirred up this mess. I took the childrens, sir."

Newsom, heading for me, stopped in his tracks. "*You* took them?"

"Sir, see, I had to. Miss Celia here, see, she wouldn't open the door to me. I be leaving the soup and bread, and going a ways away to see would she take it in and at least feed the babies, and she wouldn't even do that. Till I was eating it down my own self, so you and the misses wouldn't know how ornery Miss Celia up here being. She that much

295

don't want nothing to do with me, Master Newsom. I ain't nothing but a field hand, sir. I can't make Miss Celia see no reason."

Newsom glared at me, reddening. "Celia, you were starving the children to spite this hand that *I* picked to bring you your food?"

"No harm, sir, no harm." George shook his head and grinned, concern lifting his eyebrows and wringing his voice. "You can see, sir, the babies is fine." He nodded, showing Newsom how to agree.

I shouted, "He didn't bring us any food, Mister Newsom."

Newsom, looking from one of us to the other, answered me first. "What do you *mean*, he didn't bring any food, Celia?"

"He never knocked at my door, sir. Every word he's saying is a lie. He never left us not a morsel of food, Mister Newsom."

"Did you ever look out the door to see what was left to you, gal?"

"Every day. Every day, sir, I went out for water and never saw a thing left at my door, sir."

George nodded, defending me. "That's right, sir. She never opened her door till I had done up and took the victuals away, seeing as how they offended her and all. I'd be hoping she'd come out, go on up to the big house herself, if she was strong enough. Ask for something I ain't touched, if she wouldn't feed her children the food I carried, Master Newsom. Every day. Just like she tell it, sir. Just like she say." Nodding and smiling till I thought his lips would split.

"That's a lie," I screamed at Newsom, rising on

296

the bed and pointing a shaking finger at George. "He was eating that food himself and starving us out."

Newsom slapped me. I hadn't seen him get to the bed so fast. I lay back dazed.

I was probably still light-headed from the fever, I told myself. *Get up. Push yourself up.*

I tried. I wobbled on my elbows and lay back down. I could hear Newsom finishing a tirade. "Tired of your silly games. More faints and fits than a white woman. You're putting on airs, Celia, thinking you're better than other nigras. Better than the rest of your kind. I've spoiled you, is all. And you just about killed your fool self and your babies, because of it. I'll learn you your place around here."

George whined in a low voice, "Sir, I'm that sorry I stole them babies out this house, but I couldn't see them go hungry no more. And me getting hale and hearty, eating up the food Miss Virginia cooked for them, trying to hide from you all what Miss Celia was doing. Locking me out and such. I didn't know what to do, Master Newsom. I done the wrong thing, sir. But I did it to save them babies, sir. They don't last long without no food, Master Newsom."

Newsom jerked away from me and laid a hand on George. I lay still, waiting, but Newsom didn't but pat George on the back as he finished this story. "You did what you could," Newsom told him. "Women get flighty. White women ain't got but a half a brain to start with, and it's evident to me that nigger women ain't got that much. I'm that glad

297

you took and fed the children. You did all you could, boy."

George was grinning and nodding and bobbing up and down for Newsom now. "I'm not going take no stuff no more, sir," he said, looking into Newsom's face, eager. "I'm a come right in here every day after this and feed them babies. And her too, if you tell me so, Master Newsom, sir."

Newsom shook his head, weary now. "I don't know, George," he said. "Look, I told you that you did the right thing. Now, go on and finish with the milking and currying down my horse, or whatever. I'm tired. I've got to get up early and head back to David's. House sitting in the elements, open to the weather, over this foolishness."

When George went to pick up the basin of water he'd used to wash me, Newsom was at the fire with his back to us. George looked at Newsom's still, tired back and gauged he had the time to turn to me.

George's face was cut from wood, it was so still, staring at me, framed in firelight. He looked like he hated me and was lapping up my fear like a wild thing with its tongue shooting in and out of blood.

He stared till I dropped my eyes, wondering if I dared get off the bed and try to coax out the children from beneath it. Flee. Run. I wanted to run from here. Fever thoughts.

George went to the door and tossed the water from the basin over the scraggly grass before the little porch. All the time, Newsom kept staring into the fire, his hands clasped on his walking stick behind his back.

George brought the basin inside, put it by the fireplace, and called under the bed, "Hannah. Bobby. Your Uncle George see you tomorrow, you hear? I be right back when the sun come out to take care of you. You sleep tight, now. Night, Master Newsom."

"Good night, George. And thank you. Don't even worry about this foolishness tonight. I'll see to it."

"Yes, sir. Good night, Miss Celia."

I looked at Newsom, wondering if he would tell me to answer. He kept his back to both of us and said nothing.

I refused to lift my eyes to the sight of the face that lingered in the closing doorway. I would not look at George behind Newsom's back again.

When the door had closed, Newsom said, "Celia, what the hell have you got to say for yourself?" I thought, *If Newsom doesn't believe that George starved us out, will he believe I didn't bring on what happened in the woods?*

What would Newsom do if he thought I had any part in bringing on what George had done to me in the woods?

Whip me? Whip George?

If Newsom whipped George, what would George wait and, when he had the chance, do to me?

Why had George chosen me to hate and hurt? Because I was the only woman on the place that he could get his hands on? The only negress woman?

Soon, there would be Hannah.

With a start, I slid off the bed to look under it for my children. "Oh," Newsom spat after me, "so now you finally bethink yourself of your children. After you've gotten everyone else in an uproar all day, trying to take care of them for you."

Hannah and The Baby were curled together, asleep in the thin dust, their lids shiny with what looked like tear-swelling and firelight. "Let them stay there," Newsom said. "It's warm enough."

He was unbuttoning his shirt and breeches. He flopped the clothes open, yanked them off, and threw back the covers of the bed. I swallowed bile at the sight of him crawling across my bed to wait for me, the wrinkled pale belly streaked with strings of dark hair. He lay back, sighing. "Get your damn clothes off, Celia," he said. "I've got no more patience for your shenanigans."

I began to unbutton the dress I'd just put back together in such a hurry. I wanted to get under the bed and touch my children, comfort them. Work them out from under there and sing to them by the fire, reminding them that we had each other and we loved each other.

But I slid out of the dress, as I'd been told, before I did it.

Newsom must have fallen asleep with the lullaby. For after a long while, he snorted himself awake, startled, and cried out, as if he'd seen something frightening. Shaken, I pressed my children to me. "What is it, Mister Newsom?" I called out.

Newsom, still waking, gasped, "What? What? What was that?"

I let out a breath. "You must have been dreaming, sir," I said.

"Dreaming?" Heavy with sleep, Newsom sat up and crawled to the foot of the bed, frowning at me. "What the hell you doing down there? No, I wasn't dreaming. At least, it didn't seem like no damn dream. Not any dream that I ever had." He shook his head and forced his eyes to focus on me. Red, shot through with wrinkled veins, sparkling wet and round, they held me and showed me back to myself. "Come to bed," Newsom said. "You want to make trouble. I'll show you trouble. You come up here now."

At least, I thought as I got in on the side opposite Newsom, to give myself time to work my way over to him, *at least I had a chance to hold my children*. It was only as his knees scraped mine, shoving them apart, and the bones of his hips ground into the soft, sore places bursting deep beneath my skin, that I wondered if Newsom would be able to tell another man had just had me.

George. It couldn't be true. Could it? What had he meant by what he said on the bed?

He meant he had just had me.

Newsom had never managed to take me, when I was with his son. Would he manage it now? Would he feel the betrayal? Was some kind of sign left behind?

There were the sharp nails of his thumb and curled forefinger, the jerk of his hips, driving the nails deeper into the pulpy flesh, scratched by its own hair now, it was so tender. I bit down on my lip till I peeled away the dry skin with my teeth. I had not eaten that day, or I might have gagged and been sick right there in the bed from the worry.

Would he be able to tell?

Newsom grunted, satisfied, and his hand slid away from between the hot, working places between our legs.

He had gotten in and was pushing now, grinding down and afraid to back away, driving and driving in deeper, afraid to miss anything, afraid to not feel something, circling his hips and smashing the swollen lips that had let him in back against me, mashing apart the joints that were spread to let him in, going after what wasn't even trying to get away, chasing and panting and working, it had been so long since he had been in there, and he was grabbing up feeling through his body from mine.

He let out his shriek and fell onto me, too tired to feel me try to double up against the blow and then to work him off and crawl out from under him.

My legs were the last to follow me away. They were numb where they weren't raging with ache.

I lay, sweating in the heat from the fire, thinking I would get up and wash and dress and lie down with my children, if I could move one more time today.

This cursed day. I fell asleep remembering the fear of searching for my children. I woke myself throughout the night, calling to them. I would turn and plunge into the darkness again. The mattress. The sleep. The water and the woods.

It wasn't until I woke, and it was full morning, and Newsom was gone, that I remembered George.

Chapter Eleven: Rage

I wondered, watching my children's unsure little smiles at me and each other the next day, if I had not made too much of my fears. They were here and happy, and after all, even though I was a little afraid to question them, it seemed George had really only taken them away and fed them.

I was thinking I should wash and dress, not just in the nightgown I had thrown on before the children woke, but in the dress I'd brought from the other farm so long ago—four years? going on five?—because then I could wash the mud from yesterday's dress, only the older one was so high above the ankles as to be a bit shameless, when the door slammed open in that way that George had, and he came in.

He had on his furious face. My children smiled up at him with shaky lips, trying to remind him that he had said he cared for them.

George went straight for me.

"Had your white man, now." He lifted me from the floor and carried me through the air to the bed. He was on me and working open his breeches by the time I realized what he meant to do.

"Not in front of my children," was the first thing out of my mouth, thinking they might say something, and all my decisions about whether or not and how to tell would be made for me, and terrible things would come of it.

"*Not* in front of your children?" George shouted in my ear. How could he look straight in

303

my eye, not even inches from my face? "Oh, your white man can have you in front of your children. And your white man can drag your ass out naked to the creek to wash in front of everybody on the place." He hissed in my ear, and his voice was low and deep, growling as if we'd been arguing for hours. Days. Years. "But a *nigger* can't put you on the white man's bed and give you a little of what you need in front of your children."

"A little—"

A hand pressed to my mouth, and the fingers dug into the lips, stilling them against my teeth. All the while, his other hand still worked at his breeches. Either the buttons were open or off. Now he grabbed handfuls of the nightgown and rammed it up between our bellies.

I couldn't see the children from so high up on the bed. Maybe they had hidden under it again. Was the cabin door shut? Had they run out? Would someone hear or see and come to break this up and help me?

Whip me.

George's thick legs were between mine, the rough rolled muscles of his belly against my flat, yielding ones, and still there was more of him coming.

He kept talking his way into me, as if the weight and push of his body was not enough to take me over. "Can't stand a nigger, can you, bitch? Just can't stand *this*"—there was a thrust that shot up in me like a fist. I was sure it was a fist—"and *this*"—his mouth covered my face from nose to bottom lip and swept the whole of it with his licking tongue. The rest of what he said, I couldn't tell. Between the mouth and the weight and what I was sure was a fist between my legs, I couldn't much breathe. I kept turning my head to get away and get air, but on each side, as I turned, I was met with a fist or a spread hand to press my head still, into place. That was how I knew there was no fist inside me.

He kept ramming as he talked, licked, and sucked all over the bottom of my face. He kept mashing my face into place with his hands as I turned it.

The bed groaned and swung back and forth with the force of his swing against me. I thought of my children and hoped they weren't under the bed.

Then, suddenly, it was over. George arched his upper back away from me and grabbed and lifted my legs till I thought he would put them on his shoulders. But he didn't. He held them there, staring into my face, still swinging the bed with his shoves into me.

And then he threw back his head and hollered, and the holler ended on a shout and a laugh, and he was done. He pulled away, dropped my legs, and swung away to sit on the edge of the bed, panting.

After a while, he turned and looked at me. He smiled. "So, that's what the master gets." He slapped my aching bare bottom. "So when you going to tell him he sharing with a nigger?" George laughed again. "What say, girl? Think he like that?" George made his voice high and lifted his hands, limp at the wrists, in signs of distress. "Oh, master, I so shame I don't know what to do with

305

myself. I done had me a nigger, and I ain't never going be the same." George dropped his voice and his hands and wrenched my underside with a pinch. I leaped a little away from him. George said, "Quit that lying and faking. You know you love it. But you going have to wait for some more." He got up, buttoning his breeches and closing his shirt. "Can't all niggers lay around fucking all day like you, ho. I got fields to clear."

As he got to the door, George called back, "Get that kettle of Miss Virginia's slop off the porch and save me something to eat. And fetch your own damn water and wash that white man stink off you before I get back here for my dinner."

I don't know how long I lay still, stunned. So this was my new life. The thing George was going to use to get back at Newsom. Where were my children? They must be terrified. They hadn't even come out to me after George left. I would have to find them. Comfort them. Explain something to them. What was there to explain?

When I finally dragged my aching legs and body off the bed, I didn't look for my children, after all. The thought of touching them, me filthy from Newsom and George both, shamed me. Disgusted me. I pulled Miss Mary's gown on, not closed right but almost covering me, and limped out to the porch.

I hauled in the kettle, dragging it across the bricks and onto the floorboards. I placed it before the fire, blowing the embers up and feeding them the kindling that George must have brought in while I was passed out in the woods. Then I broke open the fragrant bread Miss Virginia had made, feeling the last wisps of its warmth caress my face.

I held out pieces to Hannah and The Baby under the bed. "Come on." I had never heard my own voice so gentle. "I know you're hungry, little ones. Come eat. It's okay. Everything's all right. Come to mama."

The Baby crawled out first, staring straight into my eyes as he blubbered, and didn't stop until he clambered up on my lap and sat on me. When I felt right to him, he turned his tearstained face to my hand and opened his mouth so I could feed him sopping bread.

As he ate, Hannah wiggled out on her elbows and knees. She was crying, but she let me dry her face with the edge of my gown and answer her questions about why did all the big men want to hurt mama. I didn't know, but we had each other and it didn't matter who tried to hurt mama, because mama was still here to take care of Hannah and Baby.

After they ate--"No, mama's not hungry. Let's save some so Uncle George won't be mad if he comes back"--we went to the creek to wash together. Getting all the way in the water was the only way I could wash yesterday's dress, the morning's nightgown, and both Newsom and George off my body all at the same time.

I wandered away from my children, a little ways into the running water, to throw up a stream of burning clear juices from my stomach. Then I washed out my mouth and splashed my face. Every time I closed my eyes in the stinging handfuls of water, I saw the faces, the bodies coming at me. The sneering lips, the rolling hips, the swelling parts. My own swollen, purple, tender parts.

No matter how long I stood in the water, I couldn't feel washed. When I got out, carrying the dress and pulling against the wet drag of the nightgown, my legs were numb but my private parts still raged like it was on fire.

Hannah asked if, seeing how the sun was out and the low sky had lifted, we might play a little tag outside for a change.

So we ran, squealing, until our freshly washed legs and clothes were muddy. Then I took them inside to wash everyone and everything in the bucket.

But it was funny. Now, after all that had happened, when I went out as the dark was gathering for more water, I didn't fear anything. Not the blackening grey, and not the loneliness of my little pudgy-limbed children, alone back there in the cabin.

George moved in. It shouldn't have been possible. But he made it happen.

Newsom came home every evening from working at David's place to help clear and score and plant the fields. He evidently ate what Miss Virginia and Miss Mary cooked for him without a word of complaint. He only came down to the cabin at his usual late hour, to put his body into mine, to spill the worst and most desperate of his feelings, and to sleep.

George had the daytimes.

Beginning in the morning, as soon as Newsom

308

was off to David's, George came in to insult and use my body. He had a few hearty words for my children, and I assured them we could be happy, despite George and Newsom, as soon as George, too, had gone.

George returned late at midday, and this could sometimes be tricky. His moods were fouler at that time than any other. He was hungry. He was angry. He was unloved.

George made quite a point, every day, about me not loving him. George pointed out that it was all my fault. It had nothing to do with his meanness, his roughness, his scaring me and my children. My not wanting him, in the first place. He was a man, and he was here, and how dared I not love him? I needed to be punished.

I waited for Miss Virginia or Miss Mary to send a message. Give me an excuse to get up to the big house and tell them, hint to them, break down and beg for help from them.

No message came.

Didn't they want sewing done for David's wedding? Didn't they need me to cook, even just for them and their father? Didn't they even wonder if I had lived through the fever?

But they never sent word. And my courage died with hearing, twice every day as George ground me into Newsom's bed, that this was all my fault, that I wanted it, that I had made it happen. That Newsom would kill me if he knew.

I didn't really think it was true. Newsom wouldn't really kill me if he knew. Would he?

Why would he?

What had I done? Been brought here. I couldn't see a thing I might have done different, ever since I had been brought here.

With the falling away of my fear of the dark and the cabin, something changed in me.

It must have. Newsom started telling me, when he came into the firelight and saw me waiting in the white tatters of my gown, that something had got hold, deep inside of me. "To look at your eyes," he would say, "I might think you had gone crazy."

"Have I?" I once asked. I wanted him to tell me yes. I wanted to tell him why. Tell him how it felt. Tell him. . . .everything. Newsom watched me thinking. Then he hurried on with, "Hell. I'm just a tired man, drinking and thinking. Don't listen to me, Celia. I ain't listening to myself."

Later that night, he put both hands around my throat and tried to choke me while he took me. I fought him off.

When he got off me, he stood near the bed and pounded my face with his fists.

While I was fighting back, I felt strong. I felt brave. I felt crazy and free of everything I had been since I had come to this terrible, killing place. Killing me from the inside. I would fight back from now on, and I would live and raise my children, and if it was George instead of Joshua that saved me from Newsom, and if it was anger and madness instead of love, at least it was working.

But once Newsom was above me, off the bed and hitting down at me, the old pain and weakness took over and drained me of fight.

When George saw my face in the morning, he

310

said, "Why the hell didn't you run? Scream out? Anything?"

I said, "I couldn't run. I can't run when I'm pregnant. It would just be another hurt to add to getting hit, when I got caught again. And scream for who? Who would care if I scream?"

George got that carved wood face he usually had, the one I hated most of all of his faces. All of which I hated. "You pregnant?" he said. "With whose baby?"

I didn't say anything. There were times I didn't bother to answer George. I didn't want to get in the habit, for one thing, and talk to him in front of Newsom. Nor did I want to make things worse for myself. George could take anything I said and use it against himself, and punish me for it for days on end.

Silence earned the beating of its own day, alone.

Only, that morning, George didn't beat me for being silent. He said, "It's Newsom's, ain't it. Even your *gut* won't have me." He put his hands to his face, sitting on the bed next to where I lay stretched out. When he pulled his hands down, a long line of spittle followed.

He raised a wet, purpled face to me. He had been crying.

He made a fist. He stood and raised it in the air till it was shaking. Till he was shaking. He gritted his teeth and watched his fist shake in the air above my belly.

The children screamed. Both of them. Instead of running to hide under the bed or under the table,

311

they both crawled up on the bed, across to me.

I watched the shaking fist, the weeping man, and thought, *I should move. I should get out from under that blow.*

But I didn't have it in me. I thought, *Let it fall. Let it end. Here and now.* Death thoughts again.

But George swung and slammed his fist into the wall so that it shook the door and swung it open, slowly, like it was waving him to come away and go to work.

Which he did. He snatched up his breeches and left.

And I let my arms slide over my children and asked them to forgive mama. Nothing was going to happen. They didn't need to be so frightened. I could have got away from mean old Uncle George at any time. Next time, I promised, I would move faster.

That afternoon, my children and me ate corn meal patties and drank creek water from a bucket, sitting together under the cherry and pear blossoms. It was a glorious, beautiful day. We didn't touch Miss Virginia's soup. We left it all for George.

But George did not come back for dinner. It was a perfect day. As it ended, we had the soup and bread for our supper.

And Mister David came to call with his father that night.

"Just stopping by," David said, "to hope you'll wish me happiness in your heart for my wedding in a few days, Celia." Wasn't this quite a speech to be giving his father's mistress slave? I glanced at Newsom, who had turned away, and said nothing.

David went on, " I know it's been rough on you and my sisters, out here without the men and the regular routine. I remember how you all got together and put a stop to that little house raising party we was having for brother Harvey." David chuckled.

David had talked his way across the porch and into the cabin. Now, coming around his father, who had stopped, head bowed, outside the firelight, Mister David finally got a look at my face. "Good God," he said. "Father, have you done this to her?"

Newsom mumbled in the dark, "I won't be questioned."

"But Father, there can be no excuse—" David's fingers were stretching, mindless, towards my face "—for so much…. This is too much." I backed a step away from his reaching fingers.

Newsom roared, turning, "I WON'T be questioned! And your new status as a propertied man does *not* give you authority to moralize to me. *You* are still my son."

Newsom thumped his walking stick into the floor and came after David. Now they stood face to face while Newsom's finger jabbed into David's chest. "You are nothing—*nothing*—that I didn't make you, you hear? You have everything because of me. You are what you are and you're marrying who you're marrying because of my work. Don't forget it, David."

I stood, head back, and watched David leave. He lingered dangerous long at the door while the twilight wrapped its purple and black around the edges of his face and his body. He stared at me, and firelight ran up and down from his eyes to his jaw,

313

where he was working to say something. I didn't have permission from his father to speak to him, so I was spared.

I could only have said I hated him. I hated him deeply. Somehow, though I didn't know how, I knew he was a part of what was killing me. *Go on away from here, David. You can't help me.*

Nobody can help me now.

For that was all I knew. That I was dying, and so was the baby within me. Sometimes it took me from my children in spurts of vomiting or shuddering with pain. The child could not live. And I would not. And what would become of Hannah and The Baby when I died?

George and the pain he loved to give, and Newsom and the misery he loved to spread, fell away into nothing whenever the thought took hold of me that I would not live to finish raising my children.

It was all the using of my body. Of that much I was sure. If my body had been my own, if Newsom had brought me here to cook, as he should have, if David had left me alone as he left his sister Mary alone, who was my same age, if they had protected me from George, who hated me, instead of from Joshua, who I still believed had once loved me…maybe I would still be alive, instead of this dying from the inside.

I was like candles. Bright before dying. Blazing with heat and light before the quiet dark.

I would do something before I died. My death would count for something. My children would live better, because I had died.

I didn't yet know quite how. But the doomed baby growing inside me, I promised myself, was the only one I couldn't save from what had been done to me.

When the men returned from clearing and sowing David's fields, I went back to cook in Miss Virginia's kitchen. It was the only way, I saw, to get more food than just her soups.

George never brought supplies, as Mister David had done. Miss Virginia did not trust George, did not like him, and would not open her kitchen door to him for any reason.

Newsom didn't bring supplies, even when he pointed out to me that my supplies had got "appalling low. What are you doing, starving the children again?"

I was going to die, anyway. Work couldn't kill me any faster. And there was no longer any reason to fear that, if I left the children alone in the cabin, something terrible would get in. Would get to them.

It had always been with them. They had been born to it. I had been born to it. How foolish I had been to fear. To hope. To try to stay alive.

I went to work and cooked Newsom's dinners and took what I wanted, as long as I could carry it home on my head.

"The spring do something for you, don't it?" It was Joshua, standing beside me on the pathway to the cabin.

Where had he come from? I hadn't seen him. I lived these days in my thoughts and didn't see much of anything.

I stared at him now and watched his eyes

follow the shape of my swelling breasts through the thinning threads of my old dress. He looked up at my eyes again, suddenly realizing that I had been watching where he was looking.

He wanted to say something. He struggled with his thoughts. His lips, full, dark, and cut along the edges with sharp dips and curves, worked on the words he couldn't bring himself to say. Had never said. Would it have ever made a difference, anyway?

I moved away from him. Did I have something to say, my own self? Was there a time, did I believe, when Joshua might have saved me? Had he refused? Or had it just been too much for him? Too much for me, too.

I moved slowly beyond him, watching him watch my body and how it moved, watching him wish he knew what to say to me, until I had to turn and look where I walked down the path beneath the falling blossoms of the fruit trees. Saving me was a ridiculous fool notion. But I didn't want to fall on the path to the cabin and break my neck. It was too soon to die, just yet. If I could help it. As I turned away, I thought I saw Joshua mouth my name. "Celia."

And I died a little more inside, knowing my hate had grown to take in Joshua, too.

I didn't have tears or sadness for Joshua. I didn't have tears for myself. I no longer even had tears for my children. Everything I had, every feeling, every thought, now went into dealing with George. For I had to deal with George every midday.

316

Newsom, "the old man," as George always called him, was changing his habits. He no longer got up early in the morning to get out to the fields. He lay abed in the cabin with me and my babies. He didn't seem to want to wake. He didn't seem to want to go. He was slow to rouse and slower to get moving.

And Newsom came back every night after supper, full of whiskey. He was only gone midday, when George was suppose to be in the fields. But who was there, any more, to make sure that George stayed in the fields when he was suppose to? Not Harvey. And not David.

Newsom had never hired an overseer. And what was he going to do if George wasn't in the fields when he finally got there? Whip him? How?

George began to sneak from his work in the midday, when Newsom sat down with his family to dinner, and to return to my cabin in the evening, when Newsom and his family were at supper.

He began to brag to the other hands that Newsom couldn't keep him where he didn't want to be, and to carry these brags back to me, testing them out. He began to say that he, George, was all the overseer there was around this place. That Newsom feared him. What did I think? Didn't Newsom fear him? Look how Newsom never asked him to account for leaving the fields.

I said nothing. He would try to beat me into talking, agreeing with him. Newsom must have seen the bruises, couldn't have been so whiskey sodden that he didn't see them, even in the firelight, even in the dark. But he said nothing about them.

And George's blows meant nothing to me anymore, either. I could bear them. Somewhere in them was the force, the rage, that would hasten my death or make something of it, I was sure.

George swore that the fact that I didn't cry, that I didn't cringe or hide, that I made the children laugh, later, at how he beat me, meant he was nothing to me. I loved the master. I was a black ho.

He asked me to kill the child I was carrying.

I looked at him in the sparkling black of a late spring night lit by fireflies. "There's no need for me to kill it. The child I'm carrying will die anyway."

He sneered. But he sounded uncertain when he said, "You talking witch's talk. Ain't no way you could know that."

I watched my Hannah and The Baby toddling and tagging each other among the fallen cherries and hanging pears, swinging, and said, "But I do know that. The baby won't live, and neither will I."

Maybe that's where he first got the idea. I know that's where I got it.

We would kill Newsom. And in the wild run for freedom, George would take my children on when I couldn't.

I wasn't sure I trusted George. I had seen what he did to Boo. I had seen what he did to me. I didn't believe he wouldn't hurt my children.

But I was dying. Everything takes on its brightest colors, like fall leaves, when it knows it's dying.

I did too. My death would blaze. My death would set things right. My death would do what I couldn't, alive. I didn't know how. But I knew it would be so.

I began to stumble when I walked up the hill to Miss Virginia's kitchen. I used to not even know it was a hill. But now, lifting my feet, one before the other, had become such a chore.

Joshua caught my arm. "Miss Celia," he said, staring into my face, "you ain't no ways well. You beautiful as ever. More beautiful, still. But you ailing. Let me help you."

I started to pull away. But as he tightened his hold, I studied his face. "Joshua," I said at last, for no rules applied to me anymore. I was dying. What more could Newsom do? "You're right. I'm sick, and it's real, real bad. If I don't get well, will you look out for my children? Keep them from falling into the wrong hands, if you could? Would you promise me that?"

He looked shaken. "If I could, you know I would. But why don't you ask Master Newsom for the doctor, Celia? If you think it be that bad. You don't want to just take it and die."

"The doctor won't watch out for my children. For that, I got to ask you. Joshua." He leaned towards me to hear how I whispered his name. "Joshua, would you run if you could?"

He got quiet and let go of my arm. I said, "Don't answer. But if there was such a thing, would you take my children? You wouldn't have to keep them when you got where you were going." I swayed on my feet, knowing my eyes were bright and wild. Joshua stayed with me just long enough to catch at me and keep me upright. Then he shook his head and jogged away, not looking back at me.

When I came back down the path with my food bundle after cooking dinner, George came out of the cabin to watch me coming.

White blossoms sprinkled from the sky and fell around me. He stood in a rich soft green of grass popped with bright spreading petals of color. Flowers were blooming.

I wanted to live.

I was going to tell George so. I just needed to tell somebody.

The closer I got, the more I could see George was worked up. Frowning. The face cut out of wood. He said, before he could even reach out and grab at me, "What was you doing talking to Josh today? Don't even bother to lie. I seen you at it."

I said nothing and passed by George into the cabin.

He followed me inside and made fast the door. That was when it came to me I couldn't see the children anywhere.

George beat me, around and around the room, pulling me from under the bed when I tried to crawl and hide, until one of the hands I didn't know, a stranger's voice, was sent from the fields to bang and holler at the cabin door, telling George that Newsom found him missing.

At that, George left me on the floor unable to rise, without a word as to the whereabouts of my children.

I had got as far as the creek, stumbling up and down the bank, pushing myself off the rocks, holding my arm slung across my belly, sloshing myself in the cool water, tamping my fever and calling out, "Hannah. Baby," when I heard the men coming in from the fields.

Someone was singing. Another voice I didn't know. I heard George calling me.

I couldn't think how to get across the water to the other side, to the woods, to look for my children, before George found me and stopped me. Shouldn't there have been a trail of stones, like a bridge? Didn't there used to be? Where was it?

I fumbled through the darkening sparkles of water, feeling for stones big and flat enough for me to crawl across on. I didn't get very far across the creek this way before I fell in.

The men must have heard the splash. They came running, calling out, "Who that? Who fell in the creek?"

I heard George shout at them to get back. But they came on with him, anyway. George waded into the water, cursing, to fish me out.

The men clustered around him to get a look at me and hear what I had to say. I looked around at these men who lived here with me on the same farm and were strangers to me. I searched the concern and tenderness that softened the lines along their mouths. One, scruffy, had a beard. His mouth hung open, slack with worry and the work to breathe, running after me. Then I found Joshua's face. Frightened. Pulling back. Scared of what had happened, of what must be happening, of what might happen next.

Would Joshua remember what I had asked of him? What had he decided? Would he look out for my children someday when I couldn't?

I told the men, "I can't find my children. I fear they are stolen." Joshua took one of the men's torches and set out across the creek into the woods. One other man followed him. The last, the oldest looking man, said he would get Boo to help him search the grounds. Call out if we found the babies first.

George carried me back to the cabin without a word. Newsom was there.

"She fell in the creek, sir," George said to him, surly, "looking for her babies."

"Those damn babies again," Newsom said. "What the hell're you planning to do with another one, Celia, if you can't keep an eye on the two you've already got?"

I lay on the bed, wet, while George worked up the fire. I put my hands gently on the wet sides of my swollen belly. "I don't have no plans for this one, sir," I said. "It won't live, no how."

George turned to look at me from the fire. He glared. Newsom had his mouth open but couldn't choose no words to say to me.

The first thing Newsom finally managed to say was, "What the hell talk is that?" Then he turned on George, as if seeing for the first time that we weren't alone together. "What you eavesdropping around in here for?" Newsom demanded. "Get on out of here and turn up those damned children."

George, rising and flowing out of the door like a cloud of smoke, didn't say a word.

Newsom came to the bed and, to my shock, put his arms around me. I cried into his shoulder until, drier and tired, I fell asleep.

I woke when I heard voices at the door. Joshua's. Other men's. George's, angry and helpless. Arguing.

Joshua and George came through the cabin door first, each one carrying a child. The children hung limp, and I was frightened. Newsom had let go of me when the voices got close. It was him who opened the door. He stood a little behind it and held out an arm to stop me when I rushed to grab my children.

They sat up in Joshua and George's arms, looking around for me. "Mama?"

"Where were they?" Newsom demanded, looking in turn at each of the four men.

The two strangers bid me good night and melted back into the darkness. Joshua said, "In a cave, Master Newsom. Way back in the woods, sir."

Hannah said, "We wanted to come home, but we didn't know how."

The Baby reached for me, and I took him from George. Joshua came close so I could hug Hannah without taking her from him. He said, "Well, now I know where that cave is, Master Newsom. If they ever get into it again, I'll know how to find them, Miss Celia. Don't you worry no more, ma'am."

George was silent.

Newsom thanked Joshua and promised him a reward in the morning. "Now go get some shut eye, you two. It's early to the fields in the morning."

Newsom was awake when I crawled from the bed in the dark to lie with my children, but he didn't call me back. And as soon as Newsom left the cabin in the morning, George came. The children stopped their play and stared at him.

"Looks like Joshua's going get your children killed, stupid bitch," George said, closing the cabin door behind him. "It's some fools can't leave well enough be."

"What do you mean?"

"I hide your kids to teach you a lesson. Give you time to think. You don't want time to think? I always did say you was a stupid black bitch of a ho. Next time, it won't be no finding your damn kids."

"George, I've already got a dying baby. You wouldn't threaten—"

"No, I wouldn't," he said. "Ain't no threat. I'm just telling you. You don't want to know."

"Know what?" But of course he slammed out of the cabin and was gone to work in the fields without answering me. I held my children and didn't leave them alone to go cook up at the Newsom house. They had potatoes baked in the fireplace and stew from a rabbit Joshua brought by that evening from Miss Virginia, on his way in from the fields. His hands lingered on mine as the pot passed between us, but he said nothing.

Newsom came in while the children were still eating. He said nothing about how did I get the rabbit or even why didn't I come cook up at the big house.

When Newsom left in the morning, George came. He was right. Newsom must have known when not to order him to the fields.

Nobody came for George.

George was hungry for the food we had saved

him but he threw out the last of the rabbit stew for spite. He stood in the doorway, glaring toward the mess he'd made in front of the porch, and said, "It's time to get rid of that damn old man. You wouldn't want me to get sick of coming down here, trying to sneak in and spend time with you. You shaming me. Got me sneaking round behind the back of a old damn useless white man. Time to get rid of him."

I said, "I can't get rid of him. I would have got rid of him long ago, if I could."

George said, "You just ain't tried. You forget all the things you and me talked about?"

Killing Newsom. Now, after the disappearance of the children and my night spent fearing their death, I had had enough of killing.

George went on, "It's up to you. But if I can't feel to home around here, because you got your old white man hanging around, shaming me, I just might decide to teach you how it feels. I just might let you come home to a empty cabin, your own self. A woman who don't want a man don't have a right to no children. It ain't no ways natural."

It took me two more days to figure out that George was threatening the lives of my children. In that time, I didn't go up to the big house to cook, anyway. I was in too much pain.

Joshua must have went to Miss Virginia and asked could he take me some supplies. She sent him with bread and buttermilk. He appeared quietly in the cabin doorway framed by gloaming, hoping to miss both Newsom and George's visiting times.

He didn't stay to eat with us. But this time, as I

325

took the food, he touched my hands. "Celia, I want you to know I would do what you ask. I would do more. *If I could*, Celia. I done always cared for you. Every chance I got, was me asking to come care for you. Nobody sent me. I want you to know that." Too late, the words to feed my starving heart came after it had died of hunger and beatings. I thought I should at last, at least, kiss his cheek. But I didn't.

And as Newsom and my children slept that second night, when I finally knew what George meant, I was sure I heard George stepping through the grass up to the open shutters, to watch us, cornered in the cabin, and rage at us and listen to us breathe.

Chapter Twelve: Cudgel

George whispered to me to come to the window.

I crept over Newsom's pale body, sprawled naked on the bedclothes, and went to George. "Get out of here," I hissed down at him standing on the bare patch where flowers used to grow. "You'll wake Newsom."

"And you'll get Newsom killed, ho," George hissed back.

I felt my face flush with anger and tiredness and the shame of wondering how long George had been at the open shutters, watching Newsom work at my body. I spat at him, "All you talk about is killing." I was dying. I might as well speak my mind.

George spat back, "You make a man so all he can think about is killing."

I reached to close the shutters. "Go to sleep, George. We're all going to die soon enough."

George's hands shot up and clamped on my wrists. He pulled me closer till his eyes were at mine. "You going make me do it, Celia. You going make me kill him, to get rid of him. You shaming me. You know what happen to a nigger kill a white?" He waited, like he thought I just might answer. When I didn't, "They string a nigger up, try to make sure he die slow. You going come watch when they string me up for killing Newsom?"

Even I could hear the contempt in my voice now. "One thing I'm sure of. I'll never live to see such a day."

George loosed one wrist and solidly smacked my face. "No, but you want to. You want me dead, don't you, black ho? Well, you come see them string me up. Watch me kicking and shitting and turning colors, dying one breath at a time like they like."

I pulled back. "George, I ain't listening to this."

George yanked me close again. The window ledge dug into the swell of my stomach. George said, "And while I'm dying, you'll be begging me to tell you one last time what I done with your kids. Only, it won't be nothing to tell, ho. They going be dead." George's teeth, smooth, large, and even, gleamed white in his smile. "Soon as I kill me Newsom, tomorrow night in your little pretty cabin here, guess what next I'm going do."

Maybe if I could get away, could close the shutters and not hear, I wouldn't be bound to do something about whatever George was planning. I yanked hard at my wrist. Pain shot up my arm. I grabbed one of the shutters and tried to slam it closed on George.

He snatched me back through the shutters towards him so that my head scraped the rough wood. He put his lips to my cheek and kissed it while he talked. "You done this to me. I'm a do it to you. You don't love me? You going make me get myself killed? Well, I'm a take me them babies you love so bad. Take them off somewheres and kill them before I die."

"George, don't--"

He mimicked me. "'George, don't.' Yes, I

328

will. And I'm going love every minute of it, too."

"You wouldn't really."

"You daring me?" He had snatched me clear over the ledge so that I balanced on the screaming pain where my body could no longer cushion the dying baby. My feet swam slowly behind me, searching and stretching for the floor. I could no longer talk.

George finished what he wanted to say. "Tomorrow. I done made up my mind. I'm a love every minute of this."

When he let me go, I sagged backwards into the cabin and caught hold of the ledge to break my fall. "George," I called, and Newsom mumbled loudly in his sleep.

George turned back from leaving the window, his eyebrow raised at me.

"What can I do to save my babies?" I leaned back over the ledge. I reached out to George, willing him to come back. Relent. Maybe I should have told him I loved him. Would that do it? How he had once cried to hear those words!

"I want to tell you, after all," I whispered, shuddering, "maybe I done learned to care for you," imitating Joshua's blessed words, passing them on to this man I hated. I was a shameless liar. A whore. Everything George and Newsom said.

George laughed. "Lying ho," he said. "But I give you this. It do feel good to a man to hear talk like that."

"Don't kill them, George," I pleaded and reached for him again. "Come here." I would touch him, kiss him, hug him. Go down on my

329

knees. Offer to do things he used to force me to do. And offer him my own neck to break, my own breast to stab. Whatever he needed. What difference could it make to me?

I don't know how much of all that I said. I realized George was talking again, a softer smile on his face, shaking his head like at a very foolish woman. "Celia, finally seeing you beg ain't doing a damn thing but making me itch to break they little necks. You always did have a soft spot for the master's bastards. I ain't forgot Boo."

"Boo? What does Boo have to do with anything? Is Boo Newsom's?"

"Wouldn't be here if he wasn't, now would he, stupid bitch? Master borrowed a woman from town for 'cooking' the first time his wife took sick."

I said, still reaching and wishing he would take my hand and let me be gentle with him, "Don't blame me for what Newsom bought me to do. George, if I can get him to leave me be--"

I watched his mean, warm-colored face sparkle with the light from the stars and the slip of moon on the creek, glow from behind him, and wished I had ever reached for him, made him think I cared for him before now.

Was it really too late?

George raised his hand, both to keep it out of my reach and to shut me up. Like he could hear what I was thinking--or had I said it out loud?--he said, "You don't give a damn about me. You never did. I know that. But I give you this, Celia. You keep that bastard Newsom out a <u>my</u> cabin and off <u>my</u> woman, and maybe I won't have no call to gut

330

his little brats. And don't let me catch you with Joshua again, neither."

"George, you know I've never touched Joshua."

"I don't know no such thing. But see that you don't take it up, then." He turned towards the creek, like he was thinking. I ached with how bad I wished I could gentle him towards me. I reached out towards him one last time. Maybe I would risk it. Run out of the cabin to him and touch his heart, make him tender towards me.

"George." He turned back to me, frowning now and impatient to be gone. But he didn't back away again from my reaching fingers. They fell just short of him.

He reached forward and took them in his strong, dry ones. His hand closed, firm and gentle, on mine.

He seemed too tired to take any more pleasure in my panic. Too sad. I was stunned. What could I say? "What about running away? Remember when we used to talk about getting us and my babies free? I could help run with them a little ways. And I wouldn't say nothing, not a word, if you had to go on and leave me behind. I know I'm dying. I just want <u>them</u> to live." If he ran with them, he wouldn't want to hurt them, would he? If only I had something to give him.

Maybe I could get something from Newsom. What, I couldn't think. Money? How would I know if I got my hands on it? What did it look like?

"Stupid ho." It took an effort, but George dropped my fingers. Then he turned his back and trotted away with that heavy jut of his butt he got when he was running.

I watched his shape disappear around the cabin. I had lost him. So big. It wouldn't take him a second to….with his hands on my babies… Oh, God, it didn't bear thinking about.

Newsom mumbled at me from inside the cabin to get away from the window. It was too hot to close the shutters. Was I out of my damn mind?

The whining rumble of Newsom's voice stilled as I lay down beside him. I stared at him in the dark for a while, feeling the tightness of my hatred for him in my stomach, growing right alongside the baby that was dying.

Through the night, my mind chased itself in circles that got tighter and tighter and more frantic.

I should have begged George harder. Maybe I should go right now and look for the barn. I knew the hands slept there--how did I know? I must have heard it sometime—but I didn't know for sure how to get to it or into it. It looked big from a distance. Could I get lost in there? Maybe I better take the lantern.

But what would I say? And what about the two men who slept in there that I didn't know? If one of them found me and talked to me, even helped me look for George, wouldn't it make George more mad and determined to kill my children?

Was that all George was really after, killing my children? Or was he after Newsom? If only I could understand.

But I couldn't still my mind and make it sort out everything I had heard from George tonight.

Maybe I could sneak out right now to wait at the barn door and ask George, when the men rose to go about morning chores. How I would hate to get the wrong man, though, and upset George. If only I knew what his first light chores were.

It suddenly swept through me how lonely and stupid I felt, not even knowing who gathered the eggs or did the morning milking around this place.

I hadn't lived. Not yet. Not really. I hadn't seen the farm. I hadn't been around, like Miss Virginia, hollering for my babies to come home from petting the baby horses and holding the baby chicks. I wouldn't even know how to find the pasture and the chicken coop.

Again that sadness hit me that I wanted to live. To start living. To walk around the place every day and call to my children and not fear beatings because I had talked to somebody besides Newsom, Miss Virginia, and George.

Was there no way out of this?

I just wanted to save my children. I would wake them and run right now, if I only knew how to get to the road and which way to go on it, once I found it. Where were people running to, when they were running to be free? George was the only person who had ever mentioned such a thing to me. But he hadn't told me nothing I could use on my own, without him.

Get away. Get away.

Hadn't Mister David said he'd like to come back and get me away from here? Surely he meant my children could come away with me, too. Maybe I needed only to wait.

How could I wait? George's rage was an unknown I couldn't plan for. Could I figure how to find Mister David's farm, on my own? No. But George had been there. He would know. Wait. Joshua had been there. Would he tell me how to find it?

I rose and reached for the ties at the neck of my nightgown, thinking to slip it off, dress, and go over to the barn to search for Joshua in the dark and ask him to tell me how to run to Mister David's.

But as my hands fumbled at the ties, I thought, *George might see me. I don't know where in the barn the men sleep. Even if I could find Joshua, if George sees me with him in the middle of the night, he might lay in wait for my children. George mentioned Joshua in particular to me.*

Maybe I would wait at my cabin door for George to come in the morning and get on my knees and say, "George, kill me. You got to hurt somebody. Then kill me."

But could I get my babies safe, first?

Maybe I could get Newsom to take them to David's.

But think of that last ugly spat between Newsom and David. Newsom would be none too happy to hear me ask about Mister David. He wouldn't even hear that I was asking about my children. Newsom was that way.

Wait! I brightened. *What about Master Harvey? I'll ask Newsom to get us over to Master Harvey's.*

What reason could I give him?

Wasn't Master Harvey's bride expecting a

334

baby? Couldn't I say Miss Mary and Miss Virginia didn't even need me, or say it was too much cooking to do around here and I couldn't get better at this rate, and how about letting me stay and cook for Master Harvey and help his wife with the baby? That's what I would say!

I sat back down on the bed with the strings hanging loose and the nightgown open at the throat while I stared at the pale still shape of Newsom. Should I wake him? Ask right now? Get my babies out of here before the sun broke over the distant edge of the land and George came back?

I didn't know for sure when it was George didn't want to see Newsom at my cabin no more. Could I be sure that tomorrow night was the most time I had to get my children away or get Newsom to leave me alone?

What if I could get myself and my children moved back into Newsom's house? That might be best. When we used to live in there, I didn't even know there was such a man alive in the world as George, until I was foolish enough to go down to the creek.

I nudged Newsom gently as the sun broke up the night with little pale shades of grey outside the shutters. I wanted him to think he was waking on his own. But he slept like the dead. I got to shoving him in the side with my hands, whispering, "Newsom. Master Newsom," but he wouldn't rouse.

So I held onto my fear, held it back, and got up and dressed myself and busied myself around the cabin, pouring wash water for the children and me—thank goodness it didn't need heating in the summer! I felt so rushed—and stirring a little mush in the kettle to get the children awake and started.

Oh, how I wished we had somewhere to run and knew how to get there. I went and stood a few minutes at the open cabin door, watching and dreading the pink spread of day.

Never mind Newsom. I would get my children up to the big house kitchen and lock them away from George. Let me just think of excuses to stay there, as the next days and nights wore on.

Could I tell them? What could I tell them, without saying anything about George? Newsom had already shown he wasn't inclined to hear me accuse George.

Sunlight spilled almost golden. I rushed the children through their washing and eating and had them almost out the door when Newsom woke.

"What the hell are you up to?" he rasped at me from the bed. "Where are you going at this time of day?"

"Sir," I said, quickly shutting the door—if George was outside, it wouldn't do to let him see me turning to talk to someone still inside—as I pulled my children back in close to my skirts. "I must get up to the kitchen."

"You ain't been up to the kitchen for three or four days. What's your hurry now?"

Was I out of supplies? I didn't have time to check. I risked a lie. "Supplies, sir. I was just stirring up gruel for the children, but I thought—"

"You thought nothing." Now Newsom looked suspicious. "Didn't my daughter tell me she told you stop bringing your babies up there?"

Here I was. Caught already, and I hadn't even gotten them out of the cabin, to say nothing of off the farm.

I shoved my babies gently toward their abandoned bowls of gruel. "Eat, little ones." Then I went onto my knees at the side of the bed. I took Newsom's hand.

His eyes got big.

"Master Newsom," I tried to get my voice and eyes less urgent, but I couldn't. "It's powerful important to me to beg you for this favor. Can you send my children and me to Master Harvey's? Please, sir."

Newsom looked thunderstruck. "Master *Harvey's?*" He snatched his hand from mine. He grabbed my hair with that free hand, tilted back my head and stared into my eyes, like maybe he could read something more there than what I had just said.

"Master *Harvey's?*" he repeated. "Since when you got your whoring mind set on Master Harvey? What the hell?"

"Sir, it's my children."

"Your *children?*"

"Yes, sir." The pain of his fingers balled up and easing hair from my scalp by the roots stung. I could hardly think. Tears washed down my face. "Can't I get them away from here, sir?"

"Away from here? You done gone crazy at last? Why should your children go away?" His face went slack and so did his grip on my hair. "Oh, I get it." He pulled back and let me go. "You likely had some birth pangs in the night, regular

337

thing, nothing to get worked up about, but you done went and made it a case for dying, like you do. I ain't never seen a nigger whore so set on dying, every least little pain she gets."

I should have known he would do this with my request. Turn it into something else. Now what could I do with it?

Agree. Push it. "Yes, Master Newsom," I said, and the tears still ran on their own. "I'm dying, and I've heard with my own ears your daughter say she's tired of feeding them, and they're good children, sir." My voice rose, trembled, cracked. "They could learn to work for Mrs. Harvey, and with her new baby and all she'd love the help, wouldn't she, sir?"

I was getting worked up. I *would* persuade him.

But he cut me off. "I done gave Harvey everything he has today, and he ain't gave me a thing back. Including gratitude. Forget it, wench. I ain't giving no free *nothing* else to that lazy, ungrateful son of mine."

Only then, I said, "But maybe if you'd let me move the children back into the big house—"

"Not you and the children nor just the children. I like my privacy away from that damn house and you're just like Virginia, trying to keep me in it."

"She's right, sir." Here it was. Here was my chance. "Please don't come down here any more."

Newsom's mouth went open on words he couldn't even think to say. He waited for something to come to him. Inspiration failed.

I tried to think quick. "You see how ill I've

been, sir." The children must have sensed something was wrong. They left their bowls and came around me, crawling into my lap and trying to take my hands down from where I reached for Newsom.

Newsom kept out of my reach. "You telling me leave you alone, girl?"

"Yes, sir. I'm begging you, sir."

Newsom's face went red. Fell. Frowned. Bloated up again.

He hauled back and slapped me. "Insolent negress!" He tumbled out of bed and steadied himself to tug on his breeches and shirt.

He was soon out of the door. It creaked only a little shut behind him. Beyond Newsom, stomping barefoot up the hill with his shirt front flapping wide and his shoes, stockings, and cane dangling from one hand, and his breeches clutched shut in the other, was the still, watching form of George.

I quickly shut the door.

I closed the shutters and waited in the dark, the warm, protecting dark, holding my children. I rocked them and whispered, "Go away, go away, go away. Go away, George. Go away, Newsom. How can *we* go away?"

George didn't come.

After a while, the tears dried and left my face tight. My rocking slowed and stopped.

George wasn't coming. Newsom wasn't coming back.

I gathered up the children, who stared at me big-eyed in the dark left by all the cracks that let in streaks of sunlight. We went to the door, opened it, watched a while, and then hurried, holding hands, up the hill. What would I say to Miss Virginia when she reminded me I'd been told not to bring my children? I couldn't think what I could say. Did I dare lie? "Your father said I could."

But luck was with me. Miss Mary was at the kitchen door, handing a bucket of slops out to Coffee for the hogs. She let me and my babies past without a word.

And I used to wish I could just say, "Good morning," to her. Goes to show how stupid I used to be.

The less said to these people, the better.

I went around the kitchen in a frenzy, putting together things to make everybody's favorites, if I could. It would be a heavy meal for summer. But it would keep me busy and in there, and give me some excuse why I had to come in so very early.

Miss Virginia tapped the back of my arm. "Celia, didn't I tell you not to bring your children in while you're cooking? And besides. I thought you were ill again. Should you even be up here, yourself? None of my children need more coughs and fevers."

I wiped my hands on my apron. I wet my lips to get to work on the words I had been practicing for her. "Miss Virginia, you're right, I'm sick. But it ain't spreading. It's on the inside. But it's taking me. I'm dying. You know that, ma'am. I came today so I could ask you, please, help me send my children to your brothers. Please, ma'am. I'm begging."

She rolled her eyes as she turned away. "Celia,

I can't--"

"Please. Oh, please, Miss Virginia."

She turned on me. "What *is* all this talk about dying? If people could just up and die to escape their problems, everybody would be dead."

My voice shook. Tears came again. "I don't want to die, Miss Virginia, ma'am. Why would I want to die? What is it like, anyway, Miss Virginia, to be dead?"

Miss Virginia recoiled from me like I was a snake. "To be dead?" she echoed. "I guess the good people fly among the clouds singing heavenly praises, and the bad people burn, and all that goes on forever. Why do you ask?"

Now I was eager. "You see, Miss Virginia," I urged her, "that's not what I want. I want to care for my children, to bathe them some more, and—oh I don't know, anything!—to just be with them, to live, more than I ever lived before. Miss Virginia, it's your father. It's...." I bit down on my knuckle. Tears slid from my eyes and nose. Here I was. Here was my chance. Now how to put what I needed into words? "Please, please have pity on me, ma'am. It's your father. Can't you get him to stop coming down to the cabin, Miss Virginia?"

I was shaken. But she was hearing me.

I wiped my face in my apron and kept talking. I reached now for Miss Virginia, who backed away. "I've done everything I can," I pleaded with her. "You don't understand, but you will, ma'am. If he keeps coming down there, he'll get hurt. Or worse will happen." I was thinking of my babies, but I could see she was thinking of someone else. Who?

She went pale and snatched her hands from mine. "How would Father get hurt? What are you saying, Celia?"

"Only, Miss Virginia," I fell to my knees, "that I'm dying and I need your father not to come down there any more."

"Enough!" Miss Virginia backed away and, when I would crawl closer, stamped her foot like to scare a stray animal away. "Good women don't *hear* this kind of thing. You have *never* respected me, Celia. Never. Now, you know as well as I that my father's affairs are his own, and it is not *proper* for you to try and drag me into the middle of this."

She bunched her skirts in her hands to keep them from tangling around her ankles as she ran from the kitchen.

I turned to the door.

I only turned because I realized with a jump that the door was open and a shadow had entered it.

But the shadow was only Miss Mary, coming back from wherever she had been.

I wondered what she'd heard. Never mind. I could start again and explain again, maybe even better.

"Your face, Celia," Miss Mary said to me. "You don't look yourself. You don't look well at all. You look. . .I don't know. . .wild-eyed. Get up from off the floor. Maybe you should go back down to your cabin."

My lips had dried so that my whole mouth crackled as I tried to lick them. "Miss Mary," I started as I crawled toward her, my tongue thick, "I came up here just to ask you and your sister

342

something. It's this. Couldn't you, please, Miss Mary, persuade your father to stay away from the cabin?" I got to my feet. I drew near her. She stood her ground and stared. "It's a danger to him, as well as to me and my children, Miss Mary."

I was close now and could see Miss Mary's shock that I had actually spoken direct to her. Had I never done so before? Well, there was no time to trouble myself about such things now. I had to press my point. Now, while Miss Mary listened.

But while I thought of how to go on, Miss Mary decided she had heard her fill. Eyes big and wild as she had just said mine was, Miss Mary said slow, "How dare you speak to me, straight to my face, you shameless nigra whore, and about such things. *Such things*. I know what you and Father do in that cabin."

Her voice died out like mine had done. I watched her. Where had I lost her? What had I said wrong? I couldn't think how to start again. Neither one of us knew what to say. Neither turned away. Hopeless now, I blurted out, "But it's your *Father*." Didn't she care?

Miss Mary shook herself and cut me off. "I will not hear such things. I will not. Now get that dinner done and get out of here. You never did know your place."

Both of the sisters stayed out of the kitchen for the rest of that morning.

And the sunlit hours flew, as did my hands, over the potatoes, over the green beans, over the bacon, over the onions, over the flour for making gravy and bread, and over the tender pink slices of

343

ham that I might get whipped for cooking up on such an ordinary day, but nothing mattered except that my children were here in the big house with me, and George couldn't get at them for one hour, for one minute, more.

Could he have meant it? would pop into my mind, calming me every now and again. *George couldn't have meant it. He could never hurt my children.* I'd seen George pick up The Baby and hug him, kiss and smell and delight in the little folds of sweet skin scent caught in the tiny soft neck. I'd seen George put his last bite of supper into Hannah's trembling mouth with his own hand, when she'd asked for more and there was none, and he didn't want her to cry. I'd seen him tell her, "Eat it slow now, baby," like he cared. Surely he would never hurt my children. It was just a threat, words said in anger. Nothing.

I'd made a fool of myself with Newsom and his daughters for nothing, that was all. Why, I would go down to the cabin and. . . .

And Newsom will come and if George doesn't kill him before my eyes, Newsom will leave and keep coming back, and the day will come when George will remind me, "I told you not to have him in *my* cabin and on *my* woman," and from then on, when I come down to the cabin, it will be empty. And by the time I die, there will be no children left to me. I will have failed them all.

Many times, I dropped what I was doing and dug my fists into my eyes, trying to shut out the pictures George's quiet threats had put there.

Maybe he didn't mean it.

But if he did?

In between stirring and kneading and mashing and cooking, I hovered over my children, playing quietly under the cutting table. Their few light little laughs lifted my worry like bubbles rising to pop in the air. They smiled at me and reached for the little warm tidbits of special food that they rarely got in such abundance as I was feeding it to them today.

I came to them again and again, just to see them peek up at me from under the cutting table, and reach for the little treats, and smile.

It was almost like death had already cut us off from each other. I couldn't understand it. But I could feel it.

It was too late. We were reaching across distances, our fingers touching over the treats, but already I couldn't feel my children. It wasn't that they were no longer real. It was me. I was slipping, and I was almost gone.

As the dinner hour drew near, I came more and more often to sit on the floor beside the cutting table and pull Hannah and The Baby into my lap and hold them. Against my heart, still beating. Against the dying baby, who rarely rolled over and kicked any more. Whether or not I could feel them, they were here, with me and real.

The sisters sent Coffee and his brother in to carry out the food to the dining table. When I heard Newsom's voice, booming at his daughters and Miss Virginia's children over the dinner, I was relieved. I had never been happy to hear his voice before, and the feeling was strange.

But this time, I thought, he's still alive. George

345

ain't got to him. Maybe George really is giving me time to figure out how to get Newsom to leave me alone.

I made up my mind that, right after dinner, I would try to talk to Newsom one more time.

His eyes bugged and he threw down his napkin and rose, quivering with rage, when I came through the doorway and asked that he not leave before I could speak to him.

"You insolent barefaced whore!" Newsom bellowed. He came around the table, folds of skin jiggling as his jaw shook and spittle sprayed, shoving me ahead of him back into the kitchen. "Don't you think I know you've been upsetting my daughters today? They won't tell me what you've said, but I guess I have a good idea, don't I?" His hand landed, open and hard, again and again on my face.

He left me with my face burning. I gathered my children and held their hands as we hurried down the hill to the cabin.

I could see in the brief light as the door swung open and closed that George was not there. I sighed, catching my breath from the run down the hill and the holding it, for fear.

Maybe everyone was right and my fears were foolish. The midday heat in the closed cabin was stifling. I might as well open the shutters.

The children were asking could they go play among the fruit trees. I knew how they loved to pick up and eat the fallen cherries, and now the ripening pears. I went to open the door for them. I could wash their little shirts and spread them to dry

346

on the grass under the high sun, by way of celebrating that they were alive.

But as I crossed the cabin, I caught sight of an odd thing out of the corner of my eye.

There, in the far corner near the window. On the other side of the bed.

A large stick, too thick around at the bottom end to be grabbed with one hand, but more slender at the top, almost like someone had shaped it, a cudgel, really, leaned against the corner walls.

How had it got there? When had it got there?

George must have brought it in while me and my children was gone out of here.

I ran and grabbed my children and turned them away, like not to look at the weapon in the corner. I bent over them, holding them and staring at it.

What could I do? George had come to hurt somebody, maybe me, or Newsom, or the children, and here was the very weapon he had brought with him, and he would be back, and it would be here, ready for him.

And he would use it.

When would he come? Where could I go? Where could I take my children away to?

"Mama?" a voice called up from where my skirt pressed into my thigh, "can't we go out?"

"No." I loosed the children so I could run to the door and shut it, but it was already shut. Still shut. I looked around and ran to slam the shutters. Shut out the light and the sight of that terrible thing in the corner thinking, *He meant it. He'll kill somebody.*

I'll ask him again to kill me. Kill me and be

done with it. I don't care how. Just get it over with.

I sat on the floor with my children, as I had up in the kitchen, and held them in the soothing darkness where, blessedly, there was nothing to see.

I sang the children into a fretful nap and thought, *I was a child when I was afraid of the dark. The dark is peace and rest. I wish I could sleep, too.*

I had not slept the night before, and soon I did sleep, hunched and holding my children. I woke to The Baby's urgent shaking of my shoulder. "Mama, pot," he said. "I got to go pot."

Even in the muted streaks of sunset, now, coming through the cabin's chinks, I could see The Baby holding his private parts and jumping from foot to foot. I pulled the chamber pot from under the bed, and soon Hannah insisted that we needed the shutters open. "Smell," she said. To my surprise, I laughed.

I was still sleepy. I had been in a panic, I remembered, but I couldn't, at the moment, think why. How foolish of me. I was a crazy woman. For there was the sweet early evening beyond the opened shutters. Nothing to be afraid of. The least little breeze swept in from over by the woods and the creek, cleaning and clearing the day's cares from the evening air and the clinging worries from my mind.

The children were thirsty. Most likely from all that rich food I had given them in the Newsom kitchen all morning. Whatever had possessed me?

In the softly falling light, I went to the bucket to dip them up some water and found that it was at the

348

dregs. Oh. I must not have remembered to go to the creek this morning, after bathing the children.

No harm done. We would go now.

All the way to the creek, The Baby tried to show me how he was learning to run without falling—which he did, over and over—and Hannah tried to show that she could turn cartwheels just like Miss Virginia's boys—which she couldn't—but as they tumbled and landed in the dewing grass, we had many good laughs.

Even the baby inside me stirred once, gently.

We scooped up our water and set aside the bucket in the grass. How fresh it was to be outside of that hot cabin. How sweet to hear the creek singing over the stones. How pleasing to watch the children tumble and laugh.

I sat on a large rough stone and reached deep into the creek. My children drank the handfuls of water from my palms. Then I rubbed it lightly down their faces and bellies and behinds, giving them their evening wash, and they shivered from the sudden cool.

As they ran among the trees, gathering the last fallen cherries and throwing stones up to dislodge the perfect pears, I gazed across the creek to the woods. If there was one cave to hide children in over there, might there be another?

Maybe, if we ran now and searched, we could find a place to hide from George.

But if we ran, and he came looking and found us, hiding from him…what would he do? It didn't bear thinking about.

And what would Newsom do? Call us running

aways. And then what? Past that, being called runaways, there was no point thinking about it.

The sun flew from the sky. This was the fleetest day of my life. I couldn't grab the hours as they slipped like frayed threads, away.

It was on the way back to the cabin that I remembered what was in there, what had frightened me earlier in the day. The club. Maybe I could use it in the cooking fire, burn it and boil up gruel over its ashes and say I didn't know it was a weapon. That's what I would do.

But as we went back inside, and my eye fell on it, standing there like a friend of George's in the corner, waiting for him, I thought better of burning it. If George came looking for it, he would never stop to listen to why it wasn't there.

Chapter Thirteen: Blaze

By the time I got my babies settled for the night, the fright and restlessness of the night before had caught up with me again. I was tired. I wanted to lay down on their pallet with them. I wanted to sleep and not wake till I was well enough to believe that both me and the baby inside would, after all, live.

I didn't see how I could rest. I had to stay awake and watch for George. But only George. Surely, after the scenes I had made in his home that day, Newsom wouldn't come again.

His daughters would ask him to spare my baby, if not my body. I would tell George all this. He would see that "the old man" didn't come. He would take comfort from that and believe that he was cared about. That I could learn to love him. That he had taken me from our hated master. That he was his own man. All that stuff he was always on about.

All would be well.

There was a rattle at the closed latch of the door. Had I bolted it?

As I went to it, a voice said at the window, "None of your nonsense. Let me in this house."

Newsom.

How could he? How could he have come again?

"Go away," I hissed at his face in the window. "Get out of here, I'm telling you. It's over. You can't touch me any more."

351

Newsom bellowed, "Says who? You and what law? I bought you, whore. You don't tell me when it's over."

His bellowing would draw George, for sure.

Newsom left the window. I heard him stride around to the door. I drew the bolt and opened it.

As Newsom's face passed by me, coming inside the cabin, I thought, *Did George see_him? Will George think I've let him touch me again?*

Not if we kept arguing. George would hear and know I was fighting.

Newsom had never heard me say that he couldn't have me. I could see the shock and outrage mount up in his face with the passing waves of color.

He shook. He bellowed. He swung at me with his cane. The blows fell, and I backed into the opposite corner.

My hands, stopping my fall against the wall, fell against George's cudgel. I closed my fingers around the slender handle.

Newsom's cane sliced through the air. I turned my face, avoiding blows and the sight of Newsom, enraged, eyes bulging, teeth bared as he spat out his curses. I heard my children wake and cry out and crawl under the bed.

I thought, I could swing this. I might hit him. I might hurt Newsom, my own self. I could do it. George would be pleased.

I swung the cudgel up from the floor. Newsom's arms were down. He leaned in towards me, ranting and spitting. The cudgel caught his jaw and his head, snapping it back.

Newsom wobbled, trying to stand, but sank to the floor and lay there.

Blood poured from his scalp. The little moonlight through the open window, for I had not laid or lit a fire, was enough to show me the spreading darkness of Newsom's blood.

He raised his head, stunned, and stared at me. He gritted his teeth, and the blood flowed in between the long white squares, staining, spreading pink, and dripping from his jaw. I thought to put down the cudgel and go to him, for surely he was in terrible pain.

Newsom reached up from the floor for me, dragging his body closer on the elbow of his other arm. The reaching fingers crooked and strained.

If he touched me....

If he touched me....

My right shoulder screamed with pain from the first blow I had dealt Newsom. I raised the cudgel now with my left, caught it with my right, coming down, to give it what added force I could, and watched it sail and bump from Newsom's skull.

Newsom's head bounced on its chin, once, again. It lay still.

He lay still.

The cudgel clattered to the floor.

I watched a long time. I waited.

Newsom didn't move. Could he be hurt bad? Very bad? All that blood....

I leaned closer towards him. Looked at the tangled, dirty hair at the top of his skull, where it dipped into the puffy, bloody line I had made above his temple. I had done that?

I had done that.

I eased myself onto the floor by Newsom, moved closer, and put his head on my lap.

I was still wearing my apron. I tried with the ends to wipe at the blood that wanted to run into his eyes.

His eyes were just a little open. The blood stuck between the lashes.

Suddenly, I screamed. I dropped his head from my lap to the floor, still screaming, in my hurry to get away. From under the bed, a voice called, "Mama?"

"Don't come out," I called. "Stay there."

I reached for the edge of the bed, as if to stop a child and push it back under, but no one came out. I saw my hand shake. It was streaked with blood.

I rubbed it on my apron and looked, reaching out, toward Newsom. He couldn't be lying there, hurt and bleeding. I hadn't meant to….

He lay so flat and pale. The slit where his eyeball showed through the lids made him look like he wasn't sleeping.

He must be dead.

And I had killed him. I had killed my master. What had George told me? I would hang.

No one must know. I could do something. What could I do?

I backed away from the body, away from that side of the bed, gathered up the damp, cooling edges of my apron in my hands. I couldn't bear to see, to feel, his blood on me anymore.

I rubbed my hands on the balled up apron. I sat in the chair at the table, afraid to light the lamp.

354

What had I done?

A thought came to me. I had saved my children. When George saw this, when George found out, he would never again threaten. I had done what he had not. I had killed Newsom. Wasn't there a time we had thought that, if Newsom was killed, we could flee in the confusion?

I had done what he had not. I had set us free. Now he only had to help us find where that freedom was.

We would run. Now George, who knew which way to run, would take my children, and maybe even me.

It was a good thing I had been afraid to light the fire or the lamp. Now I went to the door and opened it on the darkness, secure that no one would see me watching for George.

I looked out and could see stars between the heavy limbs of trees. Why didn't I ever know enough? I wished I could grab my babies and run right now.

I untied my apron, still watching out for George. He wasn't coming, and the presence in the cabin behind me, so near my children, was beginning to feel like someone else, a thought, a thing, heavy and judging me, was there.

I couldn't believe Newsom was dead.

I went back, and in the light from the windows, looked again. He was as I had dropped him. Still. His cane just out of reach of one hand. The other still bent at the fingers, like when he was reaching for me.

No. I could not have done this. I hadn't meant

to do this. I reached and shoved the balled up apron in under Newsom's head, trying hard not to touch him.

But I did touch him. His skin, clammy with the sweating he must have been doing from the heat and from his anger before he fell, was still warm. Little beads of sweat ran up onto my fingers from his forehead.

Once, when he was on top of me and didn't want to move after satisfying himself, I had reached up to wipe the sweat from his forehead before it dropped into my face. I thought of that, with him lying there so still, and said, "He can't be dead."

Then I went to the bucket by the fireplace and shoved the bloody parts of my skirt into the cool water and scrubbed them. I couldn't see it, but the water was probably pinking with the blood. *"Cold running water washes away blood better than boiling."* Only, this water wasn't running.

I wished my children and me was on the road, running.

Not people, running. Water, running. The creek. I wished I could leave the cabin and go wash Newsom's blood and sweat off me, walking against the rushing, running water of the creek.

A cry came out of my mouth, a sob, I guess. I snatched the skirt ends from the bucket, wrung them, and let them fall and cling to my legs as I went back to the door.

Where was George? Had I ever waited and wanted so for that first glimpse of George, coming to my cabin?

No. I had never watched for George, unless I

watched in fear.

Enough of fear. I would take the children away from the body, and go down to the creek to wait for a sight of George.

It was hard, forcing myself down to look under the bed, even in the dark fearing to see clear across to the other side, the still body of Newsom. But I made myself think of the children and run my eyes along in the blackness, seeking out shapes not too far from my face, and I saw them.

Crouched together. Lying on each other, asleep again.

I straightened and stood and laughed, amazed. I didn't have to take the children with me. I could leave them, now.

George wouldn't hurt my children because I had made Newsom leave me alone.

I wore my nightgown to the creek and carried the "fat-lady" dress, to wash away any more blood.

Once I got all the way to the flat stone, where I sat to lean in and dip the dress into the running water, watching it lift and float just above the current, I thought, I could wash the gown free of Newsom, and his sweat would never get in it again. So I stuck my legs into the creek and eased into the current, still holding the dress.

The cold struck me in the private parts, where they used to burn, and lifted and carried the nightgown. The heavy pull of it dragged me along in the water, hurting my feet on the stones, gripping the dress that wanted to flow away in the low water. I panicked and hurt my fingers, gripping the floating dress.

Then I dropped back my head and laughed out loud, like George after taking me particular rough. It had just come to me that Newsom wouldn't say a damn thing to me, if the dress did float away. He would never say a thing to me again.

Then I slapped my free hand over my mouth. What was I doing? Out alone in the night, laughing in the creek, with Newsom lying bloody on the cabin floor.

Bloody. Maybe I should take the wet dress back and use it like a rag to wash the blood off his head. But what if there was blood all over him, running under his chest and seeping through his clothes, mixing with the sweat and spreading places where I couldn't see it?

Too bad I couldn't drag him to the creek and hold him in the running water, like I was holding my dress, to wash clean. This thought stopped my racing, chasing brain.

I couldn't drag Newsom down to the creek. But George could.

This was it. This was the killing and the confusion that would follow. We would get Newsom down here, in the stones and the water, and by the time he was found, nobody would even know, for sure, that he had died in the cabin.

I struggled out of the creek, wringing out the edges of the gown and the sagging weight of the dress I carried, my shoulder wrenching me with the twisting, and rushed, waddling and slipping, back up to the cabin. I burst into the dark with no fear of touching Newsom. I would wash him up with the apron and drag him, myself, into the creek.

"Where the hell you been?" George said from the dark behind me.

I whirled on him, sprinkling water from the dripping gown and the dress in my hand. "Down at the creek washing off Newsom's blood. Look." I pointed over towards the other side of the bed.

"What the hell you talking about?" But he was already moving, edging his way around, looking sideways over his own shoulder like he didn't want to look head on at what was lying so still.

George knelt and stared, one hand on the bed, at the body.

What little I could see of it, hid by the bed and the black night, was too ugly for what Newsom's death meant to us. Newsom, dead, should be lovely.

The longer George sat there on his heels, studying the sprawled figure, the more my feelings swelled inside me. I knew I should have been afraid. I <u>was</u> afraid.

But there was, too, a feeling in me of being powerful proud that I had done something that filled George with so much awe. <u>He</u> had not done this. <u>I</u> had. Now we could flee.

I was tired of waiting for George to speak. I said, "There's no more time to waste. Help me carry Newsom down to the creek, so as it can look like he drowned. And you and me and my babies can get started on the road. Remember what I told you. I don't want to be a burden. When I can't run on no more, you leave me to die, if I must."

George looked up at me. Even in the darkness, I could see how his eyebrow nearest me twisted up like he was making a challenge. Again, just for a moment, I had a sick feeling at the thought of leaving my children alone with him, running on the road.

But would it be better to leave them behind here, caught between Newsom and George, without me?

I had forgot again. Newsom was already dead.

Somehow, it seemed like it just couldn't be. Like he would get up, shake his head, curse me, and amble on back up to his house, figuring out some new devilment to heckle me with.

George got up from the floor and, still watching me, left the cabin.

For a moment, I was afraid with that look in his eye that he meant to go tell someone that I had just murdered the master. "That's foolish," I told myself. "This is his chance to escape, too."

Then, just to be certain nothing went wrong, I decided again to move Newsom to the creek myself, no matter what pain it cost me in that right arm. If I had to, I would break it tonight, getting Newsom out of the cabin where my children still huddled, asleep.

When I went to pull my apron from under his head, I couldn't. He looked so very wrong. Sprawled, bloody, and still. Too still. Nothing should be that still.

Reaching with the tips of my fingers, I worked loose a few ends of the apron, a corner and a string, to tie the cloth around his head, so I couldn't see the gash, the matted strings of hair, the slit open eyes.

Pulling by his ankles, I got Newsom going.

His clothes made a rasping sound on the

360

splintered floorboards. Like his snores. Like he was working up air to speak to me. Accuse me. Damn me.

I dropped Newsom's ankles. Only then did I feel the throb in my shoulder that said maybe I couldn't really do this.

As I stood, rubbing my right arm and working up my nerve, the strain of everything I had done that night moved down from my shoulder to become a tug in my womb. The tug snapped and became pain. Sharp. Running.

I squatted on the floor to ease my shaking legs.

When the pain passed, I sat, legs bent and spread apart, sweat breaking out on my forehead and the wet nightgown cooling the rest of my body to chills and even little shivers.

For Newsom was sighing. Groaning. There was no doubt about it.

I got forward on my hands and knees and crawled around closer to his head.

Newsom's eyes was still half open. But now the lids was working, fluttering like butterflies struggling to fly.

I let out a cry and tried to get away from him.

The pain reached up on the underside of my swollen belly and clutched me back down to the floor. I couldn't get away. I turned back to Newsom to watch him return to life.

The slit open eyelids kept working. They would stop and then flutter again. The groan came again, carrying low and rising through the hot summer air, trapped in the cabin despite the open shutters, lifting the hair on my scalp in fear.

361

Newsom had seemed so dead. He must have been dead. But his death was leaving him, seeping around the room. Could I get my children out from under the bed and out of here, before…?

I didn't know before what.

I dove to the floor, reached under the bed to try and grab my babies by a foot or an arm and haul them out of there. Mumbling and sucking at mother's milk in their sleep, they pulled their little limbs away from me.

The blow to my belly of falling on the floor winded me. I rolled over on my back and covered my eyes, trying to ride out the pain and get control, again, of my thoughts.

If Newsom wasn't dead, it didn't mean he had come back from the dead. So stop that thinking. It wasn't serving no purpose but scaring me out of my wits. And I needed my wits. There must be a better way to use Newsom's living than his dying. Hadn't I had bouts of horror, this very night, that Newsom was dead by my hand? Now I could be relieved of that feeling. Think. Think. What to do?

I rolled slowly to my side and worked my way to my hands and knees again. If Newsom was alive, but so very wounded, then of course this was better for our escape. We didn't have to leave him by the creek, to be found dead. We could just souse him with water from the bucket, wash away the blood and even revive him a little, and then carry him up to his own house, claiming I heard his cries and went along the creek searching, and found him where he must have fell and cracked his head. Something like that happened just last winter, but with the other hands, not me and not George and not so late at night.

And if somebody asked what would Newsom have been doing, wandering along the creek in the dead of night?

I would say he'd come to the cabin and I had refused to let him in, and he was furious, I guess, and didn't want to go to his own bed. How should I know?

Perfect. I crawled to the bucket to drag it to Newsom and begin to tip it gently along his body.

"What now?" George hissed at me from the door. "How's that going help him burn?"

I turned to see George hefting a pile of long cut poles across the floor to the fireplace. He dumped them so hard some of them rolled, like to go under the bed and poke at my children.

I didn't have to retrieve them. George himself gathered up the rolling posts and began to stack these long cuts of wood over and around bits of kindling, like a corral in the man-size fireplace.

"Burn?" I said stupidly. Then it struck me. Of course. George still didn't know Newsom wasn't dead.

I explained, going across the space between us to lay a hand on George's working arm and make him listen. "This is even better. Let's get Newsom to his daughters, wounded like this, and they'll be nursing him for days. It will take them forever to send for Master David and Master Harvey and figure out who'll do what. You know how they do. The place will be in a uproar. We can escape with nothing hanging over our heads but running away.

363

Not murder. Come on, George. Help me souse him and get him up the hill."

George kept stacking his long posts until his fire corral was built. Then he fetched Newsom's fallen cane and the blood-tipped cudgel I'd found in the cabin—was it only that very evening?—and added them, too, to the wood in the fireplace.

All the while, I sat scooping handfuls of water across Newsom's covered head. Maybe I could revive him, and George would see that we had to do this my way.

My bloody, stiff apron kept the water from seeping away from Newsom and under the bed to my children, as I'd feared. I lifted the softened, stained apron to see if Newsom's face looked any better from the little washing I'd done.

From behind, a shove sent me falling forward up to the side of Newsom's ghastly face. I cried out "Uh!" scrambling back.

George had pushed me. "What you wetting him down for? You can see I'm building a fire." He flung me away from Newsom by my sore right arm.

"What's the fire for, George?" I asked from my corner by the fireplace, nursing the wrench in my arm and the tight squeezes starting up again in my belly.

"What you think? To burn him. You want whites crawling all over the place and finding him here?"

I came at George again from out of the corner. "No," I insisted, clinging to my relief that Newsom wasn't dead. "If you don't want to take him up to

364

his daughters, all right. But once we're running, who cares what they find left behind us in the cabin? Let them find him here. At least he'll be alive."

By now I was standing, bent over and trying to tug George away from the quiet, ugly body on the floor. George straightened suddenly, catching me off balance, and sent me spinning and flying to stretch across the bed with my head numb and emptied from a blow.

When I could think again, it was of the words George was bellowing down at me. "Always did have a soft spot for your white man, didn't you? Always wanted him, didn't you? That's why he was here. That's why you got his damn bastards crawling around my feet and rotting you from the inside."

He went on while I tried to shake my head clear and find the words to tell him that, no, I wanted Newsom dead, but even more, I wanted us all safely running. I said, trying to fix my blurry eyes on George in the dark, "You don't understand. With Newsom alive, they won't think about us for days. We could be out of here. You, me, and my babies. It's for us, George. Not Newsom."

He hawked. I raised my arm to keep the glob from landing in my face. Instead, George swung around and pelted down onto Newsom.

George started to curse him. Challenge him. Kick him. I heard the blows thud, muffled against the body. I crawled to the center of the bed, covering my head to shut out the sound and any chance of seeing what George was doing.

I had the foolish, terrible fear that George might break Newsom's ribs. Might damage his face even more than I had.

Might kill him, this time.

As the sound of George's attack on the still body died down, I began to hear how I had been whimpering into the bedclothes. That noise would bother George. Enrage him more. I bit down on my lip to make myself stop.

I heard the scratch and drag of George hefting the heavy, sagging Newsom into his arms. Maybe I looked. I know I screamed.

For another little groan worked its way out of Newsom, his head thrown back, his mouth gaped open, as he rose in George's arms.

I shoved my fingers in my mouth, to hush myself, and sat up to see what George would do, now he had heard it for himself. Newsom was alive.

George stood steady and stared down, his face still now, at the hanging head where my apron dangled back like long hair, sweeping just above the floor.

Finally, George chuckled. "Alive? I ain't sure. But we can fix that. Never you fear."

I threw myself off the bed. Reached for George. The warm, limp arm of Newsom came under my hands. "Please don't," I begged. "Don't kill him."

George shoved the body against me to make me move out of the way. He turned and was at the fireplace, going down on one knee to settle the broad, hanging body on the stacked wood.

I went to George again and this time pressed my hands to the heavy muscles working across his back. "This won't help us." My breath caught, for I was trembling with the chill of my damp clothes and my growing panic. "Don't, please," I said again.

George turned once more towards me. "Beg me some more," he said. "I love to hear you beg."

He leaned toward me. "I figured it out, you know, Celia. You and your white man thought to fool me. Beat him with my stick. He'd play dead. Didn't work, did it? I'm calling you all's bluff."

Then, somehow, he got the long poles of wood and the kindling under Newsom all lit.

The flames leapt and bit at the still body, at my face, too close, even at George's hands, not snatched back fast enough.

We both fell back from the blaze.

It roared.

Steam broke into the reddened air above Newsom's outstretched body. Newsom went rigid. He arched his back, trying to rise away from the flames below him.

He stretched his legs, like I'd seen him do in the throes of his furious pleasure. His hands curled to claws. His open mouth let out a ball of sizzling mist and black smoke, all followed by a moan that carried through the roar and bellow of the fire. His eyes flew open and stared as the lashes and lids sizzled, sparked, and melted, fixed on the sight of the flames rising around him. Turning away, I could see Newsom's shadow reach up on every bright wall around us.

"The bad people burn."

With his arm flung back across his nose and mouth and his eyes streaming tears from the smoke, George grabbed the pole I used for a poker, a piece of broken railing from Newsom's old wagon, and used it to shove back the body that wanted to climb from out its fiery bed.

George had to struggle. The stretching, stiffening, eyeless body, haloed in flames, did not want to stay put.

I tried to hide my face again in my arms on the bed, gagging on the hot stench that seared my nose and eyes, that sent bile gushing up my throat. At last I ran to the window and threw up ropy strings.

I was called back to the smoke-black room and the putrid smell of Newsom, aged, whiskey-filled, and burning, by the soft cries of my children, waked and crawling from under the bed, rubbing their eyes against the sting.

"Oh no." I got my arms around them and turned them away from the fireplace, scuttling sideways to keep my back to it, absorbing the bumps from George, who leaned in to poke at his old master and enemy, and leaned out to get away from the reach of the fire that didn't care who it pulled down into it.

I got my children outside the cabin. But we had to close the door on the flaming light inside.

I got them to go around, still with their faces in the stiff, dried folds of my nightgown, to the creek side. I wanted to get them as far as the creek, to wash the soot and the stench of Newsom's scorched flesh off of them. But dizziness brought me to the grass.

I sat, and they put their heads in my lap, like to go back to sleep. I fumbled for their lullaby, wiping their eyes and noses with the hem of my nightgown. When George stumbled from the cabin and joined us, falling heavy into the grass, like he had run hard and fast from the fire his own self, I said, "Why did you do it?"

But George, usually so quick to put me down, lay panting up at the night sky, his hands rising and falling on his heaving chest, like to still his heart, and didn't answer.

Chapter Fourteen: Trapped

George woke me from the grass while it was still night. "We got to get back to the cabin," he said.

I sat up. "No. My children will choke to death in there."

"Stupid black bitch. You want everybody to find us hiding out here and know something ain't like it suppose to be? You got to go to the kitchen in the morning from the cabin, and I got to go to the fields from the barn. Now come on."

It seemed a poor plan to me. But I went along and got the children under the bedclothes with their heads covered, against the sting of the heavy smoke, before I flapped the shutters to force air to move in and out of the cabin.

George squatted before the smoldering fireplace and used the sizzling poker to poke out bones and knock off ashes from thick muscles that hadn't burned. George smashed the bones between loose bricks of the fireplace. Some of the ones that wouldn't smash small enough, I watched, from the window, as he hid under loose hearthstones and floorboards.

Maybe he had a plan, after all, to protect me and my children until we could get away.

When he rose to leave, as the night greyed to day, he looked tired. He stank with Newsom's death. "I'll go swim in the creek," George said to me and came over to the bed, where I had sunk, dizzy and sickened, unable to stand at the window any longer.

"Will you take my dress and wash it one more time? It's covered in soot and will smell like fire. George," I reached for his arm, an old, useless habit. "I don't want to go up to the Newsom kitchen. They'll know something's happened."

George knelt and shocked me by taking me by both shoulders. He looked me in my face. "Celia," he said, "if we had took Newsom, wounded bad like he was, up to the house, how long do you think it would be before they had us strung up? You think they only string up mens like me? They string up womens and childrens too. They hang childrens to teach the big ones a lesson. Ain't nobody safe when the whites want to teach a lesson. They wouldn't a believed us, saying we found him cracked in the head by the creek. This was the only way. They can't find him, and they can't know what happened to him. Ain't nothing to find."

George licked his lips. "Did you ever love me? Even a little?" he asked so quiet I wasn't sure I heard.

I said, "I think so," and cursed myself for a stubborn fool as he took my dress and left for the creek. Why hadn't I, why couldn't I, just say to George—for my children's safety—that, yes, I loved him?

Did I think it would do any good? No. It would be one more thing for him to throw back at me. I had tried and almost managed it just the night before. And he had laughed at me. It was useless.

I drifted to sleep and woke to find my dress, damp but free of blood and soot, stretched before

371

the smoking fireplace. George had washed it and left it while I slept. I crawled to the end of the bed to reach down and get it.

But something stopped me. It felt like Newsom was there, crouching in the shadows and smoke of the fireplace, just beyond the dress, watching.

I pulled back my hand from reaching for the dress and stared into the sooty corners of the fireplace.

Of course Newsom was there. George had burned his body and buried his unbroken bones under the loose bricks and stones. But the lumps of Newsom's ashes and pieces were all still there, huddled in the open fireplace, and something more. Whatever it was, it was quietly waiting. And it was as evil as Newsom had ever been.

And angrier.

I pulled the bedclothes a little higher over my children's heads and rushed to open the door, hoping a summer breeze might stir the cabin air and break up the shadowy stink of Newsom's death.

Maybe it would be best to get the children down to the creek, wash off what we could of the cabin's smoke, and strike out from there for the woods. Escape as long and as well as we could.

Easy for me to say. I was dying. But my children? I needed to plan for them to live. No running away with a woman who didn't even know where to run to.

At the opened door, I saw Mister Coffee up a cherry tree.

Cherry-picking season had passed. Picking fruit was about the only steady chore Miss Virginia allowed her wild-running children, maybe because it was the only steady chore they liked. Mister Coffee was up the cherry tree now because it was easy to climb and, being the oldest, he could get far up where nobody had got the last cherries and rest in the morning sun, straddling a branch, kicking his legs, and oozing cherry juice down his face, just to make sure everybody saw that he wasn't sharing.

I called to him. Thoughtless, hardhead boy. Surely he could help me out of the corner I was backed into today. "Mister Coffee, would you come shovel out my fireplace? You know how bending and carrying is getting hard on me."

Coffee squinted down at me from his perch. Waited. What had I overlooked? Oh. What to give him.

Having been out of Miss Virginia's kitchen for several days, I couldn't real quick think of a good treat. I couldn't even promise one against the hope that she would for sure let me in there to cook, today. My mind flitted over my dwindling stores.

Well, here goes. I had a good bowlful of walnut meats, already cracked and cleaned and ready to treat my own children. I offered Mister Coffee those.

He accepted and just about slid straight down out of the tree. Walnuts were rare enough, seeing as how it took such work to break into the outer and inner shells, and then his mother liked to save them for mincemeat pies and such.

I sighed with relief as Coffee, bright with sunshine, burst into the cabin and fell to shoveling up the worst of his grandfather's ashes.

He took out the first bucketful, with the walnuts already sagging in his breeches pocket, and dumped it along the path to the big house, to be tread into the grass by passing feet. Being Coffee, he did not return to shovel up the rest.

But my sense of all of Newsom there and watching and waiting, glowering out at me from the fireplace corners, had been broke up enough for me to strip off the nightgown, dress, and rouse my babies.

I took them to the creek to wash again. The morning air smelled so fresh. I couldn't be sure, but I worried that anyone could smell the smoke of Newsom's burning still on us.

I broke off leaves of wild mint, basil, and thyme that grew along the creek, cooking scents, clean and cleansing, and crumbled them in my hands to scrub me and my children's hair and bodies. I dried my fresh-smelling hands on their shirts and my dress, to rub in the green scent and cut the smoke stench. We chewed some of the leaves, rinsed our mouths, chewed some more.

Then, swallowing, we set out for the big house.

Only when we got to the path, and I had to lead my children around Newsom's ashes, did I look with yearning one last time towards the creek and wish, wish, wish I'd known where and how to strike out with my children and run.

Miss Virginia let me into her kitchen. She asked did I know what had become of Newsom. I was startled and stared at her, struck dumb.

"Coffee said he was in your cabin this morning, Celia, to help you out with some chores, and figured he saw your babies asleep in your bed, but not his grandfather. Buddy woke crying in the night, and I waited up in Father's chair for him to come back. I woke still in his chair, this morning. Not hearing of where he's been all night and morning has put me in mind of your agitation yesterday. You were worried about Father."

"I was, Miss Virginia." I brushed past her, oddly angry.

She stood in the doorway and watched me go about settling down my babies and pulling out what I needed for the day's dinner. I asked, only because she was watching, "Miss Virginia, are these biscuits from your family's breakfast? May I give them to Hannah and The Baby? I'm low on stores again."

"Certainly. If Father turns up hungry for his breakfast, it will be nigh on dinnertime, anyway." Her voice was gentle.

I noticed she said "if," and I didn't like it. "If hungry," I argued with myself, fighting down the chaos of anger and panic swelling in me, "if *hungry*. Not 'if he turns up.'"

I was relieved when she left out of the doorway.

But it seemed in no time she was back, more anxious than ever. "Celia," she said. I braced myself for accusations. Miss Virginia stared at me with her eyes stretched so wide the grey was lost in the whites. "Listen to me. I've sent for Masters David and Harvey to help us hunt up Father. This isn't like him. No one's seen him in the fields, in the house, or in your cabin. And I'm remembering how anxious you were for his safety yesterday. Is

375

there anything you should tell me?" This last she said slow, weighty.

"I'm sorry for your worry, ma'am." I kept my gaze on my children, who slowly chewed their biscuits with a wary eye on Miss Virginia. Waiting for her to throw them out, no doubt.

"Celia." Miss Virginia's voice went tender. "Did you know that Mister David asked Father to give you to him before he left? They came to blows. David thought Father would kill you before he could come back for you. He meant to come back and buy you from Father, if that's the only way he could—" She had to stop a minute, gather herself. "Celia, David's my little brother." Her voice caught on a sob. I turned further away from her. I felt her draw close to me, insisting. "You've seen Hannah with Bobby. That's me and David, Celia."

She loved her brother as only a big sister could. I wanted to comfort her, but I couldn't think what was safe to say.

Miss Virginia whispered, "If Mister David were to find Father—are you listening?—hurt somewhere along the creek, I wouldn't be surprised. Are you listening to me, Celia? I remember how Father used to take his evening walk along the creek, every night after he'd had his whiskey. I worried, without a torch or a full moon, that someday Father might slip and fall. Maybe hit his head and drown. Remember that incident last winter? Maybe that's what you were trying to warn me and sister Mary about yesterday. That Father would get hurt, wandering drunk down to the negro cabin. He's gotten so old. So unsteady. His drinking has increased so." Her mouth was dry. The words dragged from it on breath that stank with worry. "When Mister David gets here, I will ask him to search with me by the creek. Surely we will find Father there. I see why I should have listened to you, Celia."

Now I understood. Miss Virginia thought David had done something to Newsom, for my sake, and that I knew. Had known. Had tried to protect her father from his son. Had tried to protect them all.

What could happen to David, if Miss Virginia persisted in her thinking? I didn't know if only negroes was hung for killing masters. George had not explained more than that. I watched Miss Virginia as she left out the kitchen door, hoping to head off Mister David when he arrived from his new farm and throw her hints at him, like she'd done at me.

My only worry about David, Harvey, and Miss Virginia, too, for that matter, was to assure that one of them bore me enough good will to take my children and protect them, if George didn't run away with them.

Protect them from the remaining Newsoms and from George.

Now that I was in the kitchen, where he'd told me to go, I could feel that this was a trap. I was trapped. George knew our only hope was to run. But he could run better without me and my children. No good could come of me waiting here. I breathed fast, clutching at my heart and moving, useless,

377

between the cutting table and the fireplace till I gave up hope and went to sit with my children.

They were so beautiful. They were so golden. They had laughter in their sun-speckled eyes and in their puffy round cheeks with the little holes punched in them to mark their smiles. I wanted to live. I wanted to raise them, watch them grow.

I touched them, their round, soft arms, and filled myself up with gazing at my children until the men came.

They came into the kitchen through the back door, mottle-face white men I had never seen.

Behind them came David and Mister Harvey. I would not look at Newsom's sons.

The leader of the mottle-face white men, the one in front with the longest gun pointing down at the ground, and the thick rope coiled and hanging down from his belt, told Miss Virginia to take my children out of the room. She came in from behind her brothers, shushed and pulled away my children from my hands. I said, "But just let me touch them one more time!"

The leader said, "You answer my questions right, gal, and you'll see your children in plenty of time."

I fell back into the kitchen chair. He made the men pull me to my feet again. The questions flew. I couldn't keep them all straight. I couldn't keep anything straight after I heard that George had sent this posse to search my fireplace for Newsom's bones.

George had blamed it all on me.

George told these men that I had threatened

Newsom. I had killed him. I had burned him.

As soon as this leader man and his followers had got to the farm this morning, George joined the search party to say he had it on good faith they was wasting any time they didn't spend searching my cabin.

I sagged in the hands of the men holding me to my feet.

Far away, I heard David shout, "Celia, you ain't got to be afraid. Everybody knows how George always went on about Father."

The leader of the posse said, "Mr. Newsom, sir, I'll thank you to remember that I'm deputized to look into this kind of thing, and I know full right well how to handle niggers. The bucks and the bitches, both."

Harvey said, "David. You don't want to get in his way."

David said, "But—"

Mister Harvey said, "Stay out of his way, David. He reports to the sheriff. There'll be time for further questions later. I'm warning you."

Did Master Harvey think, like Miss Virginia, that David had done this to get me from Newsom? Was he trying to protect David? Wild thoughts flew through my mind, and I snatched at them as they flitted away. "Yes, sirs," I said to every question, no matter who it was aimed at, thinking, yes, I'll do what these men want, and this posse will maybe ask the family what to do, and maybe now Mister David can take me away and my children will be safe.

The leader man was soothing Newsom's sons like they were his own. "These is always trying

379

times for family. Boys, gentlemen, why don't you just wait in another room, have a shot to steel your nerves, and let me handle this? I know how to get answers out of niggers. Don't take no time. But it ain't pretty. You let me handle this, boys."

He wanted the truth. I would tell it. Tell on George. Tell everything. What a relief to get ready to tell. It was over. And they would go after George. And my children would be safe. "Yes," I said, "I'll tell you everything when Master Newsom's sons go out."

There was shuffling and scraping as I saw, in a blur around me, that Mister Harvey was guiding Mister David away. I heard Mister David say, "But Powell doesn't understand…!"

Powell or Power, the leader man, now came close up in my face. "You look a here." His voice rumbled like it was low in his gut or something. "You want your kids down the road and sold, and yourself swinging in a tree from this rope here?" I shook my head no, my eyes bulging. He slapped his hand on the top of the coils of rope at his hip and rubbed them, drawing my eyes to the thing that would kill me. "It ain't no use fooling with niggers these days," he said. "It's only two ways to deal with them. Take away their kids, or take away how they get kids."

Take away my kids? After I had got set to tell everything? I sagged again, and was jerked upright again, and this time the wrench in my right shoulder jabbed at my head behind my ear.

Power or Powell must have seen me wince. "Oh, you don't like the sound of that, do you, gal?

Well let's see do you like this better," and suddenly the rope was off his hip and around my neck, and he was jerking the rope with both hands so that the smell of the soil and horses on his hands was in my face along with the scratching of the rope at my neck, my cheek, and behind my left ear.

I screamed. The men holding me tightened their grip. In the dining room, I heard Mister David and Mister Harvey break out in a scuffle. A chair toppled. Sounds of a fist fight.

What did this man want? The truth? Or something else? Panicked, I sagged again, and this time the rope bit into my windpipe and I kicked forward, unable to see how to get my feet under me.

But Power had the rope and yanked it upwards and I gagged, feeling my head lift from my shoulders and my eyes strain forward from between the lids. I was pulled to my feet by the rope. The other men held me by my arms, once I got up high enough, as I shuffled and stumbled, unable to make my legs lock and stand.

"Put her in the chair," Power said.

The men dropped me. For a minute, I was startled and panicked I couldn't see my children. I looked around, wild with worry. "My babies," I sputtered, "they were here. They were eating biscuits."

"Your babies is on the way down the road to get sold, I told you, nigger. And you're on your way to hang from a tree by the neck until dead. Now if you don't want your kids sold and yourself strung up, kicking, then you got not more than ten minutes to make me understand what happened to

Master Newsom. And I ain't going for none of your nigger double talk, here today. Out with it. Straight. What you done with him?"

"Me?" I said. "What I done with him?" My mind, reeling, blurry, raced in tighter circles than it had for the last few days. George had turned me in. It seemed that George had told them everything some way they wanted to hear. They'd found— what, now? Newsom's bones or only his ashes?— still in my fireplace. What was there to tell? Why were they asking? Something about George.

Surely George had told them everything but his part.

I was crying, trying to figure out what to say. "Sir, don't sell my children. Just tell me what it is you want to know. I'll tell you. I'll tell you anything."

Power shouted over everything I said. "Who killed Newsom?"

Surely George had not told them *he* killed Newsom. He wouldn't want me to tell them that he had wanted Newsom dead. He wouldn't have wanted me to tell them anything about him.

Why should I care, with a rope around my neck and my children on their way down the road to be sold, what George wanted? Surely he wasn't my biggest fear anymore. I said, "George did it."

Power yelled, "Get her out a that chair and let's get her up a tree. You lying black miscegenating whore. We know everything. You can't fool these white men." I was pulled from the chair by the rope around my neck.

I screamed. A fist pounded on the door from

the dining room. I heard Mister David's shout. Harvey's. My own voice wheezed against the squeeze and the tug of the rope, "Don't let them in here. Don't let them come in." Harvey would shoot me for striking his father, for letting George heft him into the flames. David would hate me for every time George had laid a hand on me. All of them would turn against my children if they heard what I must say, what I had to say, and I saw with almost relief that someone went to block the door against Newsom's sons. As the rope hauled me tighter and started me by the neck across the floor, I gagged out, "I did it! I did it! I did it!" There was no other way.

Something loosened. I dropped through the men's hands and they snatched at my dress, at my sleeves, at the rope and at my hair, trying to catch me as I fell.

I was lifted to where my feet should have been yet again and held there, clutching back now at the hands that held me, for I was afraid to fall so far that the rope would be all that met me at the end. Power smiled again, leaning in close. "That's it, gal. *How* did you kill him?"

What had killed Newsom? The club or the fire? Did they already know, and were they trying to catch me up in a lie? If they were following a story George might have told, they would want to hear that the cudgel did it. I said, "With a club."

"With a club? Where'd you get it?"

Had they seen the club? Had it burned? Where did people get the wood to make a club? "From the woods?" I asked.

"You went and found a likely stick in the woods," Power told me. And so the story grew, step by step, rebuilding the last full day and night to leave out George and put the murder and the burning all on me.

There was a lot of it I didn't understand. Like why Power wanted George left in the story only enough to be the reason I was telling Newsom to leave me alone.

I tried to take George out of all that and say that Newsom had to leave me alone because I was sick and his use of my body was killing me and my baby. But that only got more threats from Power that I wasn't telling the truth yet, and did I want another taste of rope. I was a lying jezebel whore and I knew that nothing but George's jealousy drove me to want to quit the good white man that had bought and paid for me and let me keep all my bastard pickaninny brats running around on his property.

So I had to leave George in there and hope, when he heard the story as Power wanted it, he would still hear how I had protected him as far as I could, claiming I had done the murder alone, even saying it was me who thought of the burning and carried it out, and then George would have no call to go and harm my children.

If they weren't already sold, as this Power man kept threatening. How had George gotten this posse in his power, doing what he wanted like this? Faulting me, and leaving George clean out of it.

But now I understood what they wanted, I could build the story so it made sense. If they left

George out of it, he would have time to run.

And maybe, for pity or gratitude, if George ran—no, *when* George ran—he might even take my babies to freedom with him.

Power had lied. After the story was built to his satisfaction, I did not get to see my children again.

I screamed like a wild woman dragged onto the wagon, bound with ropes and twisting my head around, every which way, looking and pleading for a last sight of Hannah and my Baby, while the gag cut into the corners of my mouth and muffled their names.

I searched the faces ranged around the wagon, below me. Miss Virginia's, grim above a box that held—could it be? Out in daylight, they looked so ghastly—the charred bits of her father's skull and unbroken bones. Coffee's face, his eyes wide and excited.

Farther away, the two negro farmhands I had never known, mouths open and slack, eyes cold, and Joshua, his eyes pleading, frightened, before he turned away from me and the wagon to run.

No sight of my children.

David's face, stricken, was the last one I saw at the gate to the Newsom farm until the wagon bumped and jolted, turning onto the road, and there was George easing out from between the trees to watch me.

He held my eyes and I grew still, struck by the hatred and the rage in his eyes. He still hated me.

What had I said that left him so enraged? Did he guess that I had tried to turn him in? Hadn't he heard that I had taken all the blame, that only I would hang?

What more could he want? What more could I have done? Suddenly, out now in bright sunlight, I saw I had been foolish to think this posse wanted the truth. I should have pleaded harder with George.

Were my children sold already, where George, who had plagued my own captivity, couldn't find them? Maybe I must wish that my children were already sold. I bowed my head.

"Every condemned criminal got to have a last look," the man next to me in the wagon said, jerking my head up by my hair. I wished that Joshua, who had been my first sight of this farm, had returned, had run alongside the wagon, to be my last sight of it, as well. But he and my children were nowhere to be seen.

And then, for the first time in five years, I saw the road that led away from Newsom's farm, taking me not to freedom, nor even to be somebody else's slave, but to hang.

Power had told me so. "Too bad you confessed, gal," he said as I was bound and gagged in the kitchen. "The Newsoms should a had the pleasure of watching the crows pick your bones on one of their trees. Well, never you worry. With this confession, they'll see you hang soon enough, I reckon."

The men holding me had laughed. "This one's for the gallows."

"Bad business, here."

"Come on. Let's hit the road."

The bright dusty road. The farms popping up

out of the green. Hands in the distance, brown people rising and turning to stare as we passed. Sunburned white people spitting at the wagon as it neared them.

After a while, weaving in the heat from the sun, I began to see more and more houses, and then bigger and bigger houses, all jammed together, with lots of people in fancy dress going in and out of them, until there was no more land between the houses where people could grow their food, but only horses, carriages, wagons, houses stacked one on the other, and more people.

When the wagon stopped, I was pulled from it and led, falling in the mud and rising from the jerk of a rope tied to all the ropes around my body, into a low, dark building that stank of body waste and that sharp sweat that smells like fear.

White men met my eye on every side, all of them viciously angry, with their hands on their guns. They talked and spit long streaks of brown at my bare feet.

And then there were bars and cages, giant ones with a few people in them. And a key scraped a lock, and fingers yanked at the knot at the back of my head, untied the gag, and I was shoved into a cage.

Darkness closed around me. Shut out the faces. The sounds of groaning and yelling.

I sank to my knees, unable to catch myself, because my hands were still bound behind my back.

But at least the rope on my neck didn't snatch me back up. Was it over? The hope, the trying, the fear?

387

Had I truly killed Newsom?

I must have. This was the hanging George had told me would happen to niggers who killed their master.

I remembered laughing in the creek the night before at the thought that Newsom was dead. Why hadn't I run? Why hadn't I dared? What did it matter where? Wasn't there a cave in the woods where we could have hid?

So George could lead Power and his men to it?

But look how fast and easy the wagon got to the road.

I didn't even know where the road was. Fast and easy for Power, but for me and my children? And once on the road, then what? Did I think no one would have followed? No one would have tried to catch us? *George wouldn't have been the first to tell that I was gone, and blame the murder on me, and everything would be the same as it is now. Except that George knows now I did everything he wanted, as far as I could. He will not harm my children.*

At some time, someone must have come into my cage and untied the ropes around my wrists and arms. I woke in pain but unbound, blinking in the dark at a tin plate catching bits of light, enough to show lumps of bread and rats upon it.

Soon, I couldn't tell when I slept, when I passed out, and when I woke. My mind was always took up, always the same, with Newsom's shadow rising from the fire, and with the remembered sunlight and scent of fresh, crushed herbs, as I turned from scrubbing my children's hair to gaze

388

into the woods across the creek, wanting to run.

I tried to remember my babies. Once, with my heart skipping light, I saw them in my mind, so clear I could touch them, sitting at the cutting table that last day, dimpled and eating biscuits. I cried out. Reached for them.

And then I cried out some more, doubling over my belly. It wrenched at me, how slow and resistant the unborn baby was dying.

If only we could have died sooner. But our jailors—for this was a jail—wouldn't let us.

A man unlocked the cage to pull away a tin plate. I asked, "When is the hanging, sir?"

"Not till a judge says it is."

And soon after that, there began days when I was pulled from the cage, bound but not gagged, and sloshed with water and left to stand until dry, even in the rain, waiting to talk to three gentlemen.

Those were cruel talks. The three gentlemen wanted me to hope. Hope to live. Hope that the unborn baby, dying, would live.

They told lies. They told truths until they sounded, to my ears, like lies. They told me George had run away, proving "the family's" suspicion that it was he, in fact, who had killed Newsom. Not me. Not David. So I could go free. All I had to do was join the family in accusing George.

Or they would be forced to accuse me. After all, I had confessed.

Run away? Run away, and not taken my children? Then, surely, if they had not been sold away from the Newsom farm, they must be in the gravest danger. For who could stop George from

389

doubling back to kill Hannah and The Baby—the hate in George's eyes—if nobody even knew where he was?

But if I accused George, like they wanted me to? And they found him and brought him back and he learned what I had done?

My children would be dead before he ran away again.

The gentlemen, brutal and stupid, pressed me to blame George for the murder, telling me all the reasons I could not have swung the cudgel, could not have burned the body, could not have known my rights.

"Do we think Mister Newsom took her aside and explained to her that a slave has the right to defend herself against being beaten to death?" they would ask each other, and answer, shouting, "The question is does she have a right to defend herself against rape. And the judge will say no."

"But she's only nineteen years old."

"Anyone can rape a negress, slave or free, nineteen or ninety."

"But not everyone can beat her to death. David is our witness. If Celia can't be persuaded to blame this nigger George, then we must go for self-defense."

"The people will not wish to hear a white man's name tarnished."

"The people have discovered Mistress Virginia's baby."

The gentlemen asked me to see "Mistress Virginia." They pleaded that she had news for me I might wish to consider.

I would not see her. I could not chance more confusion. I knew what she would say. Blame George. Spare David. Risk my children for her brother. For surely, if the court would not believe I killed Newsom, they would have to consider who besides me and George could have done it.

I was dying anyway. Let my death save my children. End the fear.

They told me there were people who felt I had been wronged. I needn't stick to the story Power wrenched from me in terror, in that kitchen, with a noose. I could tell a different story. They would listen. They would save me.

And who would save my children from George, betrayed? Where was he?

No one knew. He had got clean away. But to where?

I grew silent.

The jailor told me I would have to meet with these men, sloshed with a bucket of water and trembling, until my baby was born. Whether I talked or not. Whether I understood or not. Whether they understood or not.

Not till my baby was born could I be hanged, and then it would be over.

I told the jailor, reaching up towards the empty air in the dark of my cage, fearing to touch him, but fearing that he would leave without understanding, "My baby and me are dying, both. Don't make me listen to those men until I die. They drive me crazy with their talk. I get confused."

The baby died before me.

I woke, writhing on the cool dirt floor, as a

391

thunderstorm battered at the jailhouse and shook the bars of my cage. I heard moaning—my own?—and cries as the baby was wrenched from my body.

And as the storm raged past, the warmth of the baby and the sack that had held it slipped down between my legs and lay. Gingerly, I felt for the body and drew it towards my breast.

The head flopped. I felt it. It was too big. The neck was too small and felt snapped. The little fingers felt melted into the club-like hands. There were no toes.

There was no smell of baby skin and baby breath. Only the heavy breath of death. Blood that dried and would not run, heat that festered flesh, and strain. My newborn smelled like rot.

I held it until the jailor came, cursing the stench, with a bucket and pried my fingers from the baby's wrinkling flesh.

I heard it plop into his pail. I heard him, cursing, lock me into my cage again and trudge away.

Maybe now I could die. The baby that the law wanted was gone.

Its smell stayed on me and would not go, no matter the buckets of water thrown. My heart, my nerve, had gone in the bucket with the baby. I stopped trying to understand.

When next I was sloshed and brought before the three gentlemen, they said, "We regret the death of your newborn. But you still have two other children who need you."

What use arguing with these men that I was doing what my children needed me to do? I would die and close the story and the secrets in my grave. That much, I could still understand.

Gentlemen came late in the night, sipping alcohol from flasks they pulled from under black cloaks. "For good measure," they took a bound negro man with me to a wagon in the dark, climbed in around us, and took us through the streets and past a narrow opened gate to a small brick kitchen in a quiet courtyard. They lifted us down, chained the bound man to a knocker on the kitchen door, and shoved me inside.

A woman in lovely clean clothes came to wash me and dress me. She offered me a bowl of porridge sweet with molasses and explained that the gentlemen wanted to keep me a while and give the law time to work.

When she was gone, I felt around the walls and the mantel over the fireplace. There were no knives in this kitchen. So I dreamed, awake or asleep, of the little stump legs with no toes and the fine brittle bones of my baby's shapeless body, driving away what I remembered of the children I'd had before it.

That dead baby had become the child who awaited me.

"The good people fly in the clouds."

A baby must be good. Had it flown in the clouds? Would I see it—was I good enough?— when I died? Could I take care of it at last, flying?

And what of Hannah and The Baby? I could do no more for them. I had saved them or failed them, but I couldn't tell which.

393

Epilogue: Flight

The Reverend Boulware found his son standing at the hearth studying the flames of a low fire in his locked study. "You have done all you can, Isaac," he said. "That in itself is more commendable than a win."

"I didn't care about winning." Isaac's voice was bitter. "I wanted to save her life. She is innocent, and she will hang."

Theodorick Boulware thought for a moment. All the while, he resisted the urge to shrug, a gesture he knew his son detested.

At last he said, "At some point, son, we become the men we must, rather than the men we'd hoped to be." He could not keep himself from adding, perhaps because he himself had learned to draw comfort from this adage that his son hated above all others, "God's ways are inscrutable to even the most intelligent of us."

Isaac rasped, "God didn't condemn Celia, father. Judge Hall did. Missouri did. And in my incompetence, in my faith in a badly flawed legal system, so did I."

Reverend Boulware said, "And God let Judge Hall and Missouri and you—if you insist—carry out this injustice. Your purpose, I suppose, is to figure out what you can do to change something you have learned you cannot approve. Perhaps this is your motivating tragedy. We each have our own, son. This is what makes us, rather than the men we'd hoped to be, the men we are forced to become."

Reverend Boulware gave in to the sigh he had so far resisted before he said what he had followed his son into the study to say. "Whatever else you may choose to let this challenge make of you, son, it will not make you an outlaw. Theft is amended by return to the owner of what has been stolen. It is time to return Celia to the state of Missouri, Isaac."

"Missouri will kill her."

"She is Missouri's to execute, Isaac. If it helps you, think of it in this way: perhaps Celia dies so that many others shall not."

"I neither know nor care about others. I have known and failed Celia, father."

"You are not yet dead and forgotten, Isaac. Therefore you have not yet failed. Learn from an old man, son."

Isaac glared down at his father. "It is not I who will be executed, but Celia. When Celia hangs, I have failed."

"Then turn your thoughts to others whom you have not yet failed, and try now to ensure that you never shall fail them." The reverend held Isaac's gaze for so long that Isaac wondered for the first time if his father knew how he felt about Lise. That he wanted to own Lise, if that was all the law would allow him to do with his desire to protect and love her.

But Isaac could not have that conversation now. He hinted at it with, "I wanted to believe as you have taught me, sir, that we are all better men than this. That we are a better people than this."

Reverend Boulware's smile shocked Isaac. "And you have learned that we are not better than

395

this. Welcome to manhood, Isaac. When your society does not define you, it also cannot limit you. Welcome to freedom, son. No one but you will henceforth set your parameters. Now, what will you do with the knowledge that your people are not the good people you believed them to be when you were yet a child?"

Isaac stared at this father who, in nearly three decades, he had evidently never really known.

Into the silence, Reverend Boulware said, "Theft is corrected by return of what has been stolen, Isaac. The verdict is reached. Fair or unjust, I have your word. Celia returns to the possession of the state."

"That has condemned her."

"That has unjustly condemned her, as you say, Isaac. You are a brilliant young man, and I am a tired and old one. Something will occur to you, I have no doubt. And now, your mother and sisters are waiting for me to help them make merry this Christmas season. I will give them your excuses. Please do not discomfit yourself further. I will lock the door again behind me, as I assume you want no young women bursting in to force Christmas cheer upon you."

Reverend Boulware left, quietly closing and locking the door with his own key.

This time Isaac was sure that his father referred to Lise.

How could all the women be making merry, baking and preserving for the upcoming feast, all the while knowing that the prisoner who helped them in the outdoor kitchen would be dead before

Christmas dawned?

Virginia Newsom Waynescott sorely missed Celia's diligent efforts in her own kitchen and with all of her own and Celia's one surviving child, as Christmas drew near. Without Robert Newsom to terrify and drive them, Mary was practically no help at all in the house anymore.

Except with the children, Virginia amended. Mary was so excited about getting the children to help her sew little dolls and soldiers to give as gifts, and patch worn clothing so that it looked almost new, and plan a festive meal for the upcoming holiday that it was almost as if she were trying to get her own childhood back again.

Now Mary bounded down the hallway to David's old room, where Newsom had first brought the terrified young Celia. It was Coffee's now, but Virginia had hidden away here to face her haunting memories of Celia, a specter at their festivities even before her death.

Mary carried one of her festive, scented garlands in progress. As if enough of the bright, happy wreaths and ropes of cranberries and popped corn studded with red mistletoe and bristly pinecones did not already bedeck every wall in the farmhouse.

Mary chirped, "Oh, there you are, sister. Harvey is here to see you. I think he wants to take Hannah. May I just give her to him?"

Virginia rose, startled, from the rough little table where Celia used to always need a lantern set long before the night was so dark as it was now. "No, of course not," Virginia said. "Why should

Harvey take Hannah? She is ours. We can care for her here."

Harvey appeared in the doorway behind Mary, who turned, saw him, and disappeared to run back and have more fun with the children at their crafts.

"I know you take excellent care of Hannah, Virginia," he said. "That's not in question. Nor is that why I believe it best that I take her."

"Then why?"

"As you know, father's property has passed probate and is mine—"

"You dastard!" Virginia's voice shook. By the time she got it under control, she was stunned to feel sweat and tears cascading together down her face.

But she persisted with, "Celia has not even hung yet, and already you're claiming the spoils of this sordid business."

Harvey raised a restraining hand. "Hear me out, Virginia. You have every reason to be as upset as you are, though it behooves me to point out you will doubtless feel better, as will we all, once you've buried those damned bones of father's."

"You sound like one of those worthless attorneys. As you say, you have inherited everything. Take Hannah and take father's cursed bones, too."

"Yes, that's probably best. Do you at least want to know why I'm taking Hannah?"

"Greed."

"No. You and your children can give her the comforts of family, Virginia. But your husband isn't dead. Forgotten him, haven't you? But what if he hasn't forgotten you? And what if he hears of father's death and comes back to claim you and your children and all your property?"

Virginia thought her heart had stopped for a full beat in her chest. The pain was crushing. "Have you heard something, Harvey?"

"Let me just ask you to think about that. Either your first husband, or, who knows, what if a second man comes to ask for your hand? One who has a good farm or a good job and can help you raise those children?"

"What have you heard about these matters, Harvey?"

"As a woman, by law, your property belongs to your husband. Some man might think that includes Hannah."

Virginia was silent. So sweet and disorienting was her new freedom from her father that she had given no thought to all the constraints that still faced her as a woman in her society.

In the face of his sister's perplexed silence, Harvey said, "Any man married to you with all the best intentions might fall on hard times or hear some unfortunate gossip in town, who knows," Harvey added more gently, "and sell Hannah. Or worse. Then what was all this for?"

"Celia condemned herself to keep the posse and George from those children, I'm sure of it," Virginia said, as if Harvey hadn't already known. "And we already lost The Baby. I knew he was too weak to make it through the first frost without her."

"Does Celia know?"

"No. And please make sure no one tells her

before the execution."

"No one will. Listen, Virginia. Once the execution ends this whole thing, there might be a run on the farm. A stampede of men in a hurry to make mayhem, act up, or propose to you. It's no telling. And one of those men might just be the man who already has a claim on you and on everything he thinks you own. So let me just get Hannah out of here before somebody takes it into his head to lynch her and send her to Hell after her mother."

Virginia was openmouthed. "Harvey, what have you heard?"

"I take it I have your agreement," Harvey said and turned, calling, "Coffee, fetch me Hannah. Then go bring my horse around. I got to get home before it gets any darker, and I can't see to ride or shoot straight."

"Harvey? Will you be at the execution?"

"I think I must. Otherwise men will come to look for me and demand an explanation."

"I will be there, too."

"You needn't, Virginia. It isn't expected of you, as a woman. As a mother of small children who need you at home."

"For Celia. But I won't bring Hannah, or she'll notice that The Baby isn't there."

The gentlemen came to take me and the chained man, Wayne—so like Joshua in his strength and his fear, in giving me the gift of dreaming, *What if?*—back to jail. "We regret that the law, in your case, Celia, has failed to serve the cause of

400

justice. We lost the appeal."

In the habit of talking now, with Wayne, I asked about my living children. I had to know. Were they sold? Wherever they were, were they still alive? When George ran away, had he taken my children with him? Would anyone tell me, if he had?

The gentlemen were startled to hear me speak but rallied and assured me that my children were safe and had neither been sold nor stolen away. Master Harvey had them, they said.

I dreamed of Hannah and The Baby the next days and nights, the sunshine, the tag games, the round limbs golden with sun around my neck when I hugged them. I pictured the dead newborn in my arms, and I bent to show it to Hannah and The Baby. They smiled. We were together.

The good people fly.

Late one night, the gentlemen sent in a man in black who said that his god would forgive me. I repeated the story that everyone said would end these questions by ending my life. I screamed my confession and fell on the floor. I wanted to break my head open on the bars and end the wait. I cried for that terrible night, that last night with my children, when I still had hope, I was so stupid, and how bad and wrong it had all gone.

When I was spent screaming, the man in black told me I had repented and my death would now drive the evil from my soul.

Perhaps this last was true. For I no longer thought of the men who had used my body but only of the children who had come from it and who had

401

loved me, needed me.

And the next morning, when a sack was put over my head, and I was walked from the stench and the dark into rain, and I heard crowds of angry voices yell at me and curse me, and I rose up steps into the sky, and again I felt the rope scrape my neck, strangle my neck, burn my neck, I remembered, *Good people fly.*

Flight. I had not got my children free.

But I was at the last resolved. Whether it worked or failed, I had done all I could to save them. And I did it all alone.

I flew into the air, above the fiery pain that used to be my spine.

Selected Bibliography

Barthes, Roland. *S/Z*. Richard Miller, trans. New York: Hill and Wang, The Noonday Press, 1974.

Berlin, Ira. *Many Thousands Gone: The First Two Centuries of Slavery in North America*. Cambridge: The Belknap Press of Harvard University Press, 1998.

Brent, Linda. *Incidents in the Life of a Slave Girl*. New York: Harcourt Brace Jovanovich, 1973.

Busia, Abena. "Words Whipped Over Voids: A Context for Black Women's Rebellious Voices in the Novel of the African Diaspora." In Joe Weixlmann and Houston Baker, eds., *Studies in Black American Literature*. Greenwood, Florida: Penkeville Publishers, 1988.

Collins, Patricia Hill. *Black Feminist Thought: Knowledge, Consciousness, and the Politics of Empowerment*. New York: Routledge, 2000.

Crafts, Hannah. *The Bondwoman's Narrative*. Henry Louis Gates, Jr., ed. New York: Warner, 2005.

Davis, David Brion. *The Problem of Slavery in Western Culture*. Ithaca: Cornell University Press, 1966.

De Certeau, Michel. *The Writing of History*. Tom Conley, trans. New York: Columbia University Press, 1988.

Dodson, Howard, ed. *Jubilee: The Emergence of African-American Culture/ Schomburg Center for Research in Black Culture, New York Public Library*. Washington, DC: National Geographic, 2002.

Drapetomania Exhibit. Museum of Texas Southern University, 2008.

Eze, Emmanuel Chukwudi, ed. *Race and the Enlightenment: A Reader*. Malden: Blackwell

Publishing, 1997.

Fanon, Frantz. *Peau noire, masques blancs.* Saint Amand, France: Éditions du Seuil, 1957.

Foucault, Michel. *The History of Sexuality, Volume I: An Introduction.* Robert Hurley, trans. New York: Vintage Books, 1990.

———. *The Order of Things: An Archaeology of the Human Sciences.* New York: Vintage Books, 1970.

Franklin, John Hope. *From Slavery to Freedom: A History of African Americans.* New York: Alfred A. Knopf, 2002.

Giddings, Paula. *When and Where I Enter: The Impact of Black Women on Race and Sex in America.* New York: Bantam Books, 1988.

Harris, Trudier. *Exorcising Blackness: Historical and Literary Lynching and Burning Rituals.* Bloomington: Indiana University Press, 1984.

Holloway, Karla FC. *Passed On: African American Mourning Stories.* Durham: Duke University Press, 2002.

Hudson, J. Blaine. *Fugitive Slaves and the Underground Railroad in the Kentucky Borderland.* Jefferson, North Carolina: McFarland & Company, 2002.

Hurmence, Belinda, ed. *Before Freedom, When I Just Can Remember: Twenty-Seven Oral Histories of Former South Carolina Slaves.* Winston-Salem: John F. Blair, 1989.

———. *My Folks Don't Want Me to Talk about Slavery: Twenty-One Oral Histories of Former North Carolina Slaves.* Winston-Salem: John F. Blair, 2002.

———. *We Lived in a Little Cabin in the Yard.* Winston-Salem: John F. Blair, 1994.

James, C. L. R. *The Black Jacobins: Toussaint L'Ouverture and the San Domingo Revolution.*

New York: Vintage Books, 1989.

Kristeva, Julia. *Powers of Horror: An Essay on Abjection.* Leon S. Roudiez, trans. New York: Columbia University Press, 1982.

Lemon, Lee T. and Marion J. Reis, eds. and trans. *Russian Formalist Criticism: Four Essays.* Lincoln: University of Nebraska Press, 1965.

Lorde, Audre. *Sister Outsider: Essays and Speeches by Audre Lorde.* Freedom, California: The Crossing Press, 1982.

McLaurin, Melton A. *Celia, A Slave.* New York: Avon Books, 1993.

Morrison, Toni. *Playing in the Dark: Whiteness and the Literary Imagination.* Cambridge: Harvard University Press, 1992.

———. "The Site of Memory." In *Out There: Marginalization and Contemporary Cultures.* Cambridge: MIT Press, 1990.

Ogletree, Charles J. and Austin Sarat, eds. *When Law Fails: Making Sense of Miscarriages of Justice.* New York: New York University Press, 2009.

Oyono, Ferdinand. *Une vie de boy.* Paris: Julliard, 1970.

Rhyne, Nancy, ed. *Slave Ghost Stories: Tales of Hags, Hants, Ghosts, & Diamondback Rattlers.* Orangeburg, South Carolina: Sandlapper Publishing Company, 2002.

Slavery Exhibit. Shrine of the Black Madonna, Houston, Texas, 2007-2008.

Starobin, Robert S., ed. *Blacks in Bondage: Letters of American Slaves.* New York: Barnes & Noble Books, 1974.

Terborg-Penn, Rosalyn, Sharon Harley, and Andrea Benton Rushing, eds. *Women in Africa and the African Diaspora.* Washington, DC: Howard

University Press, 1987.

Walker, Alice. *In Search of Our Mothers' Gardens: Womanist Prose.* New York: Harcourt Brace & Company, 1983.

Walker, Margaret. *Jubilee.* New York: Harcourt, 1966.